THE ADVISOR

BY
CAPTAIN JOHN L. COOK

DORRANCE & COMPANY
Philadelphia

This book is dedicated to the countless and forgotten advisors who have fought in the jungles and rice paddies of South Vietnam, often dying for a cause now commonly considered lost. But the cause is not lost and it will never be, not as long as there are men of this stature who understand that sacrifice is the awesome and universal cost of freedom.

CONTENTS

PREFACE

My reasons for writing this book are many and quite complex. Let me admit now, in the beginning, that I cannot be objective about the Vietnamese and their struggle to survive. I feel it is impossible for anyone to spend over two years living and working with these people and remain objective. When I returned to the United States in the summer of 1970, I was deeply disturbed to discover that the true nature of this war had not been presented to the American people. It was then that I decided to make an honest effort to shed some light on a very small part of that conflict.

This is a story about one district—Di An—and how it was affected by the war. And about the people who live there—Major Chau, Lieutenant Hau, Mr. Quy, Sergeant Chi and others, people whose life and future revolve around the fortunes of war.

It isn't a pretty story; its not supposed to be. But it is true. These things happened, these people are real. My purpose is not to change the way you feel about Vietnam. I will leave that task to the newsmen who seem to know all the answers and who can neatly put all the pieces of this puzzle together in the space of a sixty-minute "special" on nationwide TV. But I will tell you about the war that gets very little attention from the news media, the war that has no major battles or any great victories. This is the war at the bottom, at the "rice roots," that goes on, day in and day out, always following the same pattern.

This is a story about the deliberate elimination of the Viet Cong Infrastructure, the shadowy political organization that decides policy for the Viet Cong and the North Vietnamese forces. It's a story about one district's fight to rid itself of this organization— systematically, methodically, without remorse.

And it's a story about the people who fight the war as naturally as they laugh and sing and hope and die. And why they think and feel and hate the way they do. And how I became involved, deeply and morally, in their struggle to free themselves from the Viet Cong. And about the success we achieved and how much it costs, and why

I would do it all over again, all twenty-five months of it, if I had to, or if I were asked.

The ideas, opinions, conclusions and collective agony expressed here do not represent the views of the United States government and should not be considered official policy. They are mine, all of them, and I have no desire to endanger my story's credibility by such an association.

Chapter One

THE ARRIVAL

There was an air of finality about the way the big 707 lifted off the runway at Travis Air Force Base, California, on that warm May night. The screaming engines severed our connections with the only world most of us had ever known, leaving it back there somewhere in the darkness and leaving us with only one firmly established prospect—a long flight. And I was prepared for a long flight too, but long before we reached Hawaii, the hours had begun to stack up, one on top of another, until the desire to stand and move about became almost unbearable. The movie had helped some. Sandy Dennis gave a very convincing performance in *Up the Down Staircase*, offering my restless mind something other than uncertainty to consume. But soon after the screen was tucked back in the ceiling of the plane, the feeling that passed for boredom returned. Or maybe it was something beyond boredom, like anticipation in reverse, brought on by the knowledge of our destination, out there in the darkness somewhere—thousands of miles in front of us— relentlessly being pursued by the indefatigable plane. Only the low, steady scream of the huge Pratt and Whitney engines remained constant, keeping me at least on the fringe of reality, as we winged our way closer to the coast of South Vietnam.

It was still dark in Honolulu when the plane landed to take on fuel. This gave all 170 of us a chance to browse through the airport terminal and have a cup of coffee or a coke at the overpriced cafeteria. For most of us, our first glimpse of the exotic isle was made less romantic by the plastic, prepackaged, commercialized world of the airport. There were a few giant goldfish in a small pond by the terminal, but they failed to generate much attention. As we walked out to reboard the plane, someone remarked that the fish must be rich, otherwise they couldn't afford to live there. This drew a weak laugh from those who heard it and we continued to march.

Straggling out of the airport, we resembled very little the role we would soon be thrust into. We didn't look like defenders of freedom nor did we bear a marked similarity to bloodthirsty killers. None of us looked like we qualified as potential heroes, either.

Rather, we resembled exactly what we were—170 American soldiers bound for duty in South Vietnam because it was the wish of the American government that we go—moral and political views aside, all of us, from private first class to bird colonel, had at least this much in common. I was just another green, inexperienced, second lieutenant in a group of twenty-four other second lieutenants fresh out of U. S. Army Intelligence School at Fort Holabird, Maryland. Our specialty was counterintelligence, that section of the organization concerned with neutralizing the enemy's intelligence-gathering network. At Holabird we had been taught the principles and techniques of the business from inside out in a very thorough, objective manner. We had been taught by professionals to be professionals but, up to the time we'd boarded the plane, it had all been academic since the one vital ingredient—experience—could not be taught, not even by the professionals. That would have to be picked up personally, "in the field," as the expression went. They had told us at Holabird how desperately our skills were needed in the war zone, trying to get us psyched up, I had assumed, so we would go charging off to the great big football field in the jungle and win the big one "for the old Gipper"—"Gipper" Johnson, that is. And the closer we got to that strip of asphalt at Bien Hoa, the more doubts I had about my indispensability.

Sleep was impossible. The best I could achieve was a sort of deep laxity and I exploited it. I returned to the surroundings I was familiar with and to faces I knew. It was easy to slip away to the mountains of southern West Virginia, to the social and cultural insulation of the tiny coal-town that would always be home. I thought about how simple and good life had been there, and I realized how much I missed it and wondered if I would ever see it again. If only I were home, I kept thinking, everything would be alright. And then I remembered reading somewhere that you can never go home again.

We flew on through the night like some giant bird trying desperately to outrun the dawn. But it caught us, about three hours from the mainland. The all-night flight made the coming day more welcome than usual, even though all we could see at first was the

2

South China Sea from 30,000 feet below us. The stewardesses had time to serve breakfast before the coastline of Vietnam came into view. As soon as the pilot announced we were over Vietnam, there was a mad rush for the windows as each of us eagerly searched for that first glimpse of land. I don't know what we expected to see—perhaps a raging battle between Viet Cong and Americans from 30,000 feet. Or perhaps an airplane dropping napalm on an enemy position. At least, I thought, there would be thousands of bomb craters as evidence we were over the war zone. But none of these things was visible. I could see nothing except the lush greenness from the jungle, as if a giant green carpet had been spread on the ground, covering all the hills and mountains and valleys. We passed over rivers that seemed undecided on which course they wanted to follow, slithering through the jungle like a snake, coiling and uncoiling for apparently no reason other than self-amusement.

As the plane descended for landing at Bien Hoa, more details came into view. Small clusters of huts became visible in the jungle clearings. Small boats plied the rivers below, some being content to drift with the current, while others moved by motor. At the lower altitude, the bomb craters pockmarked the rice paddies. Huge holes filled with water and broken, twisted trees were all that remained of past B-52 strikes—craters spaced out in straight lines like so many footsteps of a club-footed giant. Around the villages the craters were much smaller, probably caused by artillery or smaller bombs.

And as we came closer, more details were visible. A truck convoy moved along a highway, escorted by Armored Personnel Carriers. Helicopters flew beneath us, the bright sunlight reflecting from their blades.

Then the low whine of the landing gear being lowered was heard, followed by a gentle jolt as it locked in place. The landscape passed quickly by the window until it became a confused blur. The plane continued its rapid descent, barely clearing tin-roofed houses and green rice paddies, threatening to make contact with the ground short of the runway. But then the black asphalt was speeding beneath us in a great dark ribbon, ready to receive us, patiently waiting to end the long flight. The plane flared, slightly raising the nose, and a second later the wheels touched the runway. A great spontaneous "oh no" filled the cabin, but it was as much a sigh of relief as an expression of despair. As the plane taxied to the terminal, the voice on the public address system thanked us for flying Trans World Airlines, and they hoped to see all of us again soon. It was the kind of canned, routine announcement expected at the end of a commercial flight but it hit me with sudden impact, seeming strangely out of place here. I looked around me at my fellow travelers and wondered how many of them would be provided with another form of transportation on the return trip, wrapped in a plastic bag and placed in a long, metal box. By sheer statistics alone, all of us definitely would not be returning to the United States by courtesy of Trans World Airlines. This undeniable fact must have been common knowledge to the slowest, most dim-witted airline stewardess who ever spilled hot coffee, and I considered it an insult to the intelligence of the dumbest rifleman on the plane to pretend we were on a Boy Scout outing or a visit to Aunt Helen in Buffalo. Perhaps the statement bolstered the spirits of some of my companions, but I would have felt far more comfortable with a simple "good luck and keep your ass down."

The plane stopped in front of a large tin shed that looked suspiciously like our first stop. For at least thirty minutes nothing happened after the plane's engines were shut down. With the engines, the air conditioner was shut off also, and we sweltered in the rapidly rising temperature of the cabin as those in charge decided what to do with us. Finally, almost as an afterthought, the ramp was rolled into place and the doors were opened. A tall, stringy airman with three stripes on his fatigue shirt raced up the ramp and popped into the cabin. At last, I thought, they're going to get us out of here. A cheer greeted the airman but it proved to be premature for his only concern was the three full colonels on the plane. The airman escorted them to a waiting sedan parked near the tin shed and drove them away. Another ten minutes passed before an army staff sergeant boarded the plane. He carefully checked the packet of orders that had come with us from Travis. Satisfied that we were the right group and not a bunch of imposters, he asked us to follow him to the tin shed. It had been sixteen hours since we had boarded the plane in California. No matter what followed, the first part of the ordeal was over.

I had been told a lot about the climate in Vietnam and I'd even read several articles on the subject, but I was totally unprepared for the hot stifling air that waited just outside the plane. Conspiring

4

with the blinding sun to produce an almost unbearable environment, it literally took my breath away. The tin shed offered little protection from the heat, but it did deflect the direct rays of the sun. It was no better than the plane—just a different kind of agony.

"How the hell do they expect us to live in this place, much less work in it?" a young blond specialist fourth class asked his buddy. As if a formal reply was too much of an exertion, his buddy simply shrugged his shoulders to indicate he had no answer for such a profound question. Within a few minutes my uniform was wet with perspiration. The sweat ran down my back, traveled down my legs and, finally, into my new, nineteen-dollar dress low-quarter shoes.

When we were "officially" welcomed to Vietnam by the impersonal loudspeaker hanging from the ceiling, an undercurrent of moans and groans swept through the shed.

"Does that mean they really want us?" someone asked in mock seriousness.

"Yea, buddy-boy, it sure does. They been holding up the whole turkey shoot just waiting for you" came a reply from the rear.

"Well, now that I'm here, me and Westy can get this thing over with," remarked one of the lieutenants. His immodest offer to help General Westmoreland immediately drew several boos from the crowd.

"What's the most dangerous thing in the world?" asked a sergeant near the front of the shed.

"A second lieutenant with an idea," was the spontaneous reply from a dozen enlisted men, indicting all the second lieutenants present.

After the welcoming, we were divided according to the units we were assigned to. At this point, the divisions were between the two largest commands in Vietnam—United States Army Vietnam (USARV) and Military Assistance Command (MACV). The first one, USARV, was responsible for every army tactical unit in Vietnam, and included all combat divisions and independent brigades. The second command, MACV, was technically the supreme command in Vietnam, since it included the air force, navy, marine corps, army and all the advisory teams. But it was this last function, the advisory effort, that MACV was most identified with, making the terms "advisor" and "MACV" almost synonymous. On that bright May morning in 1968, I was blissfully ignorant of the difference between MACV and USARV; as far as I was concerned, they could have both been heroes in the Israeli Six-Day War and I would have been happy. However, my orders stated in big black print, INDIVIDUAL ASSIGNED TO MACV, and because of this I was sent to a special corner of the shed along with everyone else whose orders read the same.

On the other side of the shed was an unusually happy group of men. And no wonder, for they were scheduled to board the plane we'd just left. They were the lucky ones, smiling and laughing, poking good-natured fun at us.

"You'll be sorry," one of them shouted.

"Charlie's waiting for you guys. He saw your plane land." This brought laughter from the departing group but there was no laughter around me, for "Charlie" was the term reserved exclusively for the Viet Cong. Soon, I thought, these men will be on their way home, away from the heat and horrors they had lived with for the past twelve months. And in the endless cycle of events, we were their replacements just as they had been replacements for another group a year before. Their happiness was easily understandable and forgivable. They were winners of a sort, having earned this status simply by surviving, regardless of the ultimate outcome. And I was happy for them. Yet it was impossible for me not to envy them as I thought about my own chances of being in their position one year from now, wondering if I would be one of those who jeered the new troops as we were now being jeered. I felt certain this thought, or one similar to it, was on the mind of every man in my group.

There was a bond, as definite as it was unexplainable, among us new arrivals. Most of us had been thrown together just hours before at Travis, but already Travis was a long, long way in the past and the reality of Vietnam was undeniably with us. Now, it seemed that we all had to stick together since we'd all arrived together, thus assuring our safe return. Of course this was impossible and I knew it, but the old truism about strength in numbers quickly came to mind and I was reluctant to let it go.

There were some thirty-five of us herded together in the section of the shed reserved for MACV. Aside from the twenty-five lieutenants, there were a couple of captains and a few sergeants. After picking up our baggage, we boarded a long green bus with heavy wire over the windows for the four-mile ride to the 90th Replacement Battalion at Long Binh. The bus traveled through a part of Bien Hoa that had been heavily damaged during the Tet Offensive a few months earlier. Much of the rubble that had once been respectable buildings still lay as it has fallen. Jagged, bullet-riddled walls stood in grotesque patterns, contrasting sharply with the undamaged, distant skyline. Pathetic-looking little lean-tos had been thrown up among the rubble that had once been the homes of these people. Some were built with twisted tin and broken lumber taken from the debris; others were constructed with cardboard. Dirty, naked children, standing dangerously close to the road, stared blankly at the bus as it passed.

At the replacement center, our U.S. currency was taken from us and we were given Military Payment Certificates (MPCs) for the amount taken. The certificates covered all the usual denominations up to twenty dollars, and there were even five-, ten-, twenty-five-, and fifty-cent certificates. The bills were much smaller than the currency we had exchanged for them. It was often referred to as "funny money" because of the various bright colors used to mark different denominations, but I wasn't laughing at the strange pieces of paper that had been twenty-six dollars a moment before; it was all I had to last me until payday.

All of us, including those going to USARV were reunited at the replacement center, but those assigned to MACV were supposed to go to Saigon for further inprocessing. Again we were all herded together, again waiting for a bus. Apparently our coming to the 90th Replacement Center had been a mistake; only those assigned to USARV were supposed to come. It had been a long day, reaching back an ungodly number of hours to some dark and distant point over the Pacific called the International Date Line. I could have gone to sleep right there but a big, bull-necked first lieutenant kept telling us the bus was on its way and it should arrive in "a few minutes." His "few minutes" stretched into an hour and then an hour and a half. We were obviously causing his organization problems by our unscheduled presence. The last time he addressed us he said he had bad news for my little group.

"The Viet Cong have blown up the Newport Bridge between here and Saigon, and it looks like you guys will have to spend the night here," he said in a painful manner.

This statement drew a big cheer—not for the Viet Cong, but for the prospect of spending the night. The bull-necked lieutenant looked at us as if we were enemy collaborators, and then he mumbled something about picking up sheets and pillowcases from the supply room. Everyone seemed excited about the bridge, and it was the topic of discussion at the 90th's Officers Club that night.

"Sounds like we might get a little action after all," speculated Joe Adams, a classmate from Fort Holabird. "I've always wondered about how they blow bridges. Hell, if they can drop a bridge right in Saigon, nothing's sacred."

I was more concerned about the steak I was trying to cut through than Adam's conclusions when Max, another classmate at the next table, attempted to shed light on the subject.

"Know what I think? I don't think the VC did it. I think we did it and blamed it on the VC. That way the VC look bad and we look victimized. It's really a very simple technique," he said, trying to penetrate our conversation.

This was the sort of statement that had made Max famous. While at Holabird he had earned a unique reputation among the class by always being wrong, behaving as though stupidity was an admirable trait. The greatest fear we harbored, aside from getting killed, was being assigned to the same unit as Max. In fact, most of the class saw no difference between the two.

I had never had any particular liking for the fat little obnoxious-looking lieutenant and I liked him even less this night but tried to ignore him and concentrate on the steak.

"Where do you think they get this meat, Joe?" I asked.

"I don't know, but I heard they sometimes use water buffalo when they run out of beef. They figure us new guys don't know the difference," he replied.

Our conversation was interrupted by the pudgy form of Max leaning over our table.

"Did you hear my theory, Adams?" he asked in a superior tone.

"Yea, Max, I heard and so did everybody else. What's the point?"

"Well, what do you think?" Max asked.

Joe gave him a surprised look.

"Are you serious?"

"Of course I'm serious," Max retorted.

"Well in that case, I feel it's only fair to tell you that I think you're the same dumb shit you were at Holabird and I don't see any reason for your condition to change in the forseeable future. It's guys like you that make being a second lieutenant a real burden."

After that Max let the subject drop and walked away, leaving Joe and me to ponder the origin of the steak.

That night we slept in a one-room barracks-type building with about twenty-five other lieutenants and captains. Typical army bunks lined both sides of the room with an open space down the middle. There was a huge fan at each end of the room that was supposed to keep it cool but they didn't. Aside from moving the hot, sticky air around, they did little more than make noise. Joe and I flipped a coin to see who would get the top bunk and I lost. The top bunk was desirable because what little cooling effect the fans had was felt there.

Artillery was fired all night around Long Binh and there was a B-52 strike to the north of the post along about midnight. The rumblings from the evenly spaced explosions shook our flimsy building and vibrated one of the fans to the floor.

"Too goddamned close," came a sleepy mumble from the other end of the room as the fan was righted. A few other more excited comments followed, then all was quiet.

I dozed off waiting for another strike, only to be awakened by a fiery itch on my neck and face. I slapped the mosquitoes away and gingerly felt the big fat welts growing under my chin. Joe was having the same trouble above me, causing the rickety bunk to shake with each futile slap. I tried pulling the sheet over my head, but it did little good. Like so many miniature vampires, they bit on us all night, exacting a heavy price for the little sleep we got.

When I awoke the next morning, I discovered that almost everyone had beaten me to the latrine. They had said something the night before about getting up early to avoid the rush but I had forgotten. Across from me, a clean-shaven lieutenant was buttoning his shirt.

"Where's the latrine?" I asked. He pointed directly behind the building and hooked his finger to the right. Wearing only my underwear and a towel around my waist, I grabbed my shaving kit and stepped out into the bright, early morning sun. I followed the wooden walkway around the corner of our building, taking great care to avoid slipping on the soap-slicked boards.

The latrine was filled with pushing and shoving bodies, each trying to secure one of the six galvanized sinks. I saw Joe, his face covered with shaving cream, standing behind a man who had one of the sinks. He was cautiously attempting to shave around his mosquito bites while looking over the shoulder of the man in front of him and trying to find his face in the dirty mirror. When the man finished, Joe quickly moved forward, and I slipped behind him.

"How ya' feel?" I asked sleepily.

"About ten pounds lighter after them damn mosquitoes got through with me," he replied without taking his eyes from the mirror.

"Looks like they really nailed you good, Adams," Max sneered from the neighboring sink, taking apparent pleasure in Joe's sad condition.

Joe stopped in the middle of a stroke and turned to Max with the razor still on his cheek.

"Yes, Max, they nailed my ass. I guess I'm not as lucky as you are."

"What d'ya mean?" Max demanded, moving closer to Joe.

"Well, I heard a couple of them big mosquitoes talking over your bunk last night, and one of them wanted to eat you right there but the other one wanted to drag your fat ass outside. If they'd been able to reach an agreement, you wouldn't be bothering me now," Joe explained.

The veins in Max's neck stood out angrily like taut wires, and I thought for a second he was going to hit Joe. Instead, he left without shaving and I quickly moved over to his sink before someone else took it.

"Screw him if he can't take a joke," Joe mumbled, as the laughter died down behind us.

We had breakfast at the club, where the Newport Bridge was once again discussed. After breakfast we were told that the bridge had not been completely destroyed and that traffic was now moving across what remained of the span. So about noon those of us assigned to MACV boarded busses once again, this time for Saigon. Outside Long Binh both sides of the road were lined with flooded rice paddies. Only the green shoots of the rice extended beyond the water level. In other paddies, tiny farmers, dwarfed by the size of their water buffalos, prodded their large plow-pulling beasts through the narrow rows of rice.

Even before we reached the bridge, the evidence of traffic congestion was conclusive. We alternately inched our way forward in the heavy traffic and then suffered through long, hot, stifling stops—the undeniable symptoms of one-way traffic.

When we finally arrived at the bridge, I found it much larger than I'd expected. For some unknown reason I had pictured it as being quite small, but this was not the case. It had been designed to carry four lanes of traffic and I felt certain it had performed this mission quite well until the Viet Cong drastically altered the basic design. Being an arch-type bridge, it climbed at about a twenty-degree angle for approximately five hundred feet to the center. The Viet Cong had dropped a one hundred foot section of the southbound lanes into the Saigon River.

At first, it had been rumored that the damage was caused by a 122mm rocket scoring a direct hit. Later investigations, however, revealed that Viet Cong explosive experts, known as "sappers," had sneaked up the support columns from the river below and carefully placed explosives in the superstructure of the bridge. Evidence that they had found the points of greatest stress was the gaping hole they left. As we passed, I was impressed at the smoothness of the break—it looked as if someone had cut out the missing portion with a sharp knife.

From the bridge into the center of town, the volume of traffic picked up considerably. Again I was impressed, this time by the wide variety of vehicles we passed and the cargo they carried. It seemed that everything that could possibly be adapted or converted to receive wheels and the internal combustion engine was on the road that day, carrying everything from porcelain elephants to slaughtered hogs. All were making their way, with an obvious sense of urgency, to the greatest market of all—Saigon.

By far the most popular mode of transportation was the small Honda motorbike. Some of these bikes would have as many as four passengers on them as they dangerously wove in and out between the bigger, slower moving vehicles. My first reaction was a feeling of admiration at the great amount of courage and skill demonstrated by these daring operators. Since then I've come to the conclusion that what I originally considered courage is nothing more than insanity, but I still respect their skill.

As we neared the center of town, the "smog" rapidly increased. I didn't know the air pollution level in Saigon, but I felt certain it was one of the forgotten aspects of the city, failing to receive its due share of publicity because of the war. There was no question that Saigon rivaled Los Angeles in the Major League of Air Polluters. Many of the older vehicles burned (or threw out) a mixture of oil and gasoline and when two million of these air polluters were operating at a maximum output the haze hanging over Saigon during the rush hours was quite easily explained. Add to this the fact that most of the hours seemed to be rush and the problem is compounded.

In the beginning, I was naive enough to believe that there was a system for routing traffic through Saigon, and I had also expected this system to be effective to a certain degree. I was wrong on both counts. At a red light or a stop sign, everyone jockeyed for the best possible starting position, waiting for the light to flash green. And when it flashed, everything capable of moving surged forward in a big blinding, cloud of blue, white, and black smoke. God help the luckless bastard that happened to be daydreaming or girl-watching when the light changed. No quarter was asked and none was given in this harsh, swirling environment that selectively eliminated the novice and nervous driver.

As we wormed our way through this uncontrolled mass, there were a few times when I honestly thought we weren't going to make it. Yet we had one definite advantage over most of the motorists by being in a big bus. It was soon obvious that the size of the vehicle one operated in Saigon was extremely important, since size was the only quality that received respect. At any given time our driver could have wiped a dozen Hondas off the street, and, by American standards, he would have been well within his rights to have done so, as they darted in and out of the moving traffic. But in Saigon this would have been a grave mistake, for all two-wheeled vehicles had the right-of-way over all four-wheeled vehicles. Add to this the fact that pedestrians always have the right-of-way no matter what the circumstances were and you get an idea of what the motorist faced.

These were the official rules that governed vehicles, and they were duly recorded in the Great Books at City Hall. There were, however, a thousand unwritten rules known only to those who successfully navigated their way through the sea of Hondas, trucks, jeeps, 1957 Fords, and Renault taxis on a daily basis.

We finally arrived at an installation known only as Koepler Compound near the docks in Saigon. The area smelled of salt water and rotten fish. We spent a total of four days at this compound that had once served as a hotel in its glory years. Now, with most of its charm and appeal gone, it was being leased by the Army to serve as a preparation station for advisors.

We were processed with assembly-line efficiency. Our records were taken from us first, then we were issued the equipment we would need for the coming year. It consisted of four sets of jungle fatigues, two pairs of jungle boots, assorted accessories such as web gear, socks, underwear, T-shirts, foot powder, a mess kit, and other necessary items. Weapons were issued here also, and we had the option of choosing either a .45 caliber pistol or an M-16 rifle.

"What are you taking?" Joe asked as we moved into the arms room.

"I'm taking the pistol," I told him.

"Why?"

"Because I've heard that there's a lot of rifles out in the field or wherever we're going. What are you taking?"

"I guess I'll take a pistol, too, but I can't hit anything with one of them damn things. I'd feel a lot better with a pump shotgun," he confessed.

"I'd feel a lot better just knowing where I'm going," I added as we signed hand-receipts for the .45's.

'Where we were going' just happened to be the next item on our agenda. After the weapons issue, my group was sent to a tiny classroom on the second floor of the tiny hotel. A large podium stood at the front of the room bearing the name of our instructor. Beneath this name was another sign which read "VIETNAM ORIENTATION." When we were all seated, an overweight, tired-looking staff sergeant stepped up behind the podium. A large map of Vietnam hung on the wall behind him.

"Good afternoon, gentlemen," he began. "My name is Sergeant Rudinsky. In order to properly understand your assignments, which you will receive in a few minutes, a little education on Vietnam is necessary so you'll know the difference between a district and a province, a corps and a hamlet, and so on. Otherwise, your orders won't mean much to you," he explained in a machine-like, memorized tone. Then he pointed to the large map behind him and seemed to relax a little, now that the introduction was over.

"Now, I'm sure we all recognize this famous little piece of real estate," he patronized, attempting to inject an air of informality.

"Yea, it looks like Poland with a face lift," quipped a first lieutenant from the middle of the room. Rudinsky ignored the remark but the lines in his big red face hardened immediately. His eyes shot fire, prematurely killing the spontaneous laughter. Exercising tremendous self-control he continued the orientation, but this time the tone was noticeably hostile; almost intimidating. Still, there was much valuable information imparted that afternoon.

With a pointer, Sergeant Rudinsky pointed out the four corps that composed South Vietnam—One, Two, Three, Four. The numbers started in the north of the country at the so-called Demilitarized Zone (DMZ) and worked their way south. Saigon, for example, was in Three Corps. The corps were divided into forty-four provinces, averaging eleven provinces to a corps. We were told a province was the equivalent of a state in the country we had just left. The provinces in turn were further divided into districts—two hundred and thirty six in all—which Rudinsky equated to counties.

Below district, it became confusing, and Rudinsky had to rely on the chalk-board to make his point.

"This is a district, okay?" he explained as he drew a large, lopsided circle on the board. He paused for a few seconds to see if his art-work would draw any snide remarks. It didn't, and he continued.

"The district is divided up in villages," and he drew small circles inside the district to illustrate this, exposing a large wet spot under his right arm as he did so.

"Now the village is divided into hamlets, the lowest level of government in South Vietnam," he told the chalk-board as he put several lines through one of the small circles. When this was done he faced us once again. Rudinsky pulled a green, olive-drab army handkerchief from his hip pocket and mopped the beads of perspiration from his face and neck. It was hot in the room and the slow moving, over-head fans did little other than move the hot air around. Somewhere below us, a radio was blaring out the weather forecast.

"Are there any questions, gentlemen?" Rudinsky asked, his voice betraying a hint of happiness that his part of the orientation was over. There were none and Sgt. Rudinsky thanked us and left.

We were given a ten minute break to stretch, smoke and get a drink of water before we were told which province we were going to. There were several people from the personnel section in the classroom when we returned and they had what we'd been waiting for—our orders. At first I was told I was going to Tay Ninh Province, which was right on the Cambodian border, and at the time a place well known for its high level of enemy activity; I knew this much from the news reports. I stared at the official-looking documents for a long time, hoping to find something that would prove my initial interpretation wrong, but I didn't find it. A crowd had gathered around the large map at the front of the room and I walked up to inspect it, too. I was standing there numbly staring at the jagged outline of Tay Ninh hard pressed against Cambodia, noticing with growing horror how far it was from Saigon, when I felt a tap on my shoulder.

"Lieutenant Cook, sir?" the personnel clerk asked.

I'm Lt. Cook. What's wrong?" I asked defensively, afraid to imagine what else could go wrong.

"There's been a mistake in your orders, sir. You're not going to Tay Ninh. You'll be going to Bien Hoa instead. If you'll follow me downstairs, I'll give you copies of your new orders," he told me. To this day, I don't know what happened or why the change was made, but I'll always be grateful it turned out the way it did.

The first night at Koepler Compound was an eventful one. Two of us shared a room with a high ceiling, a slow, revolving fan that looked as if it was straight out of a James Cagney movie, and a shower with no curtain. Even at that it was a definite improvement over the 90th Replacement Battalion. We were on the ground floor of the four-story structure. My roommate was an infantry captain returning for his second tour, and he wasn't too happy about it. We stayed up late that night talking about life in the United States and how sweet it had been.

"This coming back business gets old after a while," the short, dark-haired captain told me as he sorted out his jungle fatigues on the bed. I asked him if he was married.

"Oh yea. This time makes number two. On my first tour in '65, I volunteered just to get away from my first wife. She was a real card-carrying bitch if I ever saw one. According to her, I couldn't do anything right. So when I got back, we got a divorce. She charged me with mental cruelty by claiming I run off to Vietnam to get away from her. Ain't that a real pisser, her charging me with mental cruelty? Well anyway, I got me a real sweet wife in Memphis and two little girls now and they make all the difference in the world." He pulled out his battered wallet and showed me pictures of a pleasant-looking, blond-headed woman nearing thirty and two babies he said were girls; I took his word for it.

"You know before, when I was married to that bitch, it really didn't make much difference one way or the other but now it does. This is going to be a long year cause I am going to be thinking about them everyday," he said, patting his wallet. Talking about his family improved his disposition considerably.

"What about you? You don't look old enough to be married," he stated.

"No, I'm single, but I guess I'm old enough to be married," I laughed.

"How old?"

"Twenty-three," I told him.

"Hell no, you ain't old enough. Wait till you're thirty and then you'll know what you want. Don't make the same mistake I made," he advised.

The conversation turned to our present situation and it seemed to depress him.

"Where you going?" he asked as he neatly folded his shirts and trousers into sets.

"Bien Hoa, where I landed," I told him.

"I know that place well. I spent a lot of time there on my first tour and tried to get assigned there again. Almost made it too. Up until today, it looked like I would be going right back up there, but they changed my orders. Don't know why they changed 'em but they did. Hell, you never know why they do things in this Army. I been in for almost twelve years, and I still don't understand the things that go on." He put the shirts and trousers in the bottom of his duffel bag, and then started sorting out his field gear.

"Where are you going now?" I asked.

"Over on the Cambodian border. A place called Tay Ninh."

About midnight, we turned in and this time I got the top bunk. It couldn't have been long after I dozed off when the first rocket hit.

16

The explosion was tremendous. By the time the second one hit, I was fully awake and terrified, aware of the captain screaming, "get down, get down."

I looked down to see where he was. He was under the bed with his mattress over him. I jumped off the top bunk just as the third rocket exploded. The impact shook the whole building and threw me against the wall. The captain kept shouting as I pulled myself off the floor, grabbed my mattress and crawled under the bed with him.

We waited for rocket number four, but it never came. I kept thinking how unfair it would be if I was wiped out during my second night in Vietnam and tried to convince myself the odds were heavily against such a thing actually happening. It didn't help much, though. Just in case we didn't make it, I wanted to tell the captain that I was supposed to go to Tay Ninh instead of him and that I wanted him to be able to return to his family in Memphis, but I didn't because it would have been awkward and embarrassing. There really was no way of explaining that sort of thing. As he had said, you never know why the Army does things the way they do.

With everything quiet, the whole idea of us being under a bed with mattresses over us seemed silly as hell and I told the captain I thought the crisis was over.

"I think we better wait just a little longer, to make sure," he replied and we did. Finally, after about an hour he declared the attack over and we crawled out and went back to bed. I was no longer sure that Koepler Compound was such a great place.

The next morning at daybreak the entire population of Koepler Compound was on the roof to survey the damage of the rocket attack. One section of town, about one hundred and fifty yards away, was still burning. Some people were trying to put it out, while others were dragging things from the ruins. It looked like about three square blocks had been burned out. This fire had been caused by the explosion of the closest rocket. The other two had landed in an area across the railroad tracks about two hundred yards away. I was surprised that they had not been closer; the night before I was certain they had hit just outside our door.

Our casualties had been extremely light. One of the guys on the second floor had cut his foot on a beer can when he jumped out of bed. He was trying to find out if this qualified him for a Purple

17

Heart. A few others, including myself, had some self-inflicted bruises, but nothing serious.

Civilian casualties had been far more serious—twelve killed and several wounded and burned. It was at this point that I realized I was witnessing a war—real war—not something far away or something that I was not involved with. What I was watching from the top of Koepler Compound was the product of this war—the senseless and useless destruction of people and property. At that time I was unable to understand the VC's motive for indiscriminate firing of rockets into heavily populated areas such as Saigon. Later, I was to learn this was one of his most effective tactics—taking the war to the people in the form of terror campaigns. It seemed unreasonable and it was. Such actions can never be dealt with rationally by Americans handicapped by a highly refined moral sense of right and wrong. There would be more rocket attacks, more bombings, more burnings, more destroyed bridges, more destruction, more sadness. This I was certain of; in fact, it was about the only thing I was certain of as I tried to assess the damage before me on that bright May morning. And for the first time since I had arrived I felt a terrible, empty, bitter sadness, but it would not be the last time I would feel this way.

After leaving Koepler Compound, I moved across town to the headquarters of the 525th Military Intelligence Group, along with the other Intelligence Officers. This compound, much bigger than Koepler, would be our home for two weeks while we attended classes at the Combined Intelligence Center located near Tan Son Nhut Air Base. It was during these two weeks that we were told what was expected of us when we arrived at our District or province.

We had been selected to participate in a new, super-secret program called ICEX—Intelligence Coordination and Exploitation—designed to eliminate the enemy's political apparatus. The formal name of this political apparatus was the Viet Cong Infrastructure, the shadowy element of the enemy's organization that controlled everything he did. It was this intercore or infrastructure, that called the shots for the Viet Cong and North Vietnamese all the way down the line. It selected targets to be hit based on their political significance, and rarely did this organization make a mistake. It could be compared to the Mafia, except the infrastructure was playing for much higher stakes—they wanted all of South Vietnam. The idea, quite simply, was to put an American Intelligence Officer in each district to coordinate the various Vietnamese intelligence agencies' attack on this infrastructure. This task would not be easy; it wasn't supposed to be. The people we would be tracking down were the leaders of the Communist Party in South Vietnam—known officially as the People's Revolutionary Party. If this party could be destroyed, then the war in South Vietnam would end because there would be no control or guidance for the enemy's main force military units. The far reaching potential of this program was unnerving, to say the least. Later, in July, 1968, the term ICEX would be dropped, replaced by a single word—PHOENIX, a word that would strike fear in the hearts of thousands of Viet Cong leaders and terrorists. But that would come later. In May of that year we were more concerned with getting the program off the drawing boards and into the districts.

At the Combined Intelligence Center, the ICEX concept was explained in detail. We also listened to lectures given by guest speakers on the tradition and culture of the Vietnamese. These distinguished looking gentlemen, most of them American civilians, attempted to explain away the mystery of the Orient. They gave the impression that the Vietnamese were vastly different from Americans and therefore had to be treated in a different manner. I supposed their contract with the State Department depended on some such startling conclusion, for they pushed it doggedly. One old fellow, for example, told us that the Vietnamese philosophy concerning death was far different from the American view. He told us that the Vietnamese provide food for the deceased to eat in the other world. However, he failed to explain the American view, whatever that is, nor did he mention our liberal use of flowers at funerals.

We were given an exhaustive list of things that were "no-no's", such as patting a child on the head, as an expression of affection. Any physical expression of emotion in public—a boy kissing his girlfriend or holding her hand for example—was definitely out, according to our cultural experts. So what did we see on our way home each evening to the 525th Compound? The park benches cluttered with young lovers, arms around each others shoulders, completely oblivious to the teachings of our highly paid and equally boring experts on Vietnamese culture.

Lectures by military personnel took up a large portion of the two weeks spent at the Combined Intelligence Center. They explained the latest enemy situation and strength, what his plans were and what he was capable of doing. In short, we were given the "big picture" in Saigon. I was soon to discover that there was a very real difference between the "big picture" they had and the way things really were down at district level. They explained how the Combined Intelligence Center could help us when we arrived at our destination. Their assets included access to specialized studies that had been completed on the different sections of Vietnam, aerial photographs for planning operations, translations of captured documents, and the latest changes and trends in the enemy's situation as it was viewed in Saigon.

Our quarters at the 525th Compound were a little crowded but adequate. Joe Adams was my bunk-mate once again. We slept in a large three-storied building which, like Koepler Compound, had been a somewhat respectable hotel at one time. At night we would go up on the roof and watch the flares that were fired every night. In the distance, far to the north, artillery was being fired. Somewhere across town there were scattered rifle shots, evidenced by the yellow tracers streaking skyward. The sporadic firing, the flares and the artillery continued almost all night.

"What do you think about ICEX?" Joe asked one night while we were lying in bed. He had been assigned to Can Tho Province in Four Corps, an area usually referred to, quite simply, as 'the Delta.'

"I don't know," I told him honestly. "The concept seems workable and it may be the only way to get the job done."

"I know that, but do you think they're really going to give the job of wiping out the infrastructure to a bunch of brand-new, green-ass lieutenants? Do you really think that's what's going to happen?" he asked.

"Yes, I think that's what's going to happen."

There was a long pause before he said anything else.

"I do too. And it really scares the hell out of me," he told me and I had a strong suspicion he was speaking for all twenty-five of us.

The bus that took us to and from the classes at the Center had heavy wire mesh over the window to prevent terrorists from throwing grenades inside. I was thankful for this security measure and hopeful it would work. However, it did distort the view I got of Saigon as we drove through town. Each time the bus passed an exceptionally attractive girl, twenty-five guys would rush to that side of the bus, trying to focus their vision through the one inch square holes in the wire. This could only be accomplished by placing one eye up to the square and closing the other. The system worked well if viewing a small object relatively close, such as a girl on a sidewalk, but it was no good for the "big picture." We became proficient at this during the two weeks in Saigon and even accepted the fact that much of what we observed in Saigon had to be framed in squares of wire.

The two weeks passed quickly, in spite of the fact that a lot of the lectures we sat through were dull and boring. Everything we saw in Saigon was incredibly new to us—the people, the shops, the language, the fact that we were in a combat zone all added to this atmosphere of newness and excitement. Although Saigon was obviously no longer the "Pearl of the Orient," signs of its former beauty and grandeur were very much in evidence. The architecture of many of the large buildings and cathedrals was reminiscent of the French occupation. The wide tree-lined boulevards, desecrated by thousands of smoke-spraying motor bikes and other offenders, had known an earlier splendor. Sand-bagged bunkers stood guard at the entrances of many, once beautiful villas. It didn't take a great deal of imagination to see another Saigon at another time, when people and traffic moved slowly, governed by dignity and sanity, through this city; a time when there was no urgency destroying the relaxed atmosphere that should come with a Sunday afternoon. But that time was gone, perhaps permanently, unable to survive the inevitable changes brought by war. However, there were two products left by the French that will survive as long as Vietnam—French bread and cognac. Nothing done by the Americans or the new generation of Vietnamese has succeeded in replacing these main stays of the Vietnamese diet.

In other areas, where there had been a smooth blending of the influences exerted on the natives by their various invaders and allies, the dominant influence was much more difficult to isolate, if in fact there was such a thing as the dominant influence. For example, a 1950 model Certion would cruise through Saigon powered by the engine from a 1967 model American jeep, supported on tires imported from Japan, with a full-blooded Cambodian at the controls, and yet the overall flavor was decidedly Vietnamese. By the time we had to leave Saigon, the city had started to grow on me.

As we prepared to leave Saigon at the completion of the two-week course, we were broken down into groups that were going to the different corps. About ten of us were assigned to Three Corps, the remainder had orders to Two Corps and Four Corps. No one was going to One Corps from this group. Once again it was time to board a bus for another trip and each time this happened, our original group grew smaller. Those of us going to Three Corps said goodbye to the others, making hasty plans to meet again somewhere, hopefully at the airport, in another year.

Chapter Two

AT BIEN HOA

There were only two of us from the original group that actually stayed in Bien Hoa Province. I was initially assigned to the team at Province Headquarters and the other lieutenant went to Duc Tu District, one of the six districts that made up Bien Hoa Province. It was there in Bien Hoa that I was exposed to the advisor-complex. The province team worked out of a smart-looking, two-story building in the middle of Bien Hoa. Up to this point, I only had a vague idea of what the average advisor did, or what was expected of him. In Saigon the stress had been placed on the intelligence effort, leaving the average advisor pretty much neglected. The whole idea of being an advisor was new to me and I had a lot of questions. Most of them were answered when Colonel Williams, the Province Senior Advisor, briefed me.

"Well, Cook, welcome to Bien Hoa," he greeted me as I entered the office. "Glad to have you on board. How about a cigar?"

I took a Dutch Masters panatella from the pack on his desk, thanked him, and sat down in a well-worn, comfortable easy chair. He was a big man, over six-feet tall, and weighed at least two hundred pounds. There was a nervous twitch around his left eye that made him appear to be winking, but it took nothing away from his command-presence. His faded, starched fatigues gave him a no-nonsense air, contrasting sharply with my bright green, wrinkled appearance. There was a large map of Bien Hoa Province on the wall behind his desk with the six district boundaries drawn in. He signed a few papers and put them in a box on this desk labeled "OUT" before he turned back to me.

"What do you think about being an advisor?" he asked, this time with a smile. He lit a new cigar and I lit mine with the match he passed to me.

"I don't know that much about it, sir, to be honest," I replied, and he laughed.

"I guess I'd better explain a little bit of what goes on around here, in that case." He put his feet up on the edge of his desk and I knew I would be in the easy chair for a long time, suddenly realizing why it was so well-worn.

"To begin with, the province team serves as headquarters for all the district teams," he pointed to the map behind him without moving his feet, "and is responsible for supporting them. Now the job I have as PSA can be held by either a military man or a civilian. If the PSA is a military man, the deputy PSA will be a civilian, or vice versa. We have civilians in the program because of the tremendous emphasis placed on pacification and civil affairs. Do you understand civil affairs?" he asked distantly.

"You mean things like public health and education, sir?" I asked, knowing it was.

"That's right. Well, it's widely believed that specially trained and high-paid civilians can do a better job in these areas than the military." A touch of cynicism crept into his voice when he told me this. "The whole advisor program comes under the control of an organization called Civil Operations for Rural Development Support. Don't worry about these fancy titles now, just call it CORDS for short. The top man for CORDS carries the rank of ambassador and works with the people in Saigon that decide U.S. policy in Vietnam. Now at corps level, the man in charge of CORDS has the title of Deputy to the Command General for Civil Operations and Rural Development Support or DEPCORDS, but just between us, he's really DEPGOD," the Colonel joked.

"Seriously though," he continued, "it's not so bad. Military advisors, like me, have a free hand in areas that are strictly military. The civilians are reluctant to tread on shaky ground, trying to keep themselves busy with such matters as food, education, and building hospitals. You're going to see a few civilians running around here and they're pretty damn good. You see, the whole idea behind an advisory team, any advisory team, is to correspond to the Vietnamese staff. We all have our counterparts on the province chief's staff. Do you know what a province chief is?" he asked.

"Is he the senior Vietnamese official in the Province?" I ventured, trying to remember what they'd told us about this position in Saigon. The colonel laughed.

"Well, in a way. You see, the province chief owns the province, damn near. Our province chief is a lieutenant colonel in the Vietnamese Army, but he's got a hell of a lot more power than any lieutenant colonel you've ever seen. He's my counterpart and I advise him. My staff advises his staff, right on down the line. In the districts, the district chiefs answer to him and the district senior advisors answer to me. I've probably got you pretty well confused by now, but it'll all fall in place after a while. Now, what questions you got?" he asked, becoming serious again.

"Well sir, to start with, where do I fit into the system? They told us in Saigon we'd be going to a district, but I was told downstairs I'd be here in Province for a while. So right now, I'm a little confused," I explained.

"You'll be here with the province team for a few days. I want to put you in Di An District, right here"—he pointed to a bulge on the western side of the province map—"but I have another lieutenant out there right now. He's leaving for Saigon in a few days and when he goes, I'll give you Di An. Okay, Cook?" he asked.

"Yes sir," I replied, considering for a second the possibility of me going back to Saigon and letting the lieutenant stay there in Di An. We talked for a few minutes more and then the colonel and I walked downstairs to meet the rest of his staff.

All things considered, life was pretty good at Bien Hoa; no one would or could deny it. We lived in a large house called the 'villa' by its occupants. Perhaps at one time, it had been worthy of this description, but it bore little resemblance to what I expected a villa to look like. I shared a room with two other lieutenants under conditions better than I'd expected, and the food was good. Parks and Weston, my two roommates, filled me in on the way of life at the villa.

"For three bucks a week you get your laundry done," Parks told me. "The mommasons come right to the villa and do it so you don't have to wait around for it. You leave what you want washed laying on the floor and it'll be done in the afternoon. Don't leave anything valuable laying out. It saves a lot of hassle. If you want something locked up, there's a safe in the bar. Give it to Weston, he's the Bar Officer."

"What about boots? Do they shine the boots, too?" I asked.

"If you want 'em to. But I'd do 'em myself the first few times, till they get broke in good. If you don't, they'll put too much polish on 'em, trying to get a shine," he advised.

Weston, a red-headed first lieutenant from North Carolina, explained how the bar fund worked.

"You can charge anything you want in the bar. Just be sure you mark it down on your page in the book. Then pay at the end of the month. That way you don't have to carry any money around with you," he explained.

"Do you guys work on the weekends?" I asked. Parks was the engineer advisor and Weston had the title of civil affairs coordinator. They looked at each other and laughed.

"Are you kidding? Hell no, we don't do anything on the weekends except maybe drive into Saigon or over to the airbase to see if there's any new stereo equipment in the PX. The only advisors that work on the weekends is them poor bastards down in the districts. Remember, you're at Province now, and nobody here does a hell of a lot," Parks told me.

"That's right," Weston reinforced, "and don't you forget it. All you got to do is look busy when you see the Old Man and don't make any mistakes like insulting the province chief and keep your nose clean, and they'll forget about you here. The name of the game here is to stay at Province. The last thing you want to do is have your young ass shipped down to a district. We get reports that there's a war going on down there."

This must have been a private joke between the two of them, but I didn't find it funny at all.

"Say, are you going to be with us permanent?" Parks asked, quickly.

"Well, right now, I'm working in the S-2 shop as the assistant intelligence advisor," I said.

"Hey, that's great; you've got it made," Parks shouted and Weston agreed, both looking a little relieved.

"But," I continued, "in a few days I'm going to take a vacancy in Di An."

After a few days in the villa, I realized that Parks had told the truth; nobody did a hell of a lot at Province. As the assistant intelligence advisor, I simply sat in the S-2 Advisor's office and read the various intelligence reports that came up from the districts. All this information was supposed to be put together in such a way that would allow "the big picture" to emerge, and Province would then be able to give guidance to those people working in the districts collecting intelligence. And for a while, I actually believed this. I was to discover later, while in Di An, this was not the case.

I had been on the Province team for nearly three weeks before I was notified that the intelligence advisor at Di An had been transferred to Saigon. This news didn't make me jump for joy, but during my time at Bien Hoa, I realized that I really wasn't needed in the Province hierarchy. I realized, too, if I ever hoped to gain any insight or understanding about the war, it would have to come from somewhere outside my contact with other Americans like myself. And, since I had no say in the matter anyway, I decided to make the best of it.

It was in the middle of June before I was introduced to Lieutenant Colonel Andersen, the senior advisor from Di An. Usually, the DSA is a major, but he had been promoted while at Di An and had been allowed to remain for the rest of his tour. I met him at the Province Headquarters and introduced myself.

"So you're Cook, huh? They told me you'd be coming to Di An," he said in a noncommital tone.

He was a big man, about forty, showing definite signs of an increasing waistline. His hair was nonexistent except for a little bit right on top, apparently left by a sympathetic barber who didn't have the heart to leave him completely bald. I felt guilty about my shaggy head which sported at least an inch of hair on top, fearful he would label me a hippy right then and there.

"You doing these people in good up here?" he asked, attempting to be gruff.

"I don't think so sir. I really don't have a whole lot to do," I replied.

"Well, we'll change that in a hurry when you get down to Di An." His fatigues were not starched as Colonel Williams's had been. They had more of a functional appearance about them as if he fit into them better and had been wearing them longer.

"You be ready to leave this damn place tomorrow morning. I've got it all squared away with Colonel Williams. Jackson'll be up after you," he ordered in the same gruff tone. Then he smiled, "You're gonna like Di An, Cook."

Sergeant First Class Robert Jackson was a powerful, well-built man with a deep, very dark suntan. His jungle flop hat was pulled low over his eyes to give some protection from the sun so that he had to tilt his head back to talk to anyone. It was obvious that he spent a lot of time on operations. His faded, well-worn jungle fatigues were almost threadbare, especially at the knees. They offered a sharp contrast to my bright green, new fatigues, the only thing that positively identified me as a "new guy"—a person that knew absolutely nothing about what was going on and had to be taught and shown everything. I was certain these thoughts were going through Sergeant Jackson's mind, but he said nothing about them.

As he helped me load my meager belongings on the jeep, he gave me an idea of what to expect in Di An.

"You'll like Di An, sir. Down there you're going to get a chance to see what this whole damn turkey shoot is all about."

I told him that was exactly what I had in mind.

"We're glad to get you, too," he continued, "we need somebody that can tell us where the little bastards are hiding. Once we find them, we can fix their wagon good."

He winked at me as if we were sharing a private joke and I smiled.

I liked him right away. There appeared to be nothing phony about him; perhaps it was the square jut of his jaw that gave me this confidence, but at any rate he knew a hell of a lot more about what was happening in this part of the world than I did, and I was prepared to learn from him all I could.

After picking up the mail from the mail room, we were on our way to Di An. Jackson's jeep had no top and the open air felt good. Five minutes out of Bien Hoa put us in open country, with rice paddies on both sides of the road. The greenness and lushness of the countryside, coupled with the clean fresh air offered a sharp contrast to Saigon and Bien Hoa with their dirt and pollution. We passed a large Chinese cemetery on the side of a hill, then more rice paddies. At a crossroads, Jackson hung a right that immediately put us in the middle of a tremendous rubber plantation. The endless rows of trees were all in perfect alignment, set out in parallel rows. I was unable to find a single tree out of place. They had grown up about thirty feet and then branched out to form a thick, green canopy of leaves on top that shut out must of the sunlight. But inside the plantation, it was open, with the space between trees never varying. The branches of the trees on the right of the road had joined with those on the left, forming a tunnel some thirty feet above. I had a very strange feeling as we travelled through this tunnel, and Jackson sensed my apprehension.

"Don't worry sir," he told me "you'll get used to it."

I doubted this ever happening, but I nodded in agreement.

When we arrived at the district, Colonel Andersen was waiting for me in front of the building that housed the advisors. Hanging from the side of the building was a nearly dilapidated shingle bearing a faded MACV crest and three words—DI AN ADVISORY TEAM. It threatened to brain some unsuspecting passerby at any moment as it swung innocently back and forth over the entrance.

"Welcome to the team, Cook. Come on in and I'll introduce you to the rest of the bunch," the colonel was saying as he nearly pulled me out of the jeep.

I followed him through a sandbagged passage way into what had to be the radio room or operations center. Maps covered two walls and three big radios took up most of the third. The first man I met here was the radio operator, Specialist Wilson. The colonel introduced us.

"How are you doing, Wilson?" I asked.

"Just fine, sir," he replied.

Wilson was a big kid, about six foot, almost two hundred pounds. He had just enough nose to keep his Army glasses from falling off his freckled face, a condition that made him appear much younger than he actually was. It was obvious that he took much pride in the immaculate appearance of the radio room. His fatigues looked like Jackson's—faded and worn—which told me he had at least survived a long time in Di An. He spoke with a slow, southern drawl, but I had a feeling it was about the only thing slow about him.

We passed on through the radio room into a room that looked like a lounge. There were a couple of bookcases against the wall, filled with paperbacks, and a big wicker coach with three matching chairs. Here I met Sergeant First Class Dalton, the medical advisor and Staff Sergeant Mason, the advisor for the Regional Force and Popular Force units in the district. Dalton was tall and thin, causing his fatigues to look loose on his frame. His face had a gaunt and haggard look which made his long nose seem even longer, and his ears protruded more than they should have, as if they were repelled by the sides of his head.

Mason was much shorter and heavier than Dalton with no

distinguishing characteristics that I immediately noticed. Again the faded fatigues that were beginning to give me a complex. Both men welcomed me to the team, and I told them I was glad to be there.

"Don't go to Saigon with Dalton. He knows all the women down there and he'll get you in trouble," the colonel said.

Everyone looked at Dalton, who was turning a little red, and laughed. The colonel's remark helped break the tension that every new man on an advisory team brings with him, and everybody relaxed a bit.

"Lieutenant Cook is our new intelligence advisor," the colonel continued. "Everything here will be new to him until he gets his feet on the ground—just like it was to all of us. He's going to need our help, so let's help him any way we can."

He looked at me and said, "If you have any questions, which you are sure to have, don't hesitate to ask us. In a few weeks you'll feel like you've been here all your life and everything will fall into place."

I thanked all of them and told them I was sure to have questions and told them again how glad I was to be in Di An.

On the wall above the couch was a poster which read, in big, bold letters, "CAUTION—VIETNAM MAY BE HAZARDOUS TO YOUR HEALTH." At other strategic places on the walls the centerfolds of past "Playboy's Playmates" were prominently displayed. They gave the place a homey atmosphere, and I decided I would get to like the place and people very much.

The colonel suggested we have a drink to celebrate my arrival. I really didn't think my arrival was such a big deal, but we followed him into the next room which just happened to be the bar. I was impressed with the bar, which was made from bamboo strips cleverly woven together. The top of the bar was a piece of polished plywood, trimmed in black imitation leather. Eight bar stools surrounded this masterpiece. The colonel served as bartender, which meant he removed six cans of Schlitz from the small refrigerator behind the bar, opened them, and gave one to each of us. We then all drank a toast to the President, the district, the Advisory Team, and finally, with the little that was left, we drank a toast to me. I got the impression that this group of men was very close knit. It was all over in a few minutes and Mason, Dalton, Wilson and Jackson, each of them with their own duties to attend to, left the colonel and me alone.

"We have a great team here, John," the colonel told me. "It won't always be easy, and you're going to see some rough times before you leave, but—" he paused briefly, then continued after finding the right words—"by God, I wouldn't want to be any other place in Vietnam than right here."

My reasons for wanting to leave Bien Hoa now seemed valid. There was an intensity about this man that made his words believable, and there was something in his eyes that said, more than any carefully chosen words could ever say, that he understood.

"Tomorrow I'll introduce you to Major Chau," the colonel said. "He's the district chief. You'll also meet his staff and some of the people you'll be working with. But right now I'm going to let you get settled and unpack your gear. Your room will be in the back"—he pointed to a place directly behind the bar—"Jackson will show you."

I followed him into the radio room where Jackson and Wilson were working on plans for artillery support of a night operation. After he was finished, Jackson helped me unload my gear and led the way to my future home. The room was small but adequate. I had a wall locker that worked and a couple of shelves over my bed.

I was happy with the room, but I wasn't happy with the design of the building. There was only one way out of my little rathole, and that was through the bar. This could have proved to be troublesome in case of fire or a mortar attack. The narrow passageway from the bar to my room was unlighted, making it necessary for me to grope along the wall until I ran into the door. The kitchen was the room beyond the bar, provided I proceeded in a straight line from the lounge. On that first day in Di An, I was convinced the building had been designed as a Chinese puzzle palace, and then leased to the Americans who weren't supposed to know the difference.

By the time I unpacked, it was supper time. I soon discovered that supper was the most important meal, because it was here that the activities of the day were discussed—usually with everyone present, which was not always the case with breakfast or lunch, due to operational necessity. Another important fact was revealed at this time—everyone had his own place at this table. The colonel sat at the end of the table, flanked by Jackson on his left, and Dalton on his right. Wilson was to the left of Jackson and Mason occupied the seat to the right of Dalton. The colonel indicated that I was to sit at the other end of the table, which I did.

My first meal at Di An was a pleasant surprise—roast beef, baked

31

potatoes, sliced tomatoes and hot rolls. The man who made all this possible was our Vietnamese cook, Thoi. Actually, Thoi was a Popular Force soldier who had been "lent" to the Advisory Team so long before that no one on the team knew exactly when he cooked his first meal for the advisors. The most plausible story I heard was that Thoi joined the first group of advisors in Di An in 1965. He still performed normal soldier duties at night, such as guard duty, but he was excluded from daily combat operations. For his services to the advisors, Thoi earned 3,500 piasters per month, roughly equal to thirty dollars. And he collected his monthly salary as a soldier, which was another 3,500 piasters. All this made Thoi quite happy.

The interpreter for the team was Sergeant First Class Luon Bao Chi, who had been supplied by the army of South Vietnam. Actually Chi was much more than an interpreter—he was a member of the team with his own place at the table, on my right. Before the war he had held a very important position with Pan American Airlines in Saigon, earning several times the salary of a Vietnamese sergeant. But he had been drafted, along with thousands of other highly trained Vietnamese and, because of his command of English, was made an interpreter.

During my first months particularly, and throughout the entire period I was in Di An, I depended very much on this extraordinary man, as did every other advisor. His first translation for me occurred right after dinner, when I remarked how much better the food was here than in Bien Hoa. It was the kind of thing you're supposed to say (common courtesy demands it) but I really meant it. Sergeant Chi immediately related this to Thoi in his native language and this pleased Thoi. He grinned from ear to ear, clearly indicating that I now had one friend in a most important position.

As Thoi cleared the table, there was some general conversation concerning the day's activities. Sergeant Dalton had been to one of the evacuation hospitals at Long Binh, where he had managed to convince a couple of the doctors that they should visit one of the villages in Di An to treat the sick. Soliciting aid from the Americans for the villagers was part of his Medical Civic Action Program. I soon discovered he was quite good at this, and that his program was one of the best in the country. Mason had taken one of the Popular Force platoons to the rifle range, and he related their progress in marksmanship to the team. Jackson spent most of the day coordinating an upcoming combined operation that would involve units of the First Infantry Division and the District Forces. Since nothing exciting had occurred that day involving either Wilson or me, he and I kept quiet.

When all had been said, everyone, except Wilson who returned to the operations room, adjourned to the bar. Sergeant Chi managed the bar which operated pretty much on the honor system. He provided a large book with each man's account listed on a separate page along with the price of the beer and mixed drinks—just like the system at Bien Hoa. When no one served as bartender, each man marked on his page what he had taken. At the end of the month Chi computed the totals, and the accounts were paid. It was a simple, efficient method that kept the bar operating. Chi explained the system to me and then turned to a blank page in the book to "open my account." With more pomp than the occasion warranted, I charged my first beer. It was fifteen cents—with no carrying charge.

About eight that evening, Wilson announced that he was prepared to show the movie. This was an additional benefit I had not expected in the district. The movies were picked up each day at the First Division Base Camp, located some three miles from our compound, and returned the following morning. Each team member was qualified to operate the projector, picked up somewhere by Dalton on one of his many "scrounging" runs to Long Binh. The duty of running the projector rotated every night, and I was informed that in due time, I would be running it with the same skill and efficiency that the other members had. I had my reservations about that time ever arriving.

That evening we saw *The Graduate*, which was a smash hit with the team. The colonel popped corn during the break between the first and second reels, while I watched the complex operation of threading the film through the projector. Wilson looked at me and smiled.

"Looks easy, don't it?" he asked.

"Hell no," I replied.

In fact, it looked impossible, but in time I managed to accomplish this difficult and important task, which I consider one of my crowning achievements as an advisor.

After the movie was over and the popcorn gone, everyone went to

33

bed except the man on radio watch. The districts were required to maintain radio contact with the Province Operations Center around the clock. Radio watch consisted of sitting in the radio room, fully awake, ready to respond to any emergency instructions sent down from Province, or passing to Province any urgent message involving the team or the district. This duty was broken up in shifts, usually two hours a night. Everyone pulled this duty except the senior advisor. As with the movie, I was told as soon as I became more familiar with the operations in the district, I would be doing this also.

Dalton had the first shift that night, so I went in and talked to him about how it worked, and he explained the emergency procedures to follow in case of an attack or some other natural disaster. He showed me how certain areas were cleared for artillery fire, explaining that no artillery could be fired anywhere in the district without the approval of the district chief. If, for example, an American unit needed artillery fire in an area, they would have to contact us, and the advisor on watch would have to get the approval of Major Chau from the Vietnamese duty officer, who was located next door. He showed me the procedure for calling a medical evacuation (or dust-off) helicopter in case someone was wounded.

As Dalton talked, I suddenly realized that our survival in the district depended on these radios. This was no training exercise, this was real—live and in color—and one mistake by the man on duty could result in a real disaster. However, just because I realized this important fact didn't make it an original thought. A sense of urgency about this small group of men influenced everything they did. If this was not always obvious, it was because they had learned to live with it; but that urgency was always there, just beneath the surface.

Long after everyone else was asleep, Dalton and I were discussing the operations of the radio room, politics on the home front and the beauty of Vietnamese women. When I finally left him and went to bed about midnight, it was with a sense of finally belonging to a unit that had a purpose that went much deeper that its own existence. And this was a most gratifying thought indeed.

The next morning, just as the colonel had promised, I met the district chief and his staff. Major Nguyen Minh Chau was impressive to say the least. Due to previous wounds suffered in

combat he was forced to walk with a cane but this in no way distract-
ed from his commanding presence; in fact, it seemed to enhance his
image. His right arm was partially paralyzed, and he didn't have
full control of his leg due to a piece of shrapnel pressing against his
spinal cord. Walking was an extremely painful ordeal for this man,
and the constant pain was reflected in the tight little lines around
his eyes. But this was the only place it showed. Because of his
position as district chief, he was a natural target for Viet Cong
assassination units, but this fact seemed to have no effect on him.
Three months after our initial meeting, Major Chau would be
seriously wounded in an unsuccessful assasination attempt by the
Viet Cong.

After I had been introduced all around by Colonel Andersen,
Major Chau invited me to his house to meet his family, but I made a
mental note to get back to Lieutenant Hau, the district intelligence
Officer, later in the day. I was surprised that he was willing to run
the risk of having his family with him in the compound; most
district chiefs were reluctant to do this. Mrs. Chau was the perfect
hostess, being well prepared for my visit. She served us small, cream
filled cakes and tea but did not join us in these refreshments. As she
moved back and forth between the living room and the kitchen, I
noticed that she was remarkably well-preserved for a woman who
had given birth to six children. Major Chau introduced me to the
young Chaus—four girls and two boys—who gave me a careful
going over, trying to determine if I was suitable for being in their
district. Apparently, I passed their test, for after a few minutes'
scrunity, they disappeared.

Although our first meeting was brief, it gave the district chief an
opportunity to look over the newest member of the Advisory Team,
and it gave me some insight into the things that motivated him—a
wife and six children. Later, when I knew him better, I would learn
other things that compelled Major Chau to become Vietnam's most
successful district chief.

After leaving Major Chau, I returned to the radio room where
First Lieutenant Tran Phuc Hau was waiting to show me his
operations. Lieutenant Hau's organization—The District Intelligence and Operations Coordination Center (DIOCC)—was located
next door to Advisory Team headquarters. It was in this center
that Lieutenant Hau "did his thing."

My only justification for being in Di An was to work in the DIOCC, assisting and advising Hau in putting together a successful attack against the Viet Cong Infrastructure. In fact, the only justification for the DIOCC's existence was accomplishing this end. And during my second day in Di An, this enormous task scared the hell out of me.

For a Vietnamese, Hau was big—about five foot eight, and a hundred and eighty pounds. His round face made it difficult for him to show any expression other than an ever-present smile. He spoke English, so there was no need for an interpreter when he introduced me to the members of the center. Each intelligence agency in the district was represented here; they had told us in Saigon that it would be this way, and it was. Hau showed me his files and explained how they processed the intelligence reports sent to the center by his agents in the hamlets and villages. Everyone was smiling a very polite, dignified smile, but I knew behind these smiles they were assessing me, wondering if this big, brand-new American could make any meaningful contributions to their fledgling operation. I was wondering the same thing when Hau picked up a piece of paper from the desk of the National Police representative and showed it to me.

"Tonight we go on ambush. Here is very good information," he said.

I looked at the paper he gave me and then handed it back.

"Can you come with me, Thieu Uy?" he asked, using the Vietnamese equivalent for second lieutenant.

It was more than a question or a simple invitation to participate in some nighttime activity; it was more of a direct challenge.

"It will be an honor for me to go," I accepted without realizing the full significance of what I was saying. This apparently pleased everyone, for they all beamed their approval.

I had been in the district less than twenty-four hours and already I'd met the district chief, his staff, and even agreed to accompany my newfound counterpart on an ambush. If this rate continued, boredom would not be a problem in Di An District.

They had warned us in Saigon about being overly optimistic toward establishing quick, personal relationships. Apparently, the Vietnamese were supposed to be hard to get to know and even harder to like, but for some reason I didn't feel Hau fit this stereotype. I realized that he had reservations about me, and it would probably be a long time before he accepted me completely, but it seemed to me that we hit it off together right away, and I was determined not to underestimate him, which was the classic mistake among too many advisors. And I planned on making every effort to learn all I could about Hau's problems. I would make mistakes; this much was certain. But I wanted my mistakes to be as original as possible.

Now it is time for coffee," Hau announced after the brief tour of the center. With Chi leading the way, we walked up the street to the local coffee shop where I was introduced to Vietnamese coffee. The shop owner, and old fellow with a Ho Chi Minh beard, greeted Hau and Chi and shook my hand. He escorted us to the back of his dimly lit establishment where the three of us sat around a small, low table on very short stools. Hau said something to the old man and a couple of minutes later, a young girl brought us three small glasses with a little tin pot on each glass.

"Do you see before?" Hau asked.

"No," I replied, "How does it work?"

"You watch and you will see," he told me pridefully.

The tin pot was a miniature "dripolator" that allowed the coffee to drip into the glass. A thick, sweet cream covered the bottom of the glass, slowly turning a light brown as it mixed with the hot coffee. As we waited for the coffee to stop dripping, I casually informed Chi that I was going on an ambush that night.

"Yes, I know Thieu Uy. Already Troung Uy tells me," Chi casually responded, lifting the tin pot off his glass. He looked at Hau and winked, and I knew then that the offer to go with Hau had been a setup. This was going to be their acid test for me, and I was glad I had recklessly accepted the invitation, although I had no idea what we would run into, or even if Colonel Andersen would approve of such a venture.

As I sipped the coffee, I thought about it all, trying to sort it out in my mind. The coffee wasn't bad; just a little stronger than what I'd been used to, but not bad. After finishing two glasses apiece, Hau paid the old man and we walked back to the compound.

When we got back, I told the colonel about agreeing to accompany Hau and his troops on the ambush that night, fully expecting to get my ass chewed out. He was packing M-16 clips.

37

"I know all about it, Cook. I'll be going, too." He smiled as he shoved the clips in his ammo pouch.

This was one shock I wasn't prepared for, since Colonel Andersen sure as hell didn't appear to fit the aggressive, "gung-ho" role. For one thing, his 220 pounds seemed to put a strain on his five-foot-ten-inch frame—a condition that could cause a lot of misery in the rice paddies. And he wasn't the youngest man on the team either; but the real shocker was the colonel agreeing to go on the ambush with so little time left in Vietnam, a condition commonly referred to as being "short." One of the most sacred of the unwritten laws governing Americans in Vietnam went something like this: "Those who are short will take no unnecessary risks." I had been taught this at Bien Hoa by my roommates; and it appeared that the ambush the colonel planned on accompanying fell clearly within the realm of an "unnecessary risk," since it was not required that he participate.

But things were not always as they appeared to be and one by one, many of my preconceived ideas about the war and its people fell by the wayside. I had formed opinions too quickly and in so doing I had made one of the most common, most serious mistakes a "new guy" was capable of making. Perhaps I had been searching subconsciously for the John Wayne type, and when I failed to find him, I was shocked. Or perhaps I thought that survival should be uppermost in everyone's mind since, at this point, it was uppermost in mine. But the truth involved neither a hero fixation nor a coward's complex. Quite simply, the colonel had given me my first lesson in dedication to duty and a cause to believe in—a cause that would later push my survival into the category of "serious consideration," permanently terminating its status as an "obsession."

The ambush was planned to take place in an area about three miles from District Headquarters. After supper, the colonel and Hau discussed such things as how many soldiers were going and the types of weapons they would be bringing. Then they showed me the area on the map—a dark green spot between the grid lines, surrounded by the little symbols used to depict rice paddies. About six o'clock we climbed aboard the district's operation vehicle, a battered and battle-scarred, three-quarter-ton truck, and proceeded to the point where we would be dropped off.

Hau and I climbed in the back of the truck with the twelve members of the Province Reconnaissance Unit (PRUs)—the bulk of our ambush force—and the colonel rode up front with the driver. I had the radio that would, hopefully, keep us in touch with the district.

The PRUs had been sent down to the district in an eighteen-man team to assist in the elimination of the Viet Cong Infrastructure. They were highly trained on conducting long range patrols, raids, ambushes, and specialized "snatch" operations, a term derived from the practice of kicking down the door of an Infrastructure member's home and snatching him. They were normally used on operations that had all the indications of making contact with the enemy; the more common, routine sweep operations were left to the more common, routine soldiers. Due to their small number and high degree of specialization PRUs were not used as regular army units. Most of their backgrounds were quite interesting and colorful. Some were former Viet Cong and North Vietnamese who, for reasons known only to themselves, had decided to switch sides. Others were former convicts who had committed a wide variety of crimes, including rape, robbery and even murder. They could have been accurately labeled social outcasts for many reasons, but there was one characteristic they all shared, a characteristic that pulled them together more than anything else. It was an uncompromising hatred for the enemy. This hatred was directly responsible for their high degree of success against both the Viet Cong and the North Vietnamese, causing them to be almost fearless in combat. Because they were considered an elite group, they were paid much more than the average Vietnamese soldier, receiving both their training and pay from the United States.

The truck we rode in had a colorful background, also. Large pieces of both front fenders and the hood had been shot away, exposing the front tires and radiator. The advisors had christened it "Claymore" since most of this damage had been caused by Viet Cong ambushes. The ambushers had employed claymore mines, a very common, popular weapon that is quite effective against people and, in this case, vehicles as well. Aside from the damage caused by the mines, there were several bullet holes in the body of the truck. The left windshield was shattered and the right one was missing altogether. Neither headlight functioned, which restricted the vehicle's usefulness to daylight hours. One headlight was broken and the other dangled uselessly by a piece of wire from the fender. Both doors had been removed to make entry and exit as rapid as possible. Only a maniac would be willing to drive such a contraption—and we had one.

At the reckless, breakneck speed of forty miles an hour, the driver managed to get us to the drop-off point in about five minutes. After we disembarked, the truck returned to the compound, since night was approaching. There was still nearly half an hour of daylight left, so we moved into a clump of palm trees to await the darkness. Once it grew dark, we would move into our ambush position. These few minutes gave us an opportunity to make final preparations and checks on equipment and weapons. Hau talked to the PRUs about their exact positions in the ambush site. In much the same way a football coach outlines a particular play, Hau drew a diagram on the ground with an M-16 round and, in the fading sunlight, explained exactly where each man would be and what he would do. They listened with all the excited anticipation of a team preparing for the big game.

I called Wilson to make sure the radio was working and also to be certain he was standing by in case we needed help. I then took the radio off my back and checked my rifle and ammo pouch, making sure my extra magazines were arranged so I could get to them in a hurry. I leaned back against a palm tree to enjoy one last cigarette. Most of the PRUs were smoking their last cigarette for the night and seemed happy and confident.

The colonel walked over to the radio and picked up the handset. "I just called Wilson and it's loud and clear," I told him.

"Good, real good." He put the handset down. "We'll be moving out in about five minutes. You feel okay?" he asked.

I nodded numbly, not really feeling anything.

"If the radio gets heavy, let me take it. Alright?"

I told him I would, and then we went over the procedure we would use to make periodic checks with Wilson. Each hour we would notify Wilson that all was well by depressing the button on the radio's handset. This would create a loud, rushing sound in the radio at district, but there would be no noise on the ambush site. If all hell broke loose, then there would be no point in maintaining radio silence, and radio communication would be more conventional and possibly more desperate.

The darkness fell on the palm trees slowly, like dew, and when only the outline of the man next to me was visible, we stood up and moved out of the clump of trees, single file. I walked ahead of the colonel and behind Lieutenant Hau. Most of the PRUs were in front of us, swallowed up by the darkness. The only sound came from the tall grass slapping against our legs. We crossed a road and then a small stream and slipped under a barbed wire fence. For about three hundred yards we followed an irrigation ditch and then passed a cluster of houses on the left. Light from kerosene lamps shown through the windows and I could see children playing in front of the houses. They were chasing each other and laughing, completely unaware of our presence or our mission.

Beyond the houses was an open space of one hundred yards and then more rice paddies. Even though it was dark, Hau was taking the extra precaution of not going directly to the ambush site. He was circling around it and approaching from the rear, making it impossible to anticipate our destination, in the event we had been observed.

Finally we reached it—a group of dry rice paddies surrounded on three sides by trees. The paddies had not been planted that year because of the Viet Cong tax collectors—the farmers had seen no reason to plan their crops and then give them to the Viet Cong, so they had simply left. Some had gone to Saigon, some to Bien Hoa, others had just vanished. Since there was no rice planted in the paddies there was no water either, which made it much more comfortable.

The PRUs took up their positions along two of the low earthen dikes built by the farmers to retain the water. The two dikes, each about two feet high, came together to form an L. Hau, the colonel, and I got behind the dikes at the point they came together, with the dikes between us and the area formed by the two arms of the L. The idea was to let the Viet Cong walk into them and then catch them in the cross fire.

Quietly, I removed the radio from my back and sat down. I felt good to be free of the extra weight. I leaned against the dike, allowing the coolness of the earth to soothe my aching legs and back. There was just enough moonlight to see the dim silhouettes of the PRUs atop the dikes. They were only a few yards away but the

41

darkness seemed to magnify the distance. Claymore mines were placed in front of the dikes, making the ambush more effective. They would be detonated electrically if there was any contact.

The colonel removed a headset for the radio from his pocket so that he could monitor the radio without it giving away our position. I checked and rechecked my ammo pouches, making sure I could find them in a hurry, and placed my right thumb on the safety lever of my M-16.

Now there was nothing left to do but wait. Everything up to this point had happened quickly, much too quickly, and now, all of a sudden, we were waiting for the enemy to come walking into our neatly laid trap.

Strangely enough, I felt neither apprehension nor fear, even though we were well prepared to destroy a number of people at any moment. There was excitement because there was anticipation, but I had felt the same excited anticipation before, while deer hunting, waiting for a big buck to appear. This time it was different; I knew it was different because we were hunting men, not deer. My mind drew this distinction for me, but emotionally they were both the same.

Mentally, I tried to place myself in the position of the Viet Cong who were out there, somewhere in the darkness, but soon found it impossible to imagine what he was thinking. It was impossible because I had no frame of reference to draw from. Perhaps, if they were out there, they were thinking absolutely nothing. I was certain he was not thinking of dying, so I pushed the thought aside and allowed the activity of the past two days to filter through my mind.

Two days ago, I had known nothing of these people I was now accompanying on this desperate mission. Now, lying in an abandoned rice paddie somewhere in Di An District, I was depending on them to see that I left this rice paddie safely. And it all seemed just a little ridiculous, too. Here we were, waiting to kill some people we had never seen. It was this possibility that bound us together more than anything else, in much the same way that business enterprises are formed—for the purpose of doing business. Our business was to kill.

I waited for something to happen that would break the awful silence that descended on the rice paddie, but at the same time I was hoping that the silence would remain to protect me. I didn't know how I would react if it were taken away and we had to do the things we had come to do.

There was a cool breeze blowing, just enough to gently sway the tops of the trees at the edge of the paddie. The breeze was refreshing, bringing the desire to sleep, to forget where I was and what we were planning. In the distance from the direction we had walked, there were rifle shots, perhaps a dozen or so. It was hard to determine just how far away they were, but there was no doubt it was gunfire.

The night dragged on. I soon discovered that it was impossible to measure time on an ambush. What seemed like hours was actually only a few minutes, with the stillness of the night slowly stretching each second. It was so quiet I could hear the ticking of the colonel's watch, above his slow, rhythmic breathing.

It was about ten o'clock when it happened. The colonel had just given Wilson the ten o'clock radio signal that all was well when the rice paddie came apart. First there was the simultaneous explosion of the claymores, followed immediately by the dull, throaty roar of the M-60 machine gun. Then the PRUs on the dikes opened fire. I could hear the explosions caused by the grenade launchers—we had three of those. I was still lying with my back against the dike, watching tracer rounds of the Viet Cong's return fire pass over the dike when the colonel started shouting.

"We've got the little sons of bitches now! We really got 'em, Cook! Crawl up there and see what's going on!"

For the first time in my life, I knew what it was like to feel paralyzing fear, a fear that forced me against the paddie dike as though each rifle shot was a rivet, stitching me to the cold, soft earth. The paralysis passed after a few seconds, but the fear remained. I was content to remain where I was with my back against the dike, hoping that the firing would stop and everything would return to normal. But the firing didn't stop, so slowly I crawled to the top of the dike for a firsthand view.

Someone had fired a hand flare and it did a fairly good job of illuminating the area inside the L. I could see a number of bodies lying still in the paddie and more crawling away. One PRU at the end of the dike was shouting orders to the others, trying to direct their fire on those still crawling.

It was a sickening sight, unequaled by anything I had ever seen. I

43

didn't look too long because we were taking fire from the edge of the paddie that was not illuminated by the hand flare. I slid back down the dike and told the colonel what I'd seen. We relayed our situation to Wilson.

Our exact location had been given to the artillery unit at the division base camp earlier in the day, so they were prepared to fire in our support. We had a choice of either high explosive or illumination rounds. The colonel told Wilson to order illumination rounds, and I crawled back up on the dike with the colonel to wait for its arrival, praying the wait wouldn't be long.

The small hand flare soon burned out, drastically reducing the level of firing but it resumed again a few seconds later when the first illumination round exploded overhead. A second after the thunderous burst, the whole world lit up. Looking up, I saw the source of our instant light swinging slowly back and forth under its parachute. As the PRUs cheered, pieces of the giant, hissing flare broke loose and fell flaming to the ground.

"Get down, goddammit," the colonel shouted, "you wanna get your ass shot off the first time out? It'll burn without you watching it."

I ducked back behind the dike and huddled close to the colonel as he talked to Wilson on the radio.

"The illum's right on the money. Keep it coming while we put the fix on their yellow asses. I don't know how many we got out there. Keep all other traffic off this net. Over."

"That's the best damn way I know of to get your head splattered all over this paddie," he screamed at me as he threw the hand set against the dike. "Now this time just peep over the top, and don't watch the goddamn flare. Watch how I do it."

We inched up the dike until we could barely see into the paddie. From this position, I could clearly see three Viet Cong at the edge of the paddie firing in our direction. The bullets smacked against the dike, spraying cold, wet dirt around the top of my head. I felt the colonel's sweaty hand on my shoulder as I pressed hard against the dike.

"We caught 'em by surprise. They didn't expect the illum this quick," he shouted in my left ear. I looked back at the Viet Cong. This time they were fully exposed to the devastating fire of our machine gunner and the rest of the PRUs. The machine gunner

44

appeared to be more effective than the riflemen as he raked the embattled area back and forth. Two of the Viet Cong folded up, followed almost instantly by the third. One of them kept screaming and another tried to crawl away. The PRUs were shouting excited orders at each other while three of them moved off the dike to attack from the left flank.

But the attack wasn't necessary; the Viet Cong had stopped firing before it came. The illumination rounds kept coming, burning huge holes in the night, and the PRUs continued to fire at the still forms in the paddie. The machine gunner moved over to my position and turned loose a final burst of fire on the Viet Cong, causing the bodies to jerk violently with the savage impact.

Then, just as suddenly as it had started, the firing stopped. The last active Viet Cong had long since stopped moving. Cautiously, the PRUs left the dikes and slowly advanced across the battle scarred paddie, followed by Hau, the colonel and me. The impact of the grenades left small craters in the ground, and the rifle and machine gun fire had chewed up the soft earth, resembling the efforts of a spastic with a pitchfork.

But more serious, permanent damage had been inflicted on the Viet Cong. Blood and pieces of torn flesh covered the ground, making it easy to trace the pathetic last minute movements of the wounded as they had struggled to get out of the killing zone. The damage we had inflicted and its intensity was incredible. Four had been killed in the initial burst of fire or immediately thereafter; those dying last had the longer trails of blood behind them. Two had been killed at the edge of the paddie attempting to escape. Apparently one had escaped, for there was a trail of blood leading out of the paddie, beyond the circle of light.

"This one's hurt bad; he won't get far," the colonel announced after examining the trail. "We should find him in the morning, out there somewhere." He pointed out to the darkness in the general direction of the trail.

The illumination continued to burst overhead as we searched for weapons and documents. One of the Viet Cong had a Chinese K-54, 9mm pistol in his pocket.

"This one is leader. Only leader carry weapon like this," Hau told me with a smile. He shoved the pistol in his belt and continued the search. The remainder of the Viet Cong had been armed with the old Chinese CKC, a 7.62mm, semiautomatic carbine. There were several blood-soaked documents on the bodies that would later aid us in identification. Hau carefully gathered all of these and put them in a small, plastic bag.

The PRUs laughed and joked as they collected the weapons and ammunition. They would be paid a handsome bounty for each enemy weapon, which made their happiness understandable. Rings, watches, and other personal items that Hau had shown no interest in were quickly pulled from stiffening hands by our eager soldiers.

"Kind of an extra incentive," the colonel explained, nodding toward the looters.

"Yea, I guess it does make 'em happy," I said.

"Hell, you think this is something, just wait till you see how they handle the tax collectors," he laughed. When the bodies had been stripped of all valuables, we returned to the dike.

One of our PRUs had sustained a minor flesh wound in the arm. It wasn't serious enough to warrant his evacuation; he could wait until morning. One of his comrades—designated the medic, since he was carrying the medic's bag—tied a field dressing around the wound that stopped the bleeding.

"We've been after these bastards for a long time," the colonel told me. "They belong to a special assasination unit. When the Viet Cong want somebody zapped for not paying taxes or for working with the Americans or police, they send these boys after them." He motioned toward the paddie, then added, "but we fixed their goddamned wagon good this time."

The colonel called Wilson and told him to shut off the illumination, adding that we had a body count of six confirmed and a possibility of seven.

"The artillery people like to know they got something for their money. The body count makes them happy, just as happy as it does us," he told me, "and it makes them respond as quickly as they did tonight. It's important for you to know this, so make note of it." I told him I would.

There was little chance of any more contact that night, but we remained where we were since there was a high risk involved in moving at night. It would be very easy to stumble into a Viet Cong ambush thus changing our status from ambushers to ambushees, and this possibility had very little appeal to me after witnessing the impact an ambush is capable of delivering.

So we waited out the night. The breeze was no longer cool, but actually cold. I had no desire to sleep, not now. Each time I closed my eyes, I could see the torn and bloody bodies and hear the firing, especially the machine gun. I had never seen a human being die before this night. In fact, with the exception of my grandfather, I had never even looked at a corpse. To me, death had always been a mysterious happening, encased in calmness and dignity, with flowers on the casket and soft organ music in the background. My grandfather had looked peaceful, lying there in comfortable softness with the casket open, showing all those who mourned his passing that there was nothing to fear from death. There had been nothing grotesque or violent about it, nothing to equate it to what I had just witnessed. I kept telling myself that if I went to sleep, I would wake up and discover that it had all been a bad dream, a nightmare. But there was an awful quality of realism about the thing we'd just done that would never let it become just a dream. The calmness and dignity of death was shattered forever, giving way to the more awesome quality of war.

The rest of the night passed without incident. The sound of planes taking off and landing at Bien Hoa a few miles to the east broke the monotonous chirping of the jungle bugs. Occasionally someone would slap a mosquito, drawing muffled reprimands from his comrades. Hau got up periodically and moved among the ambushers, shaking those who were sleeping. The colonel dozed at my side, undisturbed by sounds of the restless night.

As the first streaks of light lit the predawn greyness of the eastern sky, we prepared to move out. The PRUs moved off the dike, stretching and yawning and talking. Some were smoking and laughing, still congratulating themselves over the successful ambush. But it wasn't over yet—there was still the unfinished business of the blood trail. Now we could clearly see that it led to the edge of the paddie and into the tall grass. Hau gave the task of following the trail to two PRUs who soon disappeared in the thicket. A moment later we heard their shouts.

"They find VC," Hau translated.

They had dragged the body out of the grass by the time the rest of us got to them. He was smaller than the others and looked much younger. There were no documents on him, but he was carrying three hand grenades, one with the handle shot away. After the searching, Hau motioned to the PRUs, and they dragged the body to the center of the paddie where it was united with its other luckless comrades.

The area was searched once again but, other than the last body, we found nothing. Leaving the dead Viet Cong to be buried by the village chief, we walked away, following Hau out of the area via a different route. The sun was already beginning to burn away the early morning dew, a sure indication that the new day was going to be a real scorcher. In thirty minutes we were back on the main road, near our dropoff point the night before.

The truck arrived a few minutes later, and the PRUs rushed to meet it. They excitedly related their exploits to the driver, reenacting the whole ambush for his benefit. The machine gunner mowed down imaginary Viet Cong, while the rifle men picked off the ones he had missed. Other PRUs played the part of the Viet Cong, falling to the ground clutching their stomachs and rolling over in a realistic manner. Only after they were sure the driver understood exactly what they had done did they agree to climb aboard the truck.

There was much laughing and singing as we headed back to District Headquarters. The happiness of the PRUs was contagious and, in spite of what I had witnessed the night before, I was soon laughing with them. We patted each other on the back and told each other that we were "number one"—a phrase every Vietnamese interpreted as "very good" or "well done." There was little question that as far as ambushes go, they had performed magnificently; in fact, they had been one hundred percent effective.

About two miles from the pickup point, a large crowd had gathered near the road. Colonel Andersen motioned for the driver to stop, and we pulled off the road behind the crowd. All of us climbed down to satisfy our curiosity. Working our way through the tightly packed cluster of people, we soon discovered why they had gathered here.

Lying on the ground with their hands tied behind their backs were two men, both Vietnamese. Both had been shot several times through the head and chest. The top of one's head was torn away and his brains were scattered by the road. The other one had been

48

disembowled. Open, unseeing eyes, registering horrible fright, stared wildly at the morning sky. I suddenly remembered the shots we'd heard the night before on the ambush. The distance, direction, number, time—everything pointed here; this was where they'd come from.

I saw Lieutenant Hau talking to a woman standing by herself, away from the crowd. Her hands covered her face, and she was crying quietly. The colonel and I returned to the truck. I pulled a crumpled pack of Pall Malls from my shirt pocket, discovering only one remained unbroken. As I lit it, Hau walked over to us.

"She say VC come last night and take her husband away,"—he pointed to the one with the top of his head torn away—"they take him because they think he work for National Police. They take other man because he is friend of husband. Then they bring them here and shoot them and beat them and cut them with bayonet."

"How many Hau? Does she remember how many VC took her husband away?" the colonel asked.

"She say six, maybe seven." Then a slight smile crossed Hau's face.

"I tell her we kill VC that killed her husband,"—the smile disappeared as he continued—"but she say we kill them too late."

None of us said anything after that. I wanted to say something but I didn't. I wanted to profess some understanding that I could not possibly have. Instead, I smoked my last cigarette in silence and when it was too short to smoke, I dropped it in the dirt and ground it with my heel until it disappeared.

We waited until the PRUs had boarded the truck and we then drove back to the district. I rode up front with the colonel, having no desire to rejoin the laughing PRUs. But there was very little laughing and joking now; the atmosphere was noticeably more subdued. Over the noise of the engine, the colonel was trying to explain to me that this was the nature of war and, in time, I would get used to it.

But I wasn't listening. I was thinking about last night and this morning. It had been a long, agonizing night, marked with violence and death, exposing me to the by-products of war. And later, by the road, I had viewed the war's main product—its purpose for existing. The picture of the dead Viet Cong was replaced in my mind by the picture of the weeping widow refusing to be consoled by Lieutenant

Hau. She was right. We had been too late, therefore we had failed. The fact that this particular squad of terrorists would murder no one else gave her no comfort. How many more times would I be forced to witness the same scene with the same feeling of helpless frustration? How many more husbands would be taken from their homes at night, never to return? This had been the initiation for me, and it had been a costly one. From this point forward, I could no longer afford the luxury of viewing the war objectively or with detached disinterest. The happenings of the past few hours had suddenly made it in my war.

I was tired and sleepy when we returned to the district, but my mind wasn't ready to sleep. There was a breeze blowing, just enough to stir the trees across the street from our compound. Children belonging to the soldiers were playing in the street, and smoke from the cook fires was rising slowly from the dependent's housing behind me. It seemed difficult to believe that a war could possibly be raging in such a beautiful, peaceful place. But it was and I knew someday these children would be soldiers as their fathers were now, and that possibly tomorrow the rising smoke from the dependent's quarters could be the smoking remains of a Viet Cong attack. And the only thing holding this possibility at bay was a pitiful little handful of soldiers and the great equalizer—time. I walked back inside to my room and went to bed.

Chapter Three
THE CENTER

Because I was learning, the first few days in Di An passed quickly. And there was a lot to learn. Since I was there primarily to assist the intelligence operations, it was this area that occupied most of my time and attention.

I was spending the better part of each day in the Intelligence and Operations Center, observing Lieutenant Hau's methods of running this organization. It was here, in this small room beside the advisor's quarters, that we would conduct our experiments to prove the concept behind the Phoenix Program: that the key to defeating the enemy in South Vietnam was to destroy his political structure. We were more concerned with this structure than we were with the main force military units. To be sure, we would provide any useful intelligence we could to the American and South Vietnamese units operating in and around Di An. And we would accompany the district forces on combat operations whenever possible and prosecute the war in a military manner. But our primary purpose was to attempt to eliminate the highly organized political structure that the Viet Cong had built up in each hamlet and village over the years. This organization was a parallel structure, paralleling the legitimate government and its functions at every level. There was a Viet Cong district chief paralleling Major Chau, for example, who was responsible for every action taken by the Viet Cong in Di An. Under this man were the Viet Cong village chiefs, controlling the enemy's action in the villages. And under the villages were the hamlets with their own structure.

It was this organization that made the war "political" rather than "military," dictating every action taken by the enemy. Attacks were launched against government outposts, not to kill government soldiers, but to convince the people that the government could not protect them. Assassinations were carried out, not to eliminate the Viet Cong's enemies, but to prove to the population that the government was unable to prevent them. Each action taken by the

51

Viet Cong and the North Vietnamese had a political objective that far outweighed the military objective, for they had learned long ago that a pure military victory was impossible.

Our plan of attack called for opening a new front against the enemy. No longer was all the emphasis going to be placed on the armed Viet Cong and North Vietnamese regulars. This parallel or "shadow" government established at each level had to be eliminated, since this was the key to all military activity and acts of terror. If this could be accomplished—if we could destroy the hardcore, ideologically motivated, Communist-inspired cadres, there would be no direction or guidance for them.

We knew that the infrastructure was composed of the dedicated members of the party, the People's Revolutionary party or, more correctly, the Communist party of South Vietnam. We also knew that this organization was controlled by the Communist party of North Vietnam or the Lao Dong party. So our attack was really against the southern branch of the North Vietnamese Communist party, operating in South Vietnam. This organization had managed to gain control of a large number of the hamlets and villages in South Vietnam and, by exploiting this control, they were able to extract large amounts of money from the residents through a process known as "tax collection"—a kinder term than "robbery" but both meaning the same thing. Food was obtained in the same manner (by using terror) as was information concerning the district forces. Recruits were taken the same way. If the propaganda agents were unsuccessful in persuading young men and women to join the Viet Cong cause, they were simply kidnapped by armed squads such as the one we had destroyed.

This well-organized organization also provided hiding places and staging areas for the larger military units and provided these units with guides when they were moving through an unfamiliar area. They were responsible for planning, supervising, and directing all activities of the enemy. Simply put, the infrastructure held the key to the war—since this was a political war. By our destroying the infrastructure, the war would cease to exist. This was a fact, and we were gambling on a theory—the Phoenix Program—to get the job done.

Hau and I were trying to put the game plan together that involved all the intelligence-gathering agencies in the district. By combining them, we would have a unified, coordinated attack on the infrastructure. This was the theory I had been taught in Saigon, but it didn't mean much then, for it was only theory. But now it did, because I could see that it was possible. If all went according to plan, all of these agencies would provide the information the center needed; and by putting all the pieces together, we would have a more complete picture of the enemy's structure, allowing us to attack in a more systematic manner.

But I knew, and so did Hau, that the system would work only if all the agencies cooperated, which meant that long standing animosity and distrust among these agencies would have to cease. Traditionally the National Police and the Military Intelligence units did not get along well because neither could trust the other. There was a mutual fear that each was collecting information and "keeping book" on the other. The National Police were afraid of the military in general because the war had increased the military's size and power. The military, on the other hand, was aware of the fact that the war would not last forever, and there was widespread fear that when the war did end the National Police would turn the country into a police state, taking action against any military not in favor with the police. Obviously no progress would be made if these factions opposed each other, since we had to have the support of both. Hau understood this and eventually the police chief, Nguyen Van Tuyen understood it also, and accepted the fact that if the military won, everybody won and if the police lost, everybody lost—the infrastructure was our common enemy, and there were enough of them to keep us from fighting each other.

It became my difficult task to try to remain neutral, which meant that I was not to show any partiality toward either camp. Technically, both Hau and Tuyen were my counterparts, just as the heads of other agencies were, and I walked a tightrope between them, even though Hau was the most competent. He accepted his duties as seriously as he could, which meant that by performing his duties he was certain to incur the wrath of the Viet Cong—a condition that could cost him his life. To say that Hau was prepared to die for what he believed in would be an overstatement on my part. I did not know what he believed in at this point. Everything was hidden behind that ever-present smile, and the fact that he was fat seemed to make him smile even more; it's one of those things that seems to come naturally to fat people. He spent many hours a day in the center, reading the reports from his agents in the hamlets and villages and those from the National Police. This was unusual; in Vietnam the man in charge normally spent very little time doing what he was supposed to do—that's what subordinates were for.

Tuyen, the law enforcer, was different; he abided by tradition. It was difficult to find the snaggletoothed little man during the day and impossible to find him at night, but Hau and I decided to take a chance on finding him in his office in order to conduct some necessary business. We'd just received a report of possible Viet Cong activity in Binh Tri Village and wanted to check it out through the National Police.

We found him at his desk in the dimly lit Police Station, intensely studying the contents of a large shoebox. He was so engrossed in what he was doing that he failed to notice us, looking up only when Hau spoke to him. He seemed to be pleasantly surprised that we were there, standing up immediately and shaking our hands, excitedly pulling us close to the desk. After the greetings were over, he picked up the shoebox and dumped its contents on the desk, indicating with his hand that we were to examine them. I was mildly shocked to discover that the box had been filled with color photographs of naked women.

"Where you get?" I asked in my slowest, most broken English. I knew Tuyen's English was worse than my Vietnamese, but I could tell from his expression that he wanted to speak.

"I do Thieu Uy, I do," he repeated gleefully, pulling an expensive looking Polaroid from his desk. I looked at Hau in bewilderment, searching for an explanation. Confiscating pornography was one thing, well within the realm of a police chief's duties, but producing it was something else.

"Police Chief likes to take pictures of pretty girls. When his wife goes to Saigon to visit family, Tuyen brings girl friends here and take picture. Each time I come to Police Station, I find Tuyen has different pictures," Hau explained, casually looking through Tuyen's latest collection.

"You like, Thieu Uy?" Tuyen asked anxiously, as if my approval was important.

"I like, I like," I told him, smiling my most appreciative smile. This made him happy and he rubbed a large mole on his chin with hair sticking out of it, a sure sign that he was indeed pleased. Hau gave him a big smile, too, and this sent Tuyen into ecstasy. He pulled out a bottle of Martell cognac and three small glasses.

"Now we must drink with Police Chief," Hau informed me. "He is very happy today."

"What about the report?" I asked in reference to our purpose for coming to Tuyen's office.

"Later, we talk about report after we drink and look at pictures," Hau explained.

There was a short discussion between Hau and Tuyen and then Tuyen produced an empty film cartridge from his desk. They both examined it and then the conversation turned to me; both men seemed serious.

"Police Chief wants to know if you will help him, Thieu Uy," Hau interpreted.

"Tell him I'll do anything I can," I answered eagerly, hoping for an opportunity to foster better relations with the National Police and pleased that we were now about to discuss business. Hau gave Tuyen my reply and the police chief rubbed his mole once again.

"He would like for you to get film for his camera at PX. He cannot find on black market anymore." Hau's voice was flat and deadpan, the same tone he would have used if he was telling me the police chief was a Viet Cong agent. I sat there for a moment trying to comprehend what had just happened to me and then I nodded dumbly, giving my approval to support Tuyen's most unusual hobby.

Tuyen proved to be better at photography than at police work. Normally most police activities could be handled by Tuyen's man at the center who, for all practical purposes, ran the Police Station. For this I was grateful, and I limited my visits to Tuyen's office for film delivery only.

By the end of July the center was beginning to function as planned, primarily because Hau was unusually competent and because Major Chau was now convinced that the real enemy was the infrastructure. During the first few weeks I had observed what was happening and I had learned. In the beginning I had offered no advice, but when Hau asked what I thought of his filing system I made a suggestion.

"I think it would be much easier for us if we separated the files of the suspected members from those that we have positively identified as belonging to the infrastructure," I told him tactfully. He looked at me and smiled.

"You are right, Thieu Uy. But we have only one cabinet and it is full. If we do as you say, we will need one more. Where can we get another cabinet?"

I had suggested an improvement and Hau had agreed. We both understood it was my responsibility to provide the improvement. This was the price for giving advice; otherwise, why was I there? I was glad that I had not offered the advice before, but had waited for Hau, my counterpart, to ask for it. This way he saved face and I appeared useful—a small victory for both of us.

"Okay, Troung Uy," I told him, "tomorrow I will go to Bien Hoa and steal a cabinet from the rich Americans there. They will be happy to know that we have so much information that we have nowhere to put it." Everyone in the center laughed.

"Come," he said, "we must have our coffee." And for the first time, Hau put his hand on my shoulder and we walked up the street to the coffee shop.

Chapter Four

THE OPERATION

The rainy season in South Vietnam extends from May through November. It rains nearly every day, often two or three times in one day. And when it isn't raining the sun is boiling down, as if nature isn't content unless Vietnam is receiving something from the sky.

By the first of August my fatigues were beginning to lose their look of newness, and each day it was a little more difficult to identify me as a new guy—a change which I welcomed.

At breakfast one morning, the colonel casually asked if I would like to accompany a sweep operation that day. I had been thinking of doing just that since I'd arrived, but I wanted to get my feet on the ground in the center first, and that I was taking time. It seemed impossible that I had been in Di An a month, but I had. And I knew I had to get out and take a look at it from the ground so the maps and charts that we had in the center would be meaningful.

"Yes sir, I would like that," I told him.

"Okay then, you'll be going with Dalton and Chi," he replied, adding, "try to stay out of trouble."

Aside from being an exceptional medic, Dalton knew more about combat operations than most advisors. He had spent almost three years in Vietnam, walking through rice paddies and working in operating rooms. Most of his time in Vietnam had been spent in operating rooms at the Third Field Hospital in Saigon, where he observed the results of the war firsthand. He came to Di An from another advisory team because he had made the mistake of knowing more about being an advisor than that team's senior advisor did. That situation could not be tolerated, so Dalton was transferred to Di An and our team was far better because of it.

Phuc, our radio bearer, was also going. Phuc had been "given" to the advisors by Major Chau. At one time Phuc had been a Popular Force soldier, but that was before he had fallen victim to bacsi dai, or rice whiskey. He had not been very dependable as a soldier, and when Major Chau found out about Phuc's problem he decided to give Phuc another chance, this time with the Americans. After all, how could he screw up the job of carrying a radio? Apparently this position seemed to suit him. For about three months he had been very dependable, showing up each morning that the advisors planned on accompanying an operation. And this morning was no different; Phuc was right on time.

The first time I saw Phuc I was surprised. He had one unusual, distinguishing characteristic—all of his upper teeth were gold. It wasn't unusual to see Vietnamese with one or two gold teeth, but it was extremely rare to have a complete set. It was so rare, in fact, that I never saw it again. Phuc was proud of his teeth and he grinned a lot to show them off.

Sergeant Dalton checked his medical aid bag to make sure he had everything he might need—dressings for wounds, pneumatic splints for fractures, and morphine for pain. He carried a twelve-gauge-pump shotgun with double-0 buckshot on operations. I asked him why he did this, and his reasoning was that if he had to fire, he wanted a weapon that would put out as much lead as possible as fast as possible. Few weapons can compete with a shotgun for this. Mason had told me that Dalton carried the shotgun because it had saved his life in a fire fight with the Viet Cong in the district Dalton was in before, but Dalton didn't say anything about it and I didn't ask. At any rate, he had faith in it, and that's what counted.

Dalton was a study in detail. Everything had to be just right, and this included every detail from making sure the operation was coordinated with the artillery unit at the base camp, to the exact angle of his flop hat that he wore pulled low over his eyes.

When all was ready, Dalton, Chi, Phuc, Wilson, and I piled in Dalton's jeep and headed out. Since this was a two-company operation, trucks had been sent down from Bien Hoa to transport the troops to the dropoff point. One of the companies, the one from District Headquarters, was already in the trucks. We would pick up the other company at Binh Tri outpost, located in the area of our operation. Wilson was along to drive Dalton's jeep back. When we arrived at Binh Tri outpost, the other company was waiting.

Lieutenant Nam was in charge of the operation. He had been the deputy for security in the district for about two years, a position he held because he was extremely effective as a commander. Nam was forty-two years old, but he looked twenty-five. He had fought with the Viet Minh, the French, and now he was fighting with us.

"Fighting is all I know," he had told me. "When the war is over, I will not know what to do," he had joked once when we were drinking beer in the market place. I had laughed then and said that both of us would have nothing to do, but I realized that Nam was not joking. He feared the end of the war as much as he feared the war itself.

"When the war ends, I will not be able to trust anyone, as now. But when the end comes, we will not be able to shoot our enemies because there will be no shooting, only talking," he had explained.

At the time I had tried to dismiss Nam's remarks as the typical distrust a soldier has for all diplomacy and negotiations. Wasn't he fighting now because diplomacy had proved inadequate to handle the situation? And if this were the case—which it appeared to be—then, of course, he was justified in being skeptical about a lasting peace and a just settlement.

But Nam's feelings and understanding went beyond this point to one just outside the realm of American comprehension—or the comprehension of any outsider not personally involved in the war from the beginning. An American can never understand the war as Nam understood it, because Americans depend so much on logic, American style; and there was so much about Nam that defied logic, American style. Each day he conducted combat operations against an enemy that would eventually kill him, yet he preferred this to a situation where there was no war, for he could not trust a warless environment; it would not be safe. "Only talking," Nam had said. His contempt for the recently convened Paris Peace talks was thinly veiled behind his quick laugh.

"Talk, talk? Why we talk? There is nothing to talk about. Maybe we put three, four divisions in Hanoi, and then we talk about what North Vietnam give us if we bring them home. Then we have something to talk about. We tell Hanoi when they can have elections and who will be elected and then we bring our soldiers home," he told me. There was a pause for me to comment on this but I had nothing to say. Nam continued.

"But we have no divisions in Hanoi and because we have not, we have no good bargaining position. So you see, Thieu Uy, we must pay the price because we do not want North Vietnam."

Again the quick laugh as he added, "But, of course, you understand all this because you are an American and an officer, and you must forgive me for talking about something you know very well."

I smiled the polite smile that I was supposed to that day, slowly beginning to realize how little I really did understand about this war. Nam had a few of the answers, and I had none. But I was beginning to have a deeper appreciation of the questions, and that was a beginning.

The operation began on time, at exactly 7:00 A.M. According to the plan, we would pass through two hamlets, a rubber plantation, several swamplike marshes, and a few rice paddies. The operation was planned to terminate at noon, providing there was no contact with the enemy. If there was contact, there was no way of planning how long it would last; so we were prepared to stay all day and fight, if necessary, but the attitude of the soldiers seemed to be that this was just another sweep operation—another "walk in the sun"— and I found myself hoping they were right.

We started in the northern section of the village and worked our way south. I walked behind Phuc, keeping the radio on Phuc's back directly in front of me. Sergeant Dalton and Nam were to the right and Chi was behind me, walking with Lieutenant Nam's radio man. Occasionally Nam would shout at a soldier that was lagging behind, warning him that the Viet Cong would only shoot lazy soldiers.

Going through the paddies and marshes, the soldiers were well spread out, but the dense underbrush forced them into single-file formations after leaving the paddies. By 8:00 I was soaking with perspiration, and the sun was just warming up. Dalton was sweating also, but not as much. He was used to it, at least more than I was. A few of the Vietnamese had damp spots on their fatigues but most of them were as dry as when we started.

Some of the marshes were filled with elephant grass, a tall, knife like plant over five feet tall. As we moved through the grass, it separated us briefly, giving me a sense of isolation. I could see it moving on both sides of me, indicating where the soldiers were, but I couldn't see them. The water and mud in the marshes, coupled with the sharp grass, made the going tough. In some places the grass had fallen over, forming a shaky, jelly like mat to walk on, but the mat was full of holes, and stepping in one would put you waist-deep in the slime underneath, as more than one of the soldiers discovered.

Once we were out of the marshes, the operation became much easier. The rice paddies were no problem because we could walk on the dikes. The real danger, the one that caused chills up and down my spine, was the beautiful target we made if the Viet Cong were waiting in the thick foliage that invariably lined the edges of the paddies. Occasionally we would stop, and Chi would point out our exact location on his map so that I could relate the actual terrain to the map. We were staying well within the area planned for the operation, and Nam seemed to be pleased with the way things were going.

By 10:00 the only real enemy was the sun. With each step I could feel the sweat being sucked out of me, right through my jungle fatigues, soaking every inch of my body except the top of my head. My wet underwear was riding up my legs and beginning to rub. The more we walked, the more it rubbed, making each step a painful, searing agony. Dalton had warned me about wearing underwear in Vietnam, but I had forgotten his advice—now I was paying for it. I looked at him and he smiled, fully aware of my condition by the way I walked.

"Don't worry, sir. It happens to everybody at least once before they're convinced their underwear don't do no good out here. I've been here three years, and in three years I ain't never wore any drawers. Ain't no point in it here in this weather; they just put you in a bind and rub you raw," he told me.

I couldn't argue about either the rubbing or the rawness, but Dalton had a solution that would at least prevent further damage.

"If you'll just unbutton your pants, I'll cut the crotch outa them drawers. It'll give you some relief," he said.

I did as Dalton directed, much to the amusement of the soldiers who witnessed this embarrassing scene, and Dalton, with all the skill of an accomplished surgeon, cut the crotch out of my underwear with a scalpel from his aid bag. It gave me immediate relief, just as he had predicted, even though it was entertaining for the troops. I vowed never to wear underwear in Vietnam again, and I didn't.

About 11:00 Nam called a halt to the operation, allowing the troops to take a lunch break. We stopped by a small stream beneath a clump of palm trees. There was a group of houses nearby, and several small children, apparently from the houses, were playing in the stream. Lieutenant Nam said something to one of the boys in the stream, and the boy ran toward the houses. In a few seconds the boy returned, followed by a fat man wearing only sandals and a pair of green shorts. Nam and the fat man laughed and shook hands and talked excitedly for a while. Then Nam introduced his friends to Sergeant Dalton, Chi and me.

"My friend has lived here for a long time, and each time I pass I stop and talk with him. Today he asked us to eat with him. He like very much for advisors to eat here. I say I ask you. Okay, Thieu Uy?" Nam asked.

Our fat host smiled at me behind Nam.

"Tell him he is very kind and that we would like very much to eat with him," I replied.

It was now obvious that we would not be finished with the operation by noon, and since none of my group had brought anything to eat, this seemed like a good deal.

Some of the soldiers had brought along loaves of French bread filled with some kind of meat and wrapped in newspaper. They began to pull these sandwiches from their shirts, sharing them with the soldiers who had none. They sat in small groups around us, laughing, talking and eating.

The small boy had been sent away again, and when he returned he was carrying a basket filled with bottles of beer. Another boy behind him was carrying a basket of large glasses. Our fat friend opened the bottles and passed them around, along with the glasses.

"We have beer while women fix food," Nam said, a statement that would not have made many friends for him in the Women's Lib movement. The beer was warm and strong, a native Vietnamese beer called Ba Muoi or "33" for the sake of simplicity; they both mean the same.

Before the first round was gone, more beer arrived and halfway through the second bottle, the food was ready. A large woven mat was placed on the ground, and a small girl gave each of us a bowl and two chopsticks. I looked at the chopsticks, then at Dalton. He pointed to two U. S. Army mess hall forks that had been placed discreetly on the mat, obviously in our honor.

The first course was steamed rice, not the normal bleached white I'd always been used to, but a natural light brown. And I was surprised to discover that it had taste, too—like roasted chestnuts. Dalton and I used the forks and the Vietnamese pretended not to notice. When the rice was gone, a large bowl of boiled fish was placed on the mat. Our host expertly separated the fish with his chopsticks and served each of us a generous portion. The delicate aroma of sage wafted up from the fish, the same smell I remembered coming from my mother's pork chops; the ones she used to cook when I was a boy in the winter time when it was snowing outside and the wind was blowing. The fish, better than any I'd ever had before, tasted like it had been cooked slowly for a long time, and the sage gave it just the right amount of sharpness. The long walk had made me hungry and the beer had only increased the hunger, making me especially grateful for this meal. For the present I forgot about the discomfort caused by my underwear. When my original serving disappeared, my host ceremoniously served me more. It was here that I was introduced to nhuc mom, a poignant fish sauce used on most Vietnamese dishes. The smell was nauseating, like rotting fish, reminding me of the first day at Koepler Compound, and I had reservations about putting the thick, black liquid on my fish, afraid of spoiling the wonderful taste. But I did, afraid of offending our host if I didn't. At first it had an oily taste, like concentrated cod liver oil, but after a few mouthfuls of the nhuc mom-saturated fish, I was surprised to find that it added a certain spicy richness. I soon forgot about the smell.

During the course of the meal, I noticed one of the women serving Phuc a clear liquid from a Jim Beam whiskey bottle. Phuc was happy about this and was discussing it with Chi, pointing to the bottle from time to time and laughing.

"What is it?" I asked Chi curiously.

"The Vietnamese call it bacsi dai, but the Americans call it rice whiskey," he told me.

I knew about bacsi dai, though I had never tried it. I was only curious about what Phuc was drinking, and the subject should have ended right there, but it didn't. Seeing that I was interested in the bottle, Lieutenant Nam motioned to the woman and she brought the bottle over, placing it before me on the mat. There was a short discussion between Nam and the fat man, and suddenly, I was the center of attention.

"My friend is happy that you want to drink bacsi dai. Most

advisors say it is too strong," Nam announced.

Everyone was smiling, even Dalton. This was another test in a never-ending series of tests that face all advisors, and I knew I had to face my share; it just seemed that I was receiving my share and someone else's. But it was too late to protest. It was too late for anything short of drinking the bacsi dai and smiling, which I did in that order.

The few tastebuds that had survived the test told me that I just swallowed a mixture of rubbing alcohol and gasoline. Though they weren't able to tell the exact ratio of these ingredients, I'm sure it would have powered any internal combustion engine. Tears followed immediately, blurring my vision, but I could see the smiles on their faces. I tried to thank Nam and our host, but I couldn't speak for a few minutes.

Most of the serious side effects passed quickly but the burning sensation in my throat and stomach remained. By surviving, I had passed the test and everyone congratulated me. But I would not be fooled again; bacsi dai, like underwear, was a thing to be avoided.

"Lieutenant Nam did not tell you that most Vietnamese do not drink bacsi dai either," Chi told me. "They say it is too strong. Only the very old and strong drinkers, like Phuc, drink it."

"It's alright Chi. It's alright," I managed.

After we had thanked the fat man all around, Nam announced that it was time to move on. The troops gathered up their gear, and we walked away from the hamlet. I looked back to see the fat man and his neighbors waving goodbye to us, and I waved to them. Phuc was showing the effect of the bacsi dai as he staggered along in front of me. Occasionally he would look back and flash me a 14-karat gold smile, with the sunlight reflecting brightly from his teeth.

After leaving the hamlet, I noticed that a lot of the soldiers were carrying things under their shirts, and some had sacks on their backs. I had paid no attention to this before we stopped for lunch, but now I wanted to know what they were carrying.

"What do the soldiers have in their sacks, Chi?" I asked.

"While we eat, soldiers take fruit and other food from hamlet. Some of the sacks have chickens inside, others have rice," he told me.

"You mean they buy things from the people?" I probed, trying to make sense of this happening.

"Not buy, Thieu Uy, take," he answered.

"Why?"

It was awhile before Chi attempted to answer my last question, apparently searching for the right words that would transmit the right impression and still not violate his obligation to tell me the truth.

"The soldiers live from the land, Thieu Uy. The food they take will be their lunch on tomorrow's operation. They cannot pay because they have no money. In time you will understand how it is," he replied. His face reflected pain from being forced to answer.

But I didn't understand and the farther we walked under the hot, relentless sun, the more I could feel the anger building up inside. The people had been good to us, giving us food and treating us like guests. I had felt honored back there, a feeling that comes only with a sense of welcome and belonging. Now I discovered that our troops had stolen from them, and I knew that Nam was fully aware of this; he had to be. And, since he was in charge of the operation, he was responsible. Perhaps he could give an explanation for this, one that would be different from Chi's, because I didn't want to believe what Chi had told me. We walked along in silence, crossing more rice paddies, through a rubber plantation and past another cluster of houses. About an hour after leaving the people who had given us lunch, we arrived at the pickup point.

Sergeant Dalton called the District and officially reported the operation complete.

"Negative, negative," he told Wilson. Negative contact, negative results. A walk in the sun as had been predicted.

While we were waiting for the trucks to arrive, I asked Nam if he would explain to me why the soldiers took food from the people. It was a direct question and I knew it. I realized I was risking upsetting the delicate balance existing between the advisors and the Vietnamese, and that perhaps he would be offended by the question. But Nam wasn't offended. He was willing to talk about it, quite candidly.

"How many young men did you see back there, Thieu Uy? You see none, right? They are not there because they are either soldier or they join VC. My country is very poor and it is hard to pay the soldiers enough money. Also, the soldiers know the people know where the VC hide but the people are afraid to tell us," he said.

65

There was an air of finality about what he told me, but I knew there was more to it than this; there had to be. Nam looked at me, pleading for me to understand but I refused to accept his excuse. I waited for him to tell me more, to explain more.

"The soldiers see the people in the hamlets have much food and probably pay taxes to VC. The soldiers make operation here to protect people from VC, and because they are soldiers, they cannot own land and grow food as the people do. So the soldiers think the people owe them this; it is not much and the people understand. It is much less than the VC take and nobody is killed. Someday it will be different; I know it is hard for Americans to understand, but it only happens when my soldiers have no money," he explained, looking at me to see if I'd heard enough. I nodded, but he couldn't let it end there.

"But I am glad you care enough about my people to ask, and I hope someday you will see it as the Vietnamese see it. We are all Vietnamese, Thieu Uy, both the soldiers and the people in the hamlet."

I wanted to tell him that the Viet Cong were also Vietnamese but it would have served no purpose; he was well aware of this. And he knew it was wrong to expect too much from the people; it was not their fault, neither was it the soldiers'. It was simply the way it was. Again, my American logic was confusing me. Perhaps tomorrow would be different. Some days are better than others. The trucks arrived and we went home. . . .

Chapter Five

LEARNING

As the days passed, I became more familiar with the district, the soldiers, the advisors and the people. Colonel Andersen was leaving in September and in the little time he had remaining, he wanted me to absorb as much as I possibly could, which forced us to spend a lot of time travelling around the district visiting outposts, hamlet and village offices, and adjacent Advisory Teams.

I found that, for the most part, each team was similar to our own, at the same time maintaining a high degree of individuality. Some had better living quarters than we did, while others didn't live as well. Some advisors seemed to be very enthusiastic about their work, and others approached their mission with a lackadaisical attitude.

As I sat with Colonel Andersen at the bars of other teams, talking to other advisors, I learned much about their lives and what motivated them. I encountered many who were only marking time, waiting for the day when there would be no days left on their "short-timer's calendar," and they could return to the life they had left in the States—a life that is never really as good as it is imagined in the swamps and jungles of Vietnam, but nonetheless, the only life they had. Those who were married were only too eager to show me pictures of their wives—women who weren't quite as young or trim as they had once been and who would be just a bit older and heavier when their husbands returned from the war. But the men still thought of them as they used to be and were content to forget about the flaws and imperfections of their women, talking always about what good wives they had. Most of them were able to shut out the possibility that their wives were cheating on them at home, while speculating on the possibility that the wife of everyone else in Vietnam was doing just that. The consensus seemed to go like this: "My wife is perfect, but the wife of everyone else is not." It was a valuable lesson in rationalization for me. It seemed that the men who trusted their wives the most were the same men who spent every possible Saturday night in Saigon, while the men who were the most faithful invariably received the "Dear John" letters from the home front. I suppose there was some poetic justice to this that I failed to understand, as if what was happening here on a small scale was only a reflection of life in general.

Women were a favorite topic of discussion among the members of the Di An Advisory Team also, with Sergeant Dalton usually having more to say on the subject than anyone else. Dalton had a Vietnamese girl friend in Saigon, and he claimed he was taking her home with him when he left. Of course, he never said when he was leaving, and this deliberate oversight allowed him to avoid a definite commitment.

Often, late at night when I was on radio watch and Dalton couldn't sleep, he'd keep me company in the radio room. It was there that Dalton explained to me the way he felt about his girl friend and why.

"She understands me and treats me like a person wants to be treated," he told me. "My first wife didn't do that. She was cold, frigid. Miss Ly ain't like that. No sir, she ain't like that a'tall, and if I have a couple of drinks she don't mind. And she don't care if I'm a medic and nothing else," he explained in the slow drawl he had picked up in Arab, Alabama, where he had spent the first eighteen years of his life.

"No sir, she don't push me to be something I ain't 'cause she knows this is what I do best. And when she looks at me and smiles, it's the nicest smile you ever want to see. She's always smiling, and she don't have much to smile about either, except me and that ain't a whole lot."

It was difficult for Dalton to discuss this with me, but it seemed that he was powerless to stop. He knew that this emotion, like fear, was impossible to keep bottled up when each day could easily be his last. And when he spoke of these things, it was more of a confession than a discussion and I played the role of listener, sitting silently before him as he explained, as much to himself as to me, why he had chosen this Vietnamese woman.

"I met her in Saigon when I was at Third Field," he continued. "She lost her husband in 1966. He was an ARVN soldier and moved around a lot, so he didn't get a chance to spend much time at home."

Fearing I would get the wrong idea about their relationship, Dalton quickly cleared up the picture.

"But as long as he was living she didn't fool around none. No, sir. And when I met her we was both all alone, both needin' somebody. She needed somebody to support her, and I needed me a woman. You know how it is when you're used to havin' a woman and then don't have one anymore. It's real hard on a man."

I nodded as if I understood because right then, listening to him telling me what it was like, I thought I did. There was no declaration of undying love on Dalton's part nor did he profess that this woman would give him eternal happiness. He had lived too long in this world to be that naive or idealistic. He was only stating the facts concerning his relationship with a woman that meant more to him than anything else he possessed. And she held this present status because she filled a terrible void that Dalton could not fill alone.

Both of us knew that he would never take her back with him, providing he ever left, and perhaps she realized it, too. But Dalton was keeping the illusion as real as he could for as long as he could, fooling himself as much as anyone else. When I asked him what he would do in the end, he told me the truth.

"Well, sir, I'll tell you how I really feel about it. I would like to leave this country the way I come in and I would like to feel that I ain't changed none. I don't want to take nothing with me and I don't want to leave nothing behind," he said. I looked at Dalton and smiled and he smiled back, for we both knew this was impossible. No one ever leaves Vietnam with exactly what he brought with him; every man is both richer and poorer for being there.

What bothered me most about Dalton's conversation were the things he left unsaid. In the back of his mind, and every other advisor's, was the constant thought that he would possibly die here, and, since this was the case, what little time he had left should not be wasted or spent foolishly. With death always so close, there was nothing like living to help you forget. An opportunity missed today may never return tomorrow, and it was this sense of urgency that dictated Dalton's actions. This had to be part of the motivation that forced Dalton into the relationship with his Vietnamese woman but, because it was felt rather than understood, it was not spoken of. It would have been impossible to explain anyway, because it

69

transcended explanation, going into an area of man's very being, where words break down and lose their effectiveness.

Also, there was the personal gain factor that could not be ignored. Dalton wanted something to show for the period of his life that he was spending in Vietnam. He didn't want to feel that it was being wasted, or that he was less of a man for being there, or that he was missing any of the things he would be enjoying if he were not there. I discovered that male vanity and pride can be quite strong at times, even in combat. A woman connected him to reality, even if nothing else in the tiny, war-torn country did.

Miss Ly was vastly different from her American counterpart. As Dalton had said, she understood him and treated him as he wanted to be treated. This implied that American women did not understand Dalton and did not treat him as he wanted to be treated. He felt no need to compete with Miss Ly for a feeling of superiority. Only American women could pose this threat, and Dalton had left them far behind. Perhaps, in the simplest terms possible, this explained Dalton's motives, if anything could. I would hear these same arguments many times during my stay in Vietnam, as Americans justified their Vietnamese women and, in turn, gave up their women in America.

There was a definite increase in enemy activity during August. Hardly a night passed without at least one of the twenty outposts in the district coming under attack. It was considered unsafe to travel off the main roads with any force smaller than a platoon. With assassinations on the increase, the people became more fearful of the Viet Cong.

If there was any pattern to the enemy's actions, it was the fact that there was no pattern at all. One week it appeared that his primary target was hamlet officials, and then he would suddenly shift to killing and kidnapping young men and women, or concentrate on bombing and propaganda.

Occasionally the Viet Cong would catch a lone, American soldier in one of the hamlets, visiting his girl friend. When this happened the soldier was usually killed on the spot. It mattered very little how many times they were told to stay out of the hamlets and away from the small roadside stands that sold everything from warm Coca-Cola to combat boots; the GIs failed to heed the advice. It was hard for me to believe that an American soldier could be so incredibly stupid, but I became a believer after investigating a few of these incidents. Some of the luckier ones, the ones that had escaped, told me the hamlet "looked so peaceful," and that "everything was so quiet," they could see no harm in staying awhile, especially since the girls were "so friendly."

But they never learned, and each time something like this happened, the rating of that hamlet would drop at least one letter on the Hamlet Evaluation System. This became extremely frustrating; it took a lot of time and effort to raise those ratings, only to have them drop again when some half-drunk GI looking for a girl became a victim of the Viet Cong. And this happened more often than it should have.

The letter grade each hamlet received under the Hamlet Evaluation System was based on a very exhaustive and comprehensive report requiring the senior advisor to evaluate each hamlet in about sixteen different areas, including security, enemy activity, education, health, and the progress of the pacification effort in general. This report was updated each month to reflect the changes in these areas. The best of all possible ratings was an A. Ratings of D, E and V were considered bad, indicating varying degrees of enemy control, while Bs and Cs were considered good. During this period we had all types except A. The system was far from perfect, but it was the only method we had of evaluating the hamlets. It indicated where we needed to concentrate our efforts, clearly outlining both the weak and strong areas in Di An District. A copy of this monthly report was sent to MACV Headquarters in Saigon where those at a higher level could chart our progress and failure. This was extremely important to those men in Saigon, because control of the hamlets was vital to the government's plan of controlling the country.

We knew that the side controlling the most hamlets would also control the most people, and it would be this side that won, regardless of any other condition. This simple fact was the basis and justification of everything we did in Di An, for it was the key to victory; everything had to revolve around this basic truth.

In order to complete the Hamlet Evaluation Report, we had to visit each hamlet at least once a month and attempt to answer the questions required by the report. There were thirty-six hamlets in Di An which made this an awesome, recurring task. If there had been any enemy activity during the month, it had to be reported. If there were no school in a particular hamlet, it was reported. If there were no elected hamlet chief, it was reported. If there were no market place, it was reported. Questions concerning health and sanitation were asked. Increase and decrease in population was another category covered by the report, along with the reasons for the increase or decrease. And on and on it went.

The advisor in the district did not determine the letter grade each hamlet received, even though he supplied all the information for the determination. The grade was decided by a computer in Saigon after the report was fed into it. After this was done, the results were sent back to the advisor in the district. At times it was impossible to understand the logic used by the computer to arrive at the final letter grade. Occasionally the computer would screw up and send back the results of a district somewhere in Two Corps, but, for the most part, the system worked very well.

As district chief, Major Chau was also required to complete his version of the Hamlet Evaluation Report each month. Rarely, if ever, did his report agree completely with the advisor's. There were always areas where the situation was seen differently for different reasons, but this created no problems. In fact, differences were expected, as long as they were minor, which they usually were.

During August our forces began to receive the new M-16 rifles. Until this time, they were using the older, heavier M-14s and M1's. Some of them had been equipped with the .30 caliber carbine, the Thompson submachine gun and the .45 caliber "grease gun"—a small, light, submachine gun.

The Viet Cong units were being armed with the fully-automatic AK-47, a weapon vastly superior to the older American weapons such as the Thompson and the .30 caliber carbine. Since these older weapons had been designed exclusively for Americans, it was difficult for the Vietnamese to fire them effectively, and their weight alone created a considerable handicap on long operations.

The M-16 solved these problems. Small and lightweight, it was capable of producing a tremendous volume of fire with very little recoil. The Vietnamese had no problem reaching the trigger when the rifle was at his shoulder, an additional drawback of the older weapons since their stock had been designed for the American soldier. A fully automatic weapon, the M-16 was more than an adequate match for the AK-47. It fired a small cartridge at tremendous velocity and this allowed the soldiers to carry twice as much ammunition and a lot more confidence.

The Vietnamese loved it right away. There was an obvious improvement in morale among the troops that received this weapon, and this psychological improvement was more important than the mechanical advantages of the M-16. They now had something to believe in and by believing in this "little black gun" with a stock manufactured by Mattel Toy Corporation, they could also believe in themselves.

Day after day Jackson and Mason would take them out to the rifle range in Binh Tri Village and teach them to operate this fascinating weapon. With the aid of Sergeant Chi, Mason emphasized the importance of keeping it clean and operating. He taught them how to handle a hang fire and what to do when it jammed. They learned to fire it at night and they kept on firing it until it was as familiar to them as their hands were.

It would take a few months to arm all the soldiers in the district with the M-16, but it would be done. And as each company or platoon received it, they were given the same training the first group had received. The M-16 would not work miracles, but it would give them a tactical superiority over the enemy. The rest would have to come from them.

Chapter Six

THE GIRL IN THE TUNNEL

The new filing system I had suggested was soon set up in the center. My contribution consisted of one filing cabinet taken from Bien Hoa; it was Hau that filled it with information. We were growing closer with each passing day which meant that he had accepted me and I was allowing myself to be accepted.

Each morning, as part of the ritual, we would have Chinese soup together in the café at the end of the street. And later in the day we would have coffee there, also. On the last day of August as we were having our soup, Hau announced, "I have good information for you. I will show you when we go back."

When we returned to the center he told me that the night before, a Viet Cong had walked into one of the outposts and given himself up. Early that morning the defector had been delivered to Hau and, after he had been given some food and a pack of cigarettes, he told his story.

His name was Bay Ho and he had been a guerrilla in Dong Hoa Village for three years. He had joined the Viet Cong because he believed their propaganda and he thought they would be victorious. But now he realized this would never come to pass. He was tired of living in tunnels during the day and risking death each time he travelled at night. He was constantly wet during the rainy season, and there was never enough food.

All of this had been enough, more than enough, to try the endurance of any man. But Ho endured because he had been promised a promotion to squad leader. His political cadre leader had made the promise long ago, and when Ho asked him about it—which he did periodically—he was put off with one shoddy excuse after another. Still, Ho endured—until the promotion went to a younger man, who was far less experienced.

This had been the last straw—more than Ho could bear. He had worked long and hard for the Viet Cong, and he had been a dedicated "liberation fighter," deserving better treatment than this.

He had lost face because he had not received the promotion, and this filled him with an immediate, uncompromising hate.

Ho's appearance made his story of living in a tunnel believable. Dried mud was caked on his bare, spindly legs—exactly what you'd expect from someone sliding in and out of a hole in the ground. His only clothing was a pair of dark green, nylon shorts, a common uniform for the Viet Cong who lived in tunnels. There was nothings distinguishing about him—except an intense expression that made him appear as if his mind were in another world.

Hau asked him if he would be willing to return to his tunnel and point it out to the district soldiers. Ho's face lit up immediately, and he became greatly excited, talking and gesturing with a spontaneous zeal.

"What is he saying?" I asked Hau.

"He say that he want very much to see VC dead. They cheat him and disgrace him and he ask me if I can kill them. I tell him we would like to capture but if we cannot, then we kill them. This make him very happy."

Ho told Hau there were four people in the tunnel—the political cadre, the new squad leader, a young woman who was a tax collector, and a local guerrilla. He gave Hau their names, and a check of our files revealed information on all of them except the guerrilla, which wasn't surprising since we weren't overly concerned with the local Viet Cong guerrillas.

The political cadre was listed in our files as the Viet Cong Village Chief for Dong Hoa, a man we'd been after for a long time. We had a picture of him, and just to make sure Ho knew what he was talking about, Hau put the picture in a stack of other photographs and gave them to Ho. After sifting through the stack for a few minutes, Ho held up the photograph. He had positively identified Nguyen Van Phuc, VC Village Chief, Dong Hoa Village, and this called for an immediate operation. He was the one we really wanted—the others would be icing on the cake.

Hau told Major Chau what had happened, and the district chief gave his approval for the operation. After a brief consultation with Lieutenant Nam, it was decided that two squads would be adequate for our purpose. If more were needed, we could send for them.

While the troops were loading on "Claymore," I told the colonel about Ho and quickly filled him in on the proposed operation.

Jackson was in the radio room with Phuc, trying to teach our radio bearer a few English words. This was a real stroke of luck; normally Phuc was still in bed at this time unless he had been told the night before to be up early. I asked the colonel if Jackson and Phuc could come with me, since Phuc was only learning obscenities anyway. The colonel agreed; Jackson grabbed his rifle, Phuc grabbed the radio and we were off.

Jackson and Phuc crawled up front with the driver, and I got in the back with Hau, Ho and the troops. It was about three miles to our destination, but the holes in the road made it seem much longer. The driver obviously thought it was part of his duty to try to hit each one, and with the practice he got, he almost did. When we arrived at the dropoff point, everyone left the truck. The driver had to wait for us while we conducted the operation.

Hau and Ho had another discussion immediately after we got off the truck. Ho drew a map in the sand with a short stick and pointed to a clump of trees about two hundred yards away. The soldiers eagerly pressed in on Ho and Hau; the discussion was of vital interest to them. Ho diagrammed the tunnel, explaining as he did that there was only one entrance. This satisfied the soldiers; it would make their job a lot easier. Then Ho looked up at us and grinned. He said something that caused everyone except Jackson and me to laugh. Before I could ask what he had said, Hau translated it for me.

"Ho say that girl in tunnel is very pretty. He say she make VC very happy all the time and make them forget about other women. Do you know what this means, Thieu Uy?" he asked me.

"Yes, I know what that means," I told him and I smiled.

The sun was beginning to make itself felt as we worked our way toward the clump of trees. Our plan was to surround the site of the tunnel as soon as we were close enough for Ho to point out its exact location. After that, there was no plan; we would be forced to play it by ear. Some of the soldiers were still laughing and giggling about the tax collector's promiscuity. Hau told them to shut up. Walking very carefully in a half-crouch, we approached the area as quietly as we could.

Ho led us to two trees that stood about four feet apart and pointed to the space that separated them. Cautiously I approached the area, carefully looking for some indication of a tunnel entrance, but I could see no disturbance in the ground at all. Hau motioned to the troops and they quickly surrounded the two trees, knelt down and pointed their rifles at the spot Ho picked.

Looking around for Jackson and Phuc, I saw them kneeling at a respectable distance behind the circle of riflemen. This looked like the wise thing to do, and I slipped over to join them.

"What does it look like over there?" Jackson asked.

"Nothing," I told him, "just trees and grass and dirt."

Ho and Hau were holding another hasty conference at the inner edge of the circle when Ho rushed over and picked up what appeared to be a two-foot square piece of earth from between the trees. This was actually the tunnel cover he had ripped away, allowing us to see the entrance. Then he shouted something into the tunnel and ran for cover behind the troops. I crawled over to Hau and asked what Ho had shouted.

"He say to VC they should surrender. He tell them we are here," Hau said without taking his eyes from the tunnel entrance.

All was quiet for a few seconds, and I was beginning to think the tunnel was empty. Ho repeated his original message from his position behind the troops. More silence. While we waited, I impressed on Hau the importance of taking prisoners.

"Yes, Thieu Uy, I know. I hope very much they come out alive. But Nguyen Van Phuc have strong mind. Maybe he decide already to die here." His eyes had a distant look in them, as if he knew what the outcome would be here, and we were merely playing out parts of a tragic scenario.

Suddenly there was shouting from the tunnel. This excited everyone, even Hau. He shouted something back to the tunnel.

"They say they want to come out, and I tell them to throw out all weapons and then come out. Hands first," he said, still not taking his eyes from the tunnel.

I felt better now. Things were looking good, going the way they were supposed to, and I was about to witness my first capture. What a great day this would be for a camera man from CBS news, I thought. He could record on film, live and in color, an actual capture for showing on the home front, thus dispelling the popular myth that the Viet Cong were some kind of mystical, indestructible supermen. And if the Viet Cong were captured with tax money, we could expose them as common hoodlums to boot.

77

Ho's description of the girl had aroused my curiosity. I was eager to see this beautiful young girl that lived in a tunnel with the Viet Cong, a girl who had chosen the dangerous profession of tax collection over all the other things she could have done. I was thinking of the questions I wanted to ask her—when things began to go wrong.

A grenade, minus the pin, was tossed from the tunnel. It rolled toward a quick-thinking soldier who quickly picked it up and threw it in the trees behind him while the rest of us flattened out on the ground. As the grenade reached the highest point on its arching trajectory, time ran out on its four-and-a-half-second fuse. The violent explosion sent shock waves tearing through the trees and along the ground, ripping out huge branches and showering us with leaves, bark and chunks of wood. With my ears still ringing from the explosion, a rifle barrel was pushed out of the opening, moving from side to side in a desperate search for targets. Before the owner of the rifle could do any damage, the soldiers directed a heavy volume of fire at the tunnel entrance sending a cloud of chewed-up grass and clods of dirt skyward, forcing him back inside. Another grenade was tossed out but it failed to explode. I was glad too, for no hero rushed forward this time.

Before anyone could stop him, Ho grabbed a grenade from a soldier's belt, ran to the tunnel entrance, pulled the pin, and threw the grenade inside. I half expected to see it come flying back out at us, but it didn't. A second later, there was a dull, muffled explosion that caused a slight tremor, barely shaking the two trees above the tunnel. A small puff of dirty white smoke rolled out of the hole in the ground, and then all was quiet. A soldier ran over to the tunnel and shouted the same thing Ho had shouted, but there was no reply; I hadn't really expected one.

Two soldiers quickly stripped off their field gear and entered the tunnel, armed only with .45 caliber pistols. Jackson called the district and gave them a report of the action. Wilson wanted to know if we needed a medic.

"Tell him to have Dalton come down here if he's there, but I don't think he'll do any good," I told Jackson, who transmitted the message to Wilson.

The two soldiers in the tunnel asked for a rope. One end was dropped into the tunnel and tied around the ankle of a dead Viet

Cong. As the troops outside hauled up the grisly remains, it was greeted with a tremendous cheer.

The first body was impossible to identify from photographs; most of the head had been blown away and the left hand was missing. However, Ho was certain this was Nguyen Van Phuc because of the dark green shorts and scars on the left leg. This was believable, but it was Ho's uncontainable joy that really convinced me it was in fact, the political cadre. Ho had become a sort of instant hero to the soldiers as a result of his actions. After all, it was his handiwork that had made this possible.

The second body was in much better condition than the first. Ho identified it as the guerrilla soldier—Nguyen Van Phuc's bodyguard. He was placed along side the body of the man he had failed to protect, and the removal operation continued. This left only the squad leader and the tax collector.

Dalton arrived just as the squad leader was being dragged from the tunnel. Both his feet had been blown away by the grenade, forcing the soldiers to tie the rope around his neck.

"Looks like the boys done saved me a lota work," Dalton remarked as he quickly took in the sorry scene.

"There should be one more in there, but judging from these three, you're too late," I explained.

The footless squad leader was laid beside his two comrades and the rope was dropped into the tunnel for the last time. The soldiers gathered by the tunnel, knowing that the female tax collector was about to be hauled out. This prospect generated much more excitement than the other three had, with each soldier trying to get a piece of the rope, thus taking an active part in her removal. The concussion from the blast had removed all her clothing, which only added to the soldiers' excitement.

Ho had told the truth—she was beautiful, even in death. Surprisingly enough, there were only two fragment wounds on her body. One was in the left breast and the other in the forehead. I asked Dalton to see if there was a heartbeat, but there was none. Apparently she had been in the rear of the tunnel, protected from the full force of the blast.

With all the bodies removed from the tunnel, Hau told the soldiers inside to bring out everything that remained. There were three rifles, all of Chinese origin, and about a dozen grenades. A box of propaganda leaflets aimed at American soldiers was discovered, bearing the same old familiar theme: "Americans Go Home! Why Do You Fight and Die In Vietnam?" However, some were tailored for the black soldier, asking him why he was fighting the white man's war and warning the black soldier that the late Martin Luther King had been opposed to all forms of violence, and that they should follow the teachings of King.

Propaganda of this nature was plentiful during the months following the death of King as the Viet Cong concentrated on the black soldier, feeling that he was the weak link in the American presence. First they asked him to refuse to participate in the war, and then later they asked that he join their side. Interrogations of captured political cadres verified the fact that exploitation of the race issue was of high priority, the objective being to turn black soldiers against white, thus making both easy prey for attacking Viet Cong.

In addition to the box of propaganda, there was a smaller box of tax receipts and documents that gave us a clearer picture of the activities this particular group had been involved in. The tax receipts told us who was paying taxes in Dong Hoa Village, and how much they were paying.

This was a common practice among the Viet Cong, giving "receipts" to the people from whom they extracted rice and money, telling them the receipts would be "redeemed" when the "war of liberation" was successful. No one believed it, least of all the people who payed, but the practice continued, since it was a more practical arrangement for the people than assassination. And everyone knew that assassination was the fate of those who challenged the tax collectors.

We found a message among the tax receipts from the Province Committee Chairman to all tax collectors in the Province. The message directed them to increase their collections, explaining that the Party needed money to operate effectively. But we found no money; it had already been sent to Province. Just like us, I thought, with everything being sent up the line—except orders and directives; they always come down.

In their personal belongings, we found photographs of all the dead. One showed a young woman smiling as she posed on a motorbike. Her name—Nguyen Thi Bay—was written on the back.

It matched the name in our files, positively identifying her as a tax collector. We could now close her case; the system had worked. And Phuc's case and the case of the new squad leader could be closed, also. This had been a serious blow to the enemy and we had a right to be happy.

But I didn't feel like "being happy." I had hoped, right up to the end, that they could have been taken alive and interrogated. But more than that, I had hoped to save the girl. Her death struck me as being a greater tragedy than the others, as if, in some way, it was a more senseless loss. I had not fully accepted the fact that women played a large part in this war and that they had to be considered the enemy, just as the men were. I would soon lose this sentimental, romantic attitude and replace it with a more rational one. Soldiers cannot afford such luxuries.

It was late in the evening when it was all over and we were ready to leave. I was thinking about how I would write this in my report and wondering if it would be important to mention that Nguyen Thi Bay had been a beautiful woman who had ridden motorbikes and smiled, when Hau told me it was time to go.

"What do we do with the bodies?" I asked.

"Maybe the family will bury, maybe the Village Chief bury. Same as before in rice paddie," he answered.

Yes, same as before, I thought. Only this time a little different, perhaps. Jackson covered the girl with a blood-soaked blanket that had been in the tunnel; perhaps her own, which seemed only appropriate. He then called the district to report the operation over and told Wilson we were returning.

As we were walking back to the truck, Jackson and I discussed the day's action. Soon the conversation turned to the girl.

"She sure was pretty. It don't seem right for a girl like her to get killed. Hard to believe she'd get mixed up with them bastards," he said. His comments required a reply so I told him not be fooled by a pretty face—they're the ones you had to watch.

I knew supper would be ready when we returned and I wondered what Thoi had for us. But I really wasn't hungry.

81

Chapter Seven

DALTON

There was only one thing in the district more constant and predictable than the war, and that was sickness. The two were not always connected, and neither depended on the other to exist. Sickness and disease were not as exciting as the war, and because they weren't, they received little attention and even less publicity. Yet there were a few among us who considered human suffering and misery an enemy even more sinister than the Viet Cong, and these few had dedicated themselves to fighting this war. Dalton was one of them.

In his fight, Dalton used all the means at his disposal and constantly searched for more. When he wasn't working on a new village health station, he was usually accompanying American doctors and nurses to some remote hamlet where he was sure to find a large number of people in need of medical attention. And he would plead the case of the sick and suffering with all the skill and persuasion of an experienced trial lawyer. Yet his most valuable asset was his sincerity. When he talked to the doctors at the battalion aid stations and evacuation hospitals, they listened. And after listening, they would agree to help. This soliciting an agreement to help was his first step. His next step was taking the doctors out in the district to treat the sick. He preferred to have one "team"—usually two doctors and three nurses—"adopt" a particular village, and then have them concentrate their efforts there.

This was his master plan, and it worked very well, although it required a tremendous amount of work, salesmanship and coordination. The only time the doctors and nurses were free to come to the district was on their day off, but they did come, giving selflessly of the precious little time they had that could be called their own.

Word of Dalton's program spread quickly through the hospitals at Long Binh, and support for his campaign grew. He used every doctor and nurse that volunteered, sometimes conducting as many as seven visits to the hamlets a week. These visits, called MEDCAPS—short for Medical Civic Action Program—were part of the pacification effort. The success of the program, however, depended on the success it received in the districts, for this was where the sick were.

Part of the agreement worked out between Dalton and the doctors was that Dalton had to provide the transportation for the teams. Dalton kept his end of the bargain with a three-quarter-ton truck scrounged from some motor sergeant he refused to name. I never did get the full story behind this truck due to Dalton's reluctance to discuss it. But I suspected—really, I knew—it was a shady deal because he had carefully scraped off all the original bumper numbers and other identifying markings and painted large red crosses on both doors. He had read somewhere, or had been told, that vehicles so marked enjoyed certain privileges denied ordinary vehicles of war. But his faith in the crosses was not complete; he was convinced he needed a siren.

He talked the MPs at the base camp into giving him a siren for his EMERGENCY EVACUATION VEHICLE—it had ceased being a truck when he painted the crosses on the doors. Convincingly, he explained the importance of his program and the vital significance of the vehicle to the accomplishment of his merciful missions. There would be times, he continued, when he would need to have priority on the highway, and a siren would give him this lifesaving edge. It was a very powerful and moving argument, more than the MPs could resist. The fact that they never questioned Dalton concerning the origin of his weird-looking vehicle was proof of his sincerity and disarming personality. Who would dare question the integrity of such a saintly man?

The siren was added more from vanity than necessity, however. It allowed Dalton to boast, quite accurately, of having the only such vehicle in Three Corps. He took great pleasure in roaring down the road at a dangerous speed with the siren screaming, watching the traffic pull obediently and respectfully to the side of the road, giving Dalton priority for his nonexistent dying patient. Usually, the "emergency" was caused by ice cream scrounged by Dalton on one of his numerous liaison trips, forcing him to rush home before it melted.

When things were slow in the Coordination Center, I would accompany him on his MEDCAPS. He liked me to go with him, and he was not above offering a bribe to accomplish this. If I had something else to do, he would casually remind me that a very attractive nurse would be with that day's team, knowing this would get my assistance every time. And he needed my assistance to provide security for the teams, using me in the same manner he used the doctors and nurses.

Providing security consisted of asking Major Chau for a couple of squads of soldiers to go along with the teams as a precautionary measure against a Viet Cong attack. Nothing would have been more damaging or demoralizing to our pacification effort than having one of the MEDCAP teams annihilated. And nothing would have been more desirable to the Viet Cong. The fragile faith we were so slowly building in the government needed all the help it could get, and the most effective way of countering the enemy's propaganda was to take our case to the people and prove to them that the government could provide much more than the empty promises of the Viet Cong. And as long as the jury was still out, we couldn't afford the psychological setback of a massacre.

There was never any problem with security, even when most of the troops were committed on operations. Major Chau was well aware of the tremendous value of Dalton's program and was not about to place it in jeopardy by a lack of security. Whenever possible, the district chief would accompany the teams, acting as interpreter between the doctor and patient when we had few interpreters, which was the usual condition.

Determining where a team would go was often jointly decided by Dalton and Major Chau. They gave greater priority to the hamlets in most urgent need. If, for example, a team had recently visited their regular hamlet, Dalton would use them in another area, if the need justified it. This way he was able to utilize every volunteer, any day of the week.

It wasn't unusual for these teams to treat over a hundred patients during a single visit. Often it was late in the evening before they would leave a hamlet, but they never left until every patient had been seen by a doctor; to have done less would have been unthinkable to Dalton.

The vast majority of patients were treated by the MEDCAP teams

84

on the spot. Open sores were cleaned and bandaged; abscesses and boils were drained and dressed; infected scalps were scrubbed with surgical soap and more was given to the people to take home and use. These were some of the cases that made the doctors feel they were accomplishing something.

But there were the hopeless cases, also—enough of them to make us lose the self-satisfaction produced by the less serious patients. There was little that could be done for terminal TB and cancer patients, other than giving them something for pain and sending them home to die. Whenever possible, they were taken to the evacuation hospitals for tests and intensive treatment, but this wasn't very often since these hospitals were usually filled with combat casualities. Yet Dalton never gave up on them. He pulled every string he had and contacted every associate in each hospital, trying to find one more bed for one more dying patient. In these cases, where the odds were against him and death was already knocking at the door, he failed more often than he succeeded—but he never quit. Life to him was a fiercely sacred thing, and each death was considered a personal defeat.

All of the common illnesses were encountered—worms, open sores, skin infection, malnutrition, dysentery, scalp diseases, rheumatism and arthritis. And there were the uncommon ones too. Occasionally we would find a child with a clubfoot or a cleftpalate. These children were a pitiful sight, made more pitiful by the realization that this handicap would be carried until they died, unless something very special happened to them. It was in these cases that Dalton worked his special magic.

Due to the many years spent in hospitals, Dalton was familiar with the capabilities and limitations of surgery in these cases. He would make arrangements with the medical specialists at Third Field Hospital to perform corrective surgery, pleading each case as if his life depended on it. Dalton was able to do this because he had once worked at the hopital and personally knew most of the surgeons there. He took full advantage of these relationships, trading on his friendship shamelessly. But it worked—everytime.

Dalton was constantly on the lookout for these "special cases," enlisting the aid of every advisor and soldier to help in the search. He explained to us the importance of finding these kids before they were too old; the younger they were, the more successful the surgery would be. But finding them and getting the surgeons to operate weren't the only problems Dalton faced.

It was no easy task to persuade a Vietnamese mother and father that there were actually Americans who could make their child just like everyone else's child. At first they were apprehensive about Dalton's proposal but, with the aid of Sergeant Chi, Dalton pleaded for a chance to show them that it could be done.

Yet he always managed to persuade them and, during the month of August alone, Dalton was responsible for three successful cleft palate and two clubfoot operations. The families of these children were convinced Dalton had performed the operations himself and no amount of explaining to the contrary would shake their faith in the lanky hillbilly. To them, Dalton was just a cut above the rest of us mortals.

All of this—the MEDCAPS, the "special cases," the TB and cancer patients, the health stations—was in addition to Dalton's assigned, primary duties. He was required to see that the advisors were in good health and to treat them if they were wounded. He was also required to give advice to the District Health Officials concerning health and sanitation. This in itself was a staggering order, but Dalton went far beyond, compelled by nothing other than his own convictions to do these things. In this respect he was no different than many other advisors who felt as he did, yet he always believed there was something else he could do, something more to be accomplished. And all he wanted for himself was an occasional weekend in Saigon with Miss Ly, a small concession which the senior advisor wisely granted.

Although he was aware of the political reasons for conducting the MEDCAPS, Dalton was not motivated by them. Reluctantly, he agreed to let me use his MEDCAPS to collect information on the Viet Cong and their political structure. It was a simple screening task, whereby personnel from the Coordination Center would ask each patient questions concerning taxation, VC movement, propaganda and enemy recruitment. This procedure proved to be valuable in locating enemy units and determining their future plans.

At this point, both of our wars came close together. I was trying to rid people of the pain and suffering caused by the Viet Cong, while Dalton strived to rid them of pain and suffering, regardless of

86

politics. He had no time to consider such things as propaganda and elections and psychological operations. And he never claimed to know all the solutions to this complex war, as the lofty men in Saigon did, but he was well aware of many problems.

If virtue is its own reward, then so were Dalton's MEDCAPS. They were a means to an end, surely, but more important, each was an end in itself. It was enough that he conducted them—they needed no further justification, explanation or credit. It was my hope that when the war was over, men like Dalton who had worked, sweated and often died in the lowly hamlets without benefit of the "big picture" or the greater glory reserved for men of higher rank than he, would receive the recognition they richly deserved.

When praise is being handed out to those responsible for the successful conclusion of the war, it would not be taking too much from the generals and diplomats and chiefs of state to say, quite simply, "and Dalton, too."

Chapter Eight

A NEW BOSS

Colonel Anderson left us during the first week of September and I was genuinely sorry to see him go. I had learned a lot about the district and its problems during the short period I had known him, but I had learned even more by simply observing the things he did and following his example.

The Vietnamese gave several farewell parties in his honor, and on the last night before he left, one was given by the team. We used this opportunity to give the colonel plaques and going-away gifts. When the gift-giving was over, we good-naturedly demanded a farewell speech. At first he refused but when our demands became more insistent, he agreed.

"Hell, I don't know what to tell you guys," he opened awkwardly, looking at us through scotch-blurred eyes, "except to say that you're a damn good bunch." There was a long pause before he continued, but when he did his eyes were clear and penetrating. "We've come a long way here in Di An and we've done a good job. I learned a whole lot here and I'm goddamned proud of every one of you." He looked at Dalton and Jackson when he said this, causing both of them to turn slightly red. "This has been . . . this has been the best job the Army's ever given me. They'll give me more jobs to do but they'll never give me another one like this. I'm going to miss Di An, I'm going to miss it a lot. If it wasn't . . . if it wasn't for my family back home, by God I'd stay longer. I want you guys to believe that."

"We believe you, sir," Dalton said, speaking for all of us.

"I just want you guys to know, that's all. It don't matter to anybody else except us," he repeated. Standing there against the bar he looked older, much older, than he'd ever looked before. The lines around his mouth and eyes seemed longer and deeper, and his voice was tired. Only the pale blue eyes seemed to be ready for more of the kind of life Di An had to offer, giving the colonel's words an undeniable ring of truth.

"Now that I'm going home tomorrow and it don't matter anymore, I'm going to tell you something I've never told another living soul." We all leaned a bit closer to the bar, and Dalton quietly poured the colonel another drink.

"It's not easy to talk like this but maybe . . . maybe some of you have felt the same way. You never can tell about these things. Anyway, here it is. When I came to this team a year ago, I never thought I'd leave this place alive. I was convinced I'd die right here, but the funny thing is I didn't think about it much." He stared distantly at a spot above the bar, mesmerized by some profound thought that would not be reduced to words. "Ain't that a hell of a thing?" he finally said with a weak laugh, and not a man in the room failed to understand what the colonel was trying to tell us. He had touched, ever so briefly, the essence of war that somehow binds men together against the horrible anticipation of death. But anticipation, even of dying, dulls with time and the inescapable knowledge that nothing can really be done about it. And, once accepted for what it is, it becomes almost meaningless, leaving behind only the bond.

Understanding these things about the colonel, that he was just as human and vulnerable and afraid as the rest of us, greatly increased his value to the team. Yet it seemed terribly ironic that this would happen the night before he left. The next morning we all said goodbye and Mason and Wilson drove him to Saigon.

Colonel Andersen was replaced by Major David Allen, a rapidly balding veteran of a previous tour in Vietnam. He had served as a company commander in the First Air Cavalry Division during most of 1966. The thick horn-rimmed glasses and the marked absence of hair gave Major Allen an almost owl-like appearance. I noticed right away that he had a habit of peering over the top of his glasses, causing him to tilt his head forward at a sharp angle.

There was a lot of apprehension before he arrived, mainly generated by our ignorance of what he'd be like. And under the circumstances, the apprehension was justified, for the whole team had been molded to fit Colonel Andersen's wishes. Would his replacement go along with the way things were or would he make changes for the sake of change? Dalton had seen more senior advisors than the rest of us, so naturally his opinions on the subject were listened to with interest.

"He ought to work out alright cause he's taking over the best damn team in the country. If he makes little changes, that's okay. He don't strike me as the kind of feller that'll be making things rough for us just cause he's the boss," he told me one night shortly after Major Allen arrived. And his prediction proved to be right.

The same day Colonel Andersen left, Major Allen got us together and told us he had "heard many good things about the Di An team" while he was being processed through Bien Hoa.

"It's going to take me a few weeks to get my feet on the ground, and I'm going to depend on you guys to see that I get off to a good start with the Vietnamese," he continued.

I liked him immediately, and even tried to ignore his owlish appearance. A man honest enough to admit his limitations and shrewd enough to realize that only time can reduce these limitations has a lot going for him from the beginning. And since he was now the "new man" on the team, he had relieved me forever of that stigma, which was another reason I liked him.

But just as important as his acceptance by the team was the approval given by the district chief. He and Major Chau were pleased with each other right away, and this development caused all of us, American and Vietnamese alike, to breathe a lot easier. I had been told that the most serious and damaging situation an advisory team could undergo was a conflict between the district chief and the senior advisor.

When and if this happened, there would be little point in the team remaining, for their effectiveness would be gone. An occasional disagreement concerning ideas, policy and tactics between professional military officers was acceptable as long as the disagreement remained at a professional level. It must never, under any circumstances, be allowed to grow into a conflict of a personal nature, undermining the mutual trust and respect an advisor's success is built on.

I knew how fragile the relationship between Vietnamese and advisor really was; the closer the relationship, the more fragile it became. At times it was almost impossible to keep personal feelings from dictating some action, but the district chief and his counterpart were expected to be very diplomatic and civilized at all times. One constantly played the part of the gracious host, while the other assumed the role of an honored guest. Personality clashes could be tolerated below this level to a certain degree, but never here, for it was here that difficulties and differences must be resolved. Throughout Vietnam the pattern was the same.

The largest single cause leading to senior advisors being relieved was their inability to maintain a working relationship with the district chief. Rarely were they relieved due to incompetence, laziness, or lack of aggressiveness. Ironically, it was often characteristics such as aggressiveness and a willingness to "get the job done quickly" that led to their dismissal. For such, the blame was not entirely the unfortunate advisor's.

For years the army had subjected him to an unbending philosophy of "do it now," and "do something, even if it's wrong." As a result of his training and his experience in the army, the advisor often tried to push the Vietnamese too far too fast—in the same manner he has pushed an infantry company, if he'd ever had one—thinking that the war could be won during his relatively short tour in the combat zone.

Often the unsuccessful advisor failed to understand why the Vietnamese did not feel as he did, unable to realize that long after he had returned to the safety and comfort of the United States, they would still be fighting their enemy, just as they had for the past twenty years. And because he was not Vietnamese, he could never feel as they do about the war. He was quite capable of putting one hundred percent of his energy into the war, since his stay was short, but it's impossible to put one hundred percent effort into a conflict for twenty years. And this is what he expected.

Eventually, this inability turned to frustration, and the frustration deteriorated into distrust and hatred for the very people he had been sent to advise. When and if this stage was reached, he was removed. While the pattern of failure was relatively easy to chart, the way to success was impossible to pin down.

The successful advisor was unique in many ways. He did not have to be an exceptional commander because advising was not the same as leading. As an American commander, his will could be imposed arbitrarily; as an advisor, this was not allowed. He had to be extremely flexible and patient, willing to admit mistakes. Also, he had to be a diplomat of the highest caliber with an unusual amount of tact. Personality was extremely important. Since these characteristics are not stressed in the American Army, many advisors failed to possess them and as a result, they failed to be successful. There was no course to take or book to read that would guarantee success. He had to feel his way along, charting his course with great care, hoping to avoid the pitfalls along the way. Since on two districts were alike, he could not rely on the experiences of his peers.

But Major Allen passed most of the early pitfalls with flying colors. This was due mainly to his greatest asset—common sense. In the end, it was this uncommon commodity that separated the successful advisor from the failure. If he had this, everything was possible; without it, nothing could save him.

Chapter Nine
HILL 82

September brought with it a marked increase in the level of terrorism. The Viet Cong were reacting to the success of our coordination center and the pacification program. As the hamlet ratings began to improve and climb upward, the level of assassinations would also go up and force the short-lived improvements back down. It was a vicious cycle to say the least.

To build a school house or repair a road was a tremendous gamble, possibly costing some innocent villager his life. During this period, the Viet Cong booby-trapped school house doors and placed land mines in the road, but murder was the most common, reoccurring incident. Hau and I investigated each murder, which meant that we went to the scene and looked at the victim. We looked at twenty-three bodies during September.

The vast majority of these killings could only be classified as murder since the victims had no political connections or ambitions whatsoever. But they were committed to achieve a political objective set by the Viet Cong Infrastructure and, as such, they had to be considered "political killings" or assassinations, though I hesitate to dignify these acts by using the latter term. Occasionally there would be a note pinned to the body explaining why the Viet Cong had been compelled to eliminate this unfortunate person. The note invariably condemned the victim as an "enemy of the people" and a "lackey for the puppet government and the American imperialists." Rarely, in fact, was this the case.

Usually the victim was an ordinary villager, no better or worse than anyone else, guilty of no crime. He died because he was unfortunate enough to be chosen as an example—a bad example—to the rest of the people in that village. According to the enemy's philosophy, it was perfectly acceptable for the victim to be selected at random to make a very specific point. Their reasoning, which was logically absurd, went something like this: Perhaps a village has been too sympathetic to the government or has refused to pay all the taxes levied by our tax collectors. These are considered very serious offenses and must be rectified immediately. In such cases, anyone in this village shall serve as an example to whip the rest of the population back in line, male or female, old or young.

Hau and I saw all of them at one time or another, proof that it made very little difference who was murdered as long as the desired results were achieved. The note pinned to the body was nothing more than a thinly veiled warning to everyone else that the same act could be repeated—against anyone. If no one was really safe, then everyone was a potential victim. Admittedly, the logic was simple, and it was designed to be that way. Considering the enemy's objective, it was extremely effective, but not completely without its disadvantages.

The number of murders also indicated to a certain degree, that the Viet Cong were losing control of the population. In the terrible, twisted logic that war produces, these murders were also used to evaluate the success of the pacification effort, and the price we paid for this success was the poor, broken bodies Hau and I examined.

Based on the information gathered, it appeared that most of these acts were being committed by one unit. It was very difficult to obtain information on this group for obvious reasons—those who talked and were later identified by the Viet Cong were singled out for special torture before being killed.

Yet, bit by bit, we painstakingly pieced together the information we had. Each murder would give us a little more than we had before, but such vital intelligence as the size of the unit and its leader was almost impossible to confirm. When we did receive reports on the location of this group, it was always different from the previous reported location. Ambushes were placed around hamlets that we felt were most likely targets for attack, but nothing happened on the nights the ambushes were there. It was frustrating to know there would be other murders and terrorist acts committed and not be able to prevent them; there was no consolation in trying. Each report received was carefully checked out "on the ground" by the PRUs or Popular Force soldiers. Finally, a pattern began to evolve.

From all indications we had, this unit was operating around the area of Noi Hoa Mountain, officially designated Hill 82. A more rugged, densely foliated place could not be found anywhere in the district. Several operations had been conducted around this mountain, but none had proven successful. Now, with the reports and indications we had, it was obvious that this region would have to be searched carefully, systematically, and far more often.

The elimination of this group had grown to be an obsession among us, making objectivity impossible. We had examined the results of its actions day after day, and each day our resolve to destroy this band grew a little stronger. I found it impossible to get "used to this sort of thing," regardless of its frequency. Murder became commonplace only because the Viet Cong committed it so often, but the helpless, useless feeling I got from looking at their victims never became common. This outrage was magnified by the naturally gentle nature of the Vietnamese. Their willingness to adopt a benign acceptance concerning these atrocities was extremely painful to witness. The funerals invariably left me with an empty, unconsolable sorrow. The mourners expressed no hate or bitterness, only sadness, and the sadness was everywhere. Grief and mourning and women crying became commonplace only because the Viet Cong made it so. This, too, was a sight I could never "get used to," making me hope that each funeral I attended caused by the terrorists would be the last. There was something about the anguishing, searching stares of the survivors that compounded these tragedies, and when the stares were directed at me, they became silent appeals for help. And then the helplessness would flood over me. This senseless circle of murders, funerals and stares continued through most of September. Then, on the twenty-seventh, we received a report that would hopefully short-circuit this circle.

One of Hau's agents reported that he had, quite by accident, discovered the terrorists' base area, and that he had observed five men returning to their base. At the time he reported this information, it was less than two hours old. He explained that three of the men were armed with AK-47 rifles, and the other two appeared to be unarmed. When Hau asked how it was possible for him to come by this extra-ordinary knowledge, the agent told us that the VC had passed by his hiding place at a distance of less than five feet. He had even overhead their conversation concerning a delinquent taxpayer in Tan Hiep Village, indicating that this taxpayer would be their next victim.

Now, for the first time since tracking this unit, we had a valid reason to be optimistic. When disappointment follows disappointment in a seemingly endless pattern, optimism isn't easy to come by, but this time it was. Hau told Major Chau, and an operation was immediately arranged. Major Allen was notified, and he suggested that I accompany the operation. The newest member of the team, Captain Wentworth who had arrived only two weeks earlier, was also selected by Major Allen to go along.

Two platoons of Regional Force troops were loaded aboard "Claymore" and another truck loaned to us by the province. In five minutes we were ready to roll. Even Phuc had been easy to find, which could only be interpreted as a good omen.

While we had been preparing to leave, Major Allen called the base camp and asked to have a couple of helicopter gunships standing by in case we became involved in more than we could handle. This proved to be a very smart move.

Due to the ruggedness of the terrain surrounding Hill 82, the trucks had to be parked nearly a mile from the point where Hau's agent had seen the Viet Cong, forcing us to approach on foot. Hau briefed the troops before we left the trucks so they would know what to expect, or not to expect, depending on the outcome. When this was done, we slowly worked our way around the base of the mountain, faithfully following the informer. At this point, all of us were placing ourselves in the hands of this man. He could have very easily led us into a carefully laid trap. I didn't think abut it at the time, but I did later, and it caused me to break out in a cold sweat.

We approached the area from the west. This was the most difficult route, but it afforded far more cover than the eastern approach, which was through completely open terrain. The undergrowth of tangled brush and vines was so thick it forced us to move in single file almost all the way. We broke out of the thicket and followed a deep ravine for approximately five hundred yards. It had been formed by the water rushing off the mountain during the rainy season, but now it was completely dry. After crawling out of the ravine, we crossed the floor of an abandoned stone quarry and followed a small trail that led to a ledge overlooking another, more densely-foliated ravine. Finally, we had reached it—it was in this ravine that our agent had seen the Viet Cong.

It had taken nearly an hour of hard, steady walking to reach this point. I pulled out my map of the district, the one Sergeant Chi had given me, and tried to determine our exact location, but it was impossible to do with any degree of accuracy. The map did not show the stone quarry, and the quarry extended below and to the west of us. The ledge we were on was all that remained of a ridge that had once extended from the top of the mountain to the ravine we had just travelled. The ridge was represented on the map but the quarry had cut through it in several places, making it impossible to pinpoint our location on the ridge.

This situation would make artillery fire dangerous, if it were needed. I discussed this with Hau and Captain Wentworth, trying to get their opinion on how we should proceed. It was at least two hundred yards to the bottom of the ravine and another two hundred yards up the ravine to the base camp. The only way in was the ravine—Hill 82 cut off all other possible routes. After studying the ravine for a few minutes, Hau made his decision.

"I send one platoon down to bottom of hill and have them sweep up to where VC be. Other platoon stay here and fire down," he announced.

It was really about all he could do with the troops he had. While Hau explained this to the platoon leaders, I called the district and reported the situation. I asked for the gunships too, knowing that if I waited until they were really needed they would be too late. A moment later Wilson told me they would be overhead in about ten minutes. We watched the platoon move cautiously up the ravine and enter the brush surrounding the suspected base camp. The other platoon took up positions on the crest of the ridge and waited. Ten minutes began to seem like a hell of a long time.

I thought about the ambush I'd been on with Colonel Andersen and how confident he'd been. He'd had all the answers that night and the U. S Artillery had made the ambush successful. Now *I* was responsible for whatever support we got, and this realization made the waiting more painful. I tried to dismiss this thought, but my mind kept creating different situations that called for different reactions. Suppose there were no Viet Cong in the ravine at all? This would piss-off the pilots and we'd be accused of screaming "wolf." Or even worse, suppose a gunship was shot down supporting us. What was I supposed to do then? Or what if I had to call in artillery with nothing more than the obsolete map? These would have to be my decisions if the situation presented itself, for Wentworth was too new to make them. I was supposed to know, and this scared me more than anything else.

From my vantage point on the ledge, it was impossible to tell who fired first, but in a matter of seconds, the whole ravine was vibrating with gunfire, exploding grenades, and unrestrained, desperate screams. Wild, misguided bullets bounced off the rocks, forcing us back over the ledge toward the quarry.

"What we get?" Wentworth asked, more excited than scared.

"I don't know," I answered with more composure than I felt.

Along with Hau, we crawled back up the ledge and peered down into the ravine. We could see that three of our troops had been hit and four or five others were trying to drag them back down the ravine. What was left of the platoon was returning the Viet Cong's fire, but they were at a miserable disadvantage crouching on the floor of the ravine, with little cover to be had.

The platoon on the ledge could offer little assistance because of the foliage. Our problem was compounded by the well-entrenched positions commanded by the Viet Cong at the very end of the ravine, behind rocks and boulders that had rolled off the mountain. They also possessed at least one machine gun, and it was keeping our troops pinned down. At this point, it was anybody's guess how many we were up against, but it was obviously more than the original five that had caused us to launch the operation.

Seeing we had some wounded, Wentworth called the district and requested a medical evacuation helicopter, commonly known as a dust-off, and explained our problems. It was obvious we would have trouble getting the wounded up the side of the hill, taking at least two Vietnamese to carry each casualty. I knew a large crowd would make a beautiful target for the machine-gunner, and I found myself wondering what Colonel Andersen would do in this situation. I had never imagined such a thing happening, much less prepare for it. Andersen's logical mind would've found a logical solution, and then I suddenly realized that an American could do the job with little difficulty. It wasn't a question of choice—there were no options, other than the option of increasing our casualties by doing nothing. And yet the very idea of my leaving the relative safety of the ledge to attempt a rescue seemed insane. But worse than this was the unbearable agony of doing nothing, contributing nothing, while people—my people—were dying.

With Wentworth busy with the radio, I scrambled down the side of the ravine, ran to the first wounded, scooped him up and started back up the hill. The hill was steeper and the soldier heavier than I'd expected, and the loose rocks made firm footing impossible. I imagined the machine gunner, with the back of my head in his sights, squeezing the trigger. And there was nothing I could do about it but keep going, trying not to panic. After reaching the top, I waited a few seconds before going back. My legs were warm and slightly numb from the strain, but they were also shaking from fear. I didn't want to go back. Going back a second time was definitely insane—but the situation demanded it. I kept seeing Andersen's face, older than before, with the long, deep wrinkles, telling us that he never expected to leave Di An alive and that after a while he didn't think about it. I stumbled down the ravine for the second time, giving the machine gunner another chance. Reaching the bottom, I realized how much the first trip had tired me. It was all I could do to get the badly wounded soldier in my arms. He'd been hit in the stomach and was unconscious from either loss of blood or shock. I looked at the third soldier and realized another trip wouldn't be necessary—the glassy eyes and frozen grimace told me he was dead. The second struggle up the slope was much slower than the first, and I expected any second to be blasted into eternal blackness. I was exhausted almost beyond fear by the time I reached the ledge, allowing the soldiers there to take the wounded man from me and move him down to the quarry where the dust-off could land safely. The first wounded soldier had already been taken there.

Captain Wentworth marked the landing zone with a smoke grenade and the helicopter, which had been hovering out of range, swooped down in the quarry like some giant bird of prey, picked up the wounded and was gone, all in a matter of seconds. As the dust-off was leaving the quarry, the gunships I'd requested were overhead. It seemed incredible that both trips to the bottom of the ravine and the evacuation had taken less than ten minutes.

"Pine Spuds Eight, this is Rebel 32," came the smooth, level voice from the radio.

"Rebel 32, this is Pine Spuds Eight," I replied, holding the handset close to my mouth so I wouldn't have to repeat.

"Roger, Spuds Eight. We're overhead. Where you want the goodies?"

"32, this is Spuds Eight. Wait one while I get my people out of the area."

"Roger, Spuds Eight."

Hau had heard the conversation, but I explained this latest development anyway.

"If you can move the platoon back down the ravine, away from the VC, the helicopters can fire rockets." I used my hand to simulate a rocket leaving the helicopter and Hau got the picture. A big, broad grin divided his round face.

"Okay, Thieu Uy. Okay. Can do," he laughed. Using his radio, he quickly relayed this news to the platoon leader in the ravine.

"Rebel 32, Spuds Eight. My people are disengaging at this time. The end of the ravine is all yours," I told the invisible voice from the helicopter, trying to match his degree of smoothness.

"Roger, Spuds Eight. Can you mark the spot with smoke?" came the voice again.

"Rebel 32, Spuds Eight. I'll give it a try."

This had to be done; there was no getting around it. The enemy's position had to be marked with smoke, a necessary precondition known only too well to those of us who played this deadly game. This would insure the safety of our own troops and, at the same time, make it easier for the gunships to concentrate their firepower. From my position on the ledge, I could see the whole operation—the Viet Cong's position, our troops moving back down the ravine, and the impatient gunships overhead, waiting to kill. Under these conditions, the simple request from the gunships to "mark the spot with smoke" was not so simple at all. It involved flinging a smoke grenade into the Viet Cong's camp, necessitating exposure once again to the machine gunner.

"If you handle the radio, I'll see if I can give 'um what they want," I told Wentworth, pointing up to the helicopters.

Taking two green smoke grenades from one of the troops, I crawled along the ledge until I was as close to the Viet Cong's position as I could get. Pulling the pin on one of the smoke grenades, I hurled it as far as I could in the enemy's direction. The machine gunner promptly blew away a large chunk of the ledge directly in front of me, forcing me back over the ledge as another burst of fire ripped through the spot I'd just abandoned. Somehow, I couldn't picture Andersen doing this. Using the lip of the ledge for cover, I crawled back to where Hau and Wentworth were waiting. Wentworth had been talking to the pilots.

"What they say? Do they see it?" I asked anxiously, hoping the first shot would be enough.

"They identify green and it's their baby now," he told me, still holding the handset to his ear in case more conversation was necessary.

In spite of the fear and fatigue I'd been subjected to, I was excited about the prospect of watching the helicopters attack the Viet Cong's position. I'd just settled down with Hau and Wentworth to watch the show when the first gunship made a low approach directly over us, immediately drawing fire from the ravine. This proved to be the most serious mistake in a long list of mistakes the enemy had made that day, for aside from incurring the wrath of the pilot, it pinpointed exactly at least one enemy position. Firing at Lieutenant Hau's platoon was one thing, but taking on the gunship armed with rockets capable of penetrating the thick vegetation was something else. The gunship quickly banked to the left and made an approach directly up the ravine. Once locked in on the rising smoke, the helicopter hovered almost motionless over our troops below and began the bombardment.

Leaving a thin trail of white smoke, the first rocket streaked toward the valley. It followed an invisible line, drawn unalterably by the green smoke from my grenade. And when they came together, the combination resulted in an explosion so powerful it shook the entire ledge. Small trees and bushes that had once composed dense foliage were slowly lifted into the air, turned end over end and lazily returned to earth. The first rocket was followed immediately by the second, and third, and fourth. They savagely ripped away the protective cover of vegetation, clearly exposing the large boulders we had suspected the enemy of using for protection. The intensity of the attack was beyond anything I'd imagined.

When the first helicopter had expended both pods of rockets, his partner, who had circled patiently overhead, continued the devastating attack. The firing from the valley had ceased. The machine gun, that had made so much noise a few moments before was now silent. He was outgunned in a duel that had been hopeless from the beginning. The only sound now was the deafening impact of the rockets, and the only smoke was black—from their explosions.

101

It was all over in less than two minutes. When the last gunship had fired his last rocket he sprayed the area with machine gun fire. When this was completed, I thanked them very much for their assistance.

"Roger," came the same, flat reply, "glad to have the opportunity." And I knew he meant it.

I watched them disappear in much the same way the grateful rancher watched the Lone Ranger and Tonto disappear after fighting off an attack of wild Indians. And, like the rancher, I never had a look at the face of my saviour, but I was just as thankful.

When the smoke had cleared, we had a view of a completely rearranged ravine. From the ledge we could see bits and pieces of trees and rocks and bodies strewn carelessly about the floor of the valley. By the time we scrambled down the side of the ravine the platoon that had remained there during the attack was searching the area.

By a rough estimation, there must have been at least twelve Viet Cong at the base camp when the shooting started. Nine bodies that could be considered intact were lying about the area with parts for at least three others scattered on the ground and in the remaining trees. The twisted wreckage of a .51 caliber machine gun was almost hidden under the twisted wreckage of its last operator. Tattered rags of clothing hung on the tree branches, and small puffs of black smoke oozed from the loose earth, filling the air with the sharp smell of cordite. Splintered stocks from once serviceable Chinese rifles were intermingled with splintered tree limbs and pulverized rocks.

The destruction rained down by the gunships had been quick, efficient, and complete. And as we searched through the debris I was awed by the realization that I had called in and directed this punishing attack—I had brought power to bear and the end result of that power now lay before me. I should have felt some compassion for these poor wretches that had triggered such liberal doses of destruction, but I didn't. The only emotion I felt was fear. There had been little time for it earlier, but now there was, and it made me tremble. It was a more profound, personal fear than I had experienced on the ambush. This time I was forced to realize how thin the line really was that separated me from these lifeless, broken things in the ravine. And the realization that this same line was

102

controlled by something as absurd as fate was a most sobering thought.

At the time I did not associate my actions with the larger aspects of the war such as a free Vietnam controlled by a democratic form of government. If the free Vietnam and the democratic form of government were aided by my actions that day, this would be very noble, but at best that lay somewhere in the future at a level beyond my influence and control. Instead, I was thinking in very small, very concrete terms, on a scale I could handle. The more immediate results that I could relate to concerned a delinquent taxpayer somewhere in Tan Hiep Village who would not die that night simply because he was a delinquent taxpayer. He would not have to give his life to this band of terrorists in order to serve as a bad example for the other residents of Tan Hiep. This unnamed and unknown man had been granted a reprieve, for the time being, and this thought was satisfying indeed.

The soldiers collected the bodies and pieces of bodies and placed them in one pile. This would make burial easier and it gave some order to the confusion caused by the rocket attack. In a small cave behind the rocks we found a metal box filled with documents directly linking this group with the recent outbreak of assassinations. Photographs were taken of the dead to aid us in positive identification. When all was finished, we were ready to leave.

"What about the bodies?" Wentworth asked.

I had asked the same question on the ambush and at the tunnel, knowing the answer extremely well. I looked at Hau expecting him to answer, but he only smiled.

"We leave them here, sir. Maybe the relatives will come and claim them. If not, the Village Chief will take care of it," I told him.

As we climbed out of the ravine and headed home, I thought about this. It seemed that all advisors asked the same questions. Hau had a right to smile.

Chapter Ten

THE BOMBING

The destruction of the "Chau Thoi Gang" did not mean an end to terrorism in the district, although things were quiet for a few days afterward. September gave way to October in an orderly manner, and I was hoping the new month would bring a little peace and quiet. The recent summer and fall had been hard on all of us. What we needed was a chance to rest, and if we were lucky, we would have that chance in October. It didn't turn out that way, though it was a beautiful dream.

I was beginning to feel like a veteran now, with all of four months behind me in the district. The days passed quickly because there was much to do, but the nights I stayed up to pull radio watch were endless. During these nights, I would try to solve the problems we were confronted with and the problems that lay ahead.

My one ever-present desire at this time was to make our Intelligence Center successful enough to eliminate every trace of the Viet Cong's political structure in the district. Above everything else, I wanted to destroy their control in the hamlets and villages, and I was willing to employ whatever means necessary to achieve this. I knew that until this point was reached I would not be able to relax, or "let up," and if this was not accomplished before the end of my year, then I would stay another year, or two more years, or however long it would take. Already the thought of going home was secondary, pushed far back in the shadows of my mind, behind the matters I considered to be of a higher priority. The sense of urgency that existed in Di An made it impossible to devote much time to anything other than the enemy's elimination. All other problems and issues paled by comparison as Di An fought to survive.

This cause, the survival of the district, was a cause worthy of my undivided support, and this was what I was prepared to give. The fact that this cause could cost me my life had little effect on me at the time—not because such an expenditure wasn't important but because there was no time to consider it. My total commitment to

104

the enemy's destruction was the result of many factors, not the least being revenge.

In the beginning, when I was idealistic, I had hoped that there was possibly another alternative short of total destruction, perhaps something similar to peaceful coexistence, whereby the Viet Cong could be made to see the fallacy of their convictions and stop the killings and bombings. But I soon realized I wasn't being realistic. I discovered that these acts were simply tactics employed by the enemy's political organization and that, according to his doctrine and ideology, they were considered perfectly legitimate means to achieve a predetermined end. There can be no compromise or peaceful coexistence with an organization that commits atrocities and fails to realize or accept the fact that it is commiting them.

I knew if this situation continued, the life would be choked out of Di An in a systematic, machine like manner, reducing it to an area inhabited by people little more than automatons, no longer capable of molding their own lives. There would be one victor in the end, and to this victor would go the district; to seriously believe in any other possibility was a display of sheer idealism or paralyzing stupidity or both. And unless the Viet Cong reign of terror was brought to an end, it would succeed. In the end, it became very personal, as if I had been the victim, as if our own dirty little district war was not connected to the bigger, dirtier war that surrounded us.

Because we had felt all the human emotions one is capable of feeling toward an enemy—hate frustration, pain, outrage, helplessness, and fear—there was nothing dehumanizing about the way we conducted our dirty little war. To me, the enemy was real—not simply some nameless, faceless figure running through the jungle. After collecting information on a member of the Infrastructure for months, he became a very real person—an individual with his own individual characteristics. I could not afford to be objective about him; I knew him too well. Perhaps in a bomber at 30,000 feet above the jungle or in a plush office, far removed from the sound of war, I could think of him in abstract terms, with logic and rationalization applied to his deeds. But here I could not. And late at night, while everyone else was sleeping, and I commanded the radio room, I thought about these things, trying to come up with ways of making our operations more effective. We were succeeding, but we needed to succeed more.

There was no question that Hill 82 had been a tremendous morale booster for all of us, and that it had been a serious setback to the Viet Cong. Neither was there any question as to how the enemy would react to this. With the same certainty that night follows day, he would, at a time and place of his own choosing avenge his comrades that had fallen at Hill 82. There was little else we could do about this except wait. And the wait wasn't long.

The time was 7:30 in the morning on the seventeenth of October, and the location was the market place, less than a hundred yards from our compound. Just as we were sitting down to breakfast, the day was blown apart by a blast that shook the whole building. Coffee cups were overturned and plates of bacon and eggs were rattled into our startled laps. The fact that the blast came from the market place was a bad sign.

Instinctively, Dalton grabbed his medical bag and headed for the door with Major Allen, Sergeant Chi and me right behind him. From the street we could see a dark, almost black cloud of smoke hovering over the market. With Chi leading the way, we cut through the back alleys, taking the most direct route to the scene of the explosion, not really knowing what to expect and unprepared for what we found.

Even before we got to the market place, we were exposed to a hideous sight. A woman was running up the street, obviously in shock, with the tattered remnant of her left arm hanging uselessly from the shoulder. Dalton quickly placed a tourniquet above the elbow, and Chi told a woman peering from a nearby doorway to watch her until help arrived. We ran on to the market proper and found it in complete confusion.

The area designated the market was a very wide, rectangular-shaped piece of ground between two rows of shops or streets. Normally, the area served as a street, but during the early morning hours, traffic was diverted down the only other street in Di An, and the mobile merchants did their business in the square. In the morning between six and eight o'clock, the market bustled with activity as the women did their shopping for the day.

On the morning of seventeen October, there was activity of another sort. Fruit and vegetables littered the market and were splattered against nearby walls. Screaming, bleeding women and children were everywhere. Those that were able to walk did so, their faces mirroring incomprehensible horror. Others crawled in senseless circles. Several people were lying motionless among the destroyed stalls. These were beyond help. Dalton did what he could for a bloody little girl, while Chi talked to a group of crying women.

"They tell me a woman brings basket to market and she put it over there," he said, pointing to a particularly battered section of the market. "Then she go away and leave basket and everything blow up."

This was the revenge for Hill 82 that we knew was coming, but I hadn't expected this. There were eight dead that I could see, with possibly more buried under the debris. Chi had managed, with the aid of those unharmed, to round up the wounded and keep them from wandering away. Major Allen ran back to the compound to call for evacuation helicopters for the seriously wounded and for more medical supplies. I stayed with Dalton and helped him with the bandaging. Major Chau arrived shortly, and his presence had an immediate stabilizing effect. He had the dead moved to one side, which helped Dalton as he crawled from one bloody form to another, doing what he could. The dead included three children, an old man, and four women—one pregnant.

There were about thirty wounded, half of which were serious. I recognized a soldier who had been with us at Hill 82. He had gone to the market that morning for a loaf of French bread, and now he was lying on his back in the center of the market whimpering softly. His left foot had been blown off, and his leg was shattered to the knee, yet he still clutched the bread. Major Allen returned, driving Dalton's ambulance, followed by Wilson driving the major's jeep.

"Choppers are on the way," he told us, "we'd better be getting these people down to the pad."

Our "chopper pad" was nothing more than an open field on the edge of the town. When it wasn't being used by helicopters, it served as a pasture for local cattle. Only the seriously wounded were taken to the landing pad; the others were taken to the aid station on the base camp. Dalton's ambulance was used for the short ride, and when it was full, we used jeeps. At the pad Chi explained to the families that the wounded were being taken to American hospitals. They understood, and no one opposed our plan. Their faces reflected the same helpless, silent plea I had seen so many times before and had never quite gotten used to. While we waited for the helicopters, Dalton administered morphine to the most painfully wounded, eliminating most of the screaming. But there wasn't enough for everybody.

When the choppers appeared overhead, I directed them onto the pad with the radio on the back of Major Allen's jeep. Once on the ground, the loading of the wounded proceeded in a rapid, orderly manner. Relatives of the wounded insisted on helping with the loading, as if to be personally assured that their mother or brother or sister was, in fact, on the way to the hospital. One pathetic little woman kept forcing her baby in my arms, pleading with me to place it aboard the helicopter. I tried to make her understand that there was no point in evacuating her baby, that her baby was dead, but the noise of the helicopter and its prop wash made it impossible for her to understand me. Finally, she was led away, still fiercely clutching her dead child, and the loading continued.

The loading didn't take long. When the last victim was placed aboard the chopper, the door slid shut, and the chopper was ready to go. Slowly it lifted off the pad, straining under the burden it was carrying, hovering for a few anxious seconds over the pad to make sure it could handle the load. Once satisfied he could make it, the pilot increased the pitch of the main rotor, and the helicopter ascended into the clear blue October sky, reluctantly at first, then with ever-increasing speed until it was only a dot on the horizon. Then it was gone.

Now there was nothing else we could do. Dalton gathered up what remained of his supplies and put them in his bag. We were covered with blood from head to foot.

"What now?" he asked.

"Let's go home," I said; Dalton, Chi and I piled in the major's jeep. I knew no one would argue with the suggestion.

Riding back past the ruined market, Dalton asked me why it had happened. He asked me because he thought I knew everything that went through the enemy's mind, since I was supposed to know more about the enemy than anyone else. He wanted to know what the Viet Cong hoped to accomplish by doing something like this. I wanted to tell him this was their revenge for Hill 82, but he wouldn't understand that. He was looking for a reason that contained a certain degree of logic, but not this—not this attack against people who knew nothing of Hill 82. I wanted to tell him that in a political war you must take the war to the people because this is how you gain support, but I knew this would be unacceptable to a man who had given so much of himself to these same people.

Or perhaps Dalton knew all of this already. Perhaps he was familiar with Mao Tse-tung's theory of warfare—that all political power must flow from the barrel of a gun. It was possible that he understood all of this but refused to believe it, expecting me to have a different explanation. But I had no logical answer; I found it as unacceptable as Dalton did.

Political doctrine and ideology that motivated the Viet Cong could be explained very well in the antiseptic environment of a classroom or on the sterile pages of impressive-looking textbooks, for they dealt only with abstract thought. When this same doctrine and ideology is practiced in the market places of South Vietnam, a new dimension, not presented in the classroom or textbook is added, and this new dimension makes it all unacceptable. What is added in the market places is reality, a reality that infects the doctrine, making it malignant.

Reality is bits and pieces of innocent civilians scattered in a haphazard manner about the streets, and blood-splattered survivors screaming for their dead. Reality is a woman unable to accept the fact that her child is no longer alive and that the hopes and dreams she had for that child are dead too. Reality is pain and blindness and disfigurement. Reality is, quite simply, concrete and permanent, destroying all it touches—until there is nothing left to destroy.

Reality is an inherent part of the political belief of the Viet Cong but, like a bastard child, it is always explained and excused in kinder terms than the truth allows. Their propagandists explain such atrocities as acts of "liberation" performed, ironically enough, by the "People's Liberation Forces." Such actions as the destruction of a market place are considered "necessary" by the enemy, not for his own good but for the good of the people.

But all of this was not answering Dalton's question. He had asked "why," and I was still a long way from an acceptable "because." He was not interested in the political aspects of the war; his war was with pain and suffering and death. And he had just lost a very big battle.

"I don't know why, Jack," I answered honestly, "war is hell."

It seemed appropriate—as if it was the only acceptable answer—yet woefully inadequate.

Already it had been a long day, and it wasn't even nine o'clock.

October became a month of shattered hopes and dreams, a month in which we suffered eighteen assassinations, each one as senseless as the next. Each day there were operations, and each night there were ambushes; the contest was constant, unrelenting and ugly. . . .

Chapter Eleven

THE SHOOTING OF MAJOR CHAU

On the twentieth of October Major Chau was shot.

It never should have happened, at least not the way it did. He and Major Allen were returning from the base camp, where they had been invited to have dinner with the brigade commander and his staff. It had been an enjoyable occasion and, when it was over, the commander attempted to persuade Major Chau to spend the night at the base camp. When Major Chau politely refused, the commander insisted on sending an escort of armored personnel carriers back to the compound with him. But Major Chau politely refused this offer also, explaining to the commander that his own troops would provide an escort once he was outside the main gate.

With this understood, Major Allen and Major Chau left the base camp. On the way home, everything went wrong. Before they could reach the point where the escort waited, shots were fired from the darkness beside the road, and Major Chau slumped forward in the jeep. Only one bullet found its mark. It passed through the back of the front seat and ripped into the district chief's back.

Immediately, Major Allen called the district and gave us the grim news. As he was rushing home with his bleeding counterpart, Captain Wentworth called dust-off control in Long Binh, and an evacuation helicopter was on the way in seconds. Hau and I took a platoon of troops to secure the landing pad in case the Viet Cong planned on getting the chopper, too. By the time Major Allen arrived at the compound, the helicopter was only five minutes away—just long enough to pick up Major Chau's wife.

They got to the landing pad just as the chopper was making his slow descent. At an altitude of one hundred feet, the pilot flooded the pad with his landing light, then settled safely to the ground. Major Chau was rushed to the waiting helicopter, where a corpsman was waiting to begin an immediate blood transfusion. Dalton and Mrs. Chau quickly climbed aboard, and in thirty seconds the helicopter lifted itself into the night. All of this, the attempted assassination and the successful evacuation, had taken place in less than twenty minutes.

It was a night of tragedy and a night of miracles. It was a miracle that Major Allen—who had been slightly wounded, also—was still able to drive out of the ambush. It was a miracle that the dust-off arrived so soon, thus saving the district chief's life. The tragedy was obvious; At a time when we could not afford to lose him, Major Chau was gone, but as devastating as this blow was, it was offset by the fact that he would recover. In the months ahead, the Viet Cong would pay a very dear price for bungling the job of killing this man.

At the 93rd Evacuation Hospital at Long Binh, Major Chau underwent emergency surgery. He was on the operating table for three hours, while a team of surgeons cut into his stomach and back to remove the bullet, repairing in the process, most of the damage caused—another miracle. The bullet bypassed all vital organs, missing the spinal cord by a quarter of an inch. When the operation was complete, they sewed him up with stainless steel stitches.

For three weeks he was flat on his back in the recovery ward, consuming only what could pass through the plastic tubes attached to the ever-present bottles hanging above his head. At least twice a week I would visit him, and his face would register a feeble smile. He looked strangely out of place, lying there in the hospital bed—a man who had been so active, now completely inactive, his dark brown skin contrasting sharply with the white sheets. He was the only Vietnamese in the recovery ward, and this only added to his sense of displacement. But his spirits were high. During my visits, which I kept brief, he talked constantly of going home and how much had to be done there.

"We must hunt down the VC, Thieu Uy," he insisted.

It was pointless to tell him not to think of that now, to think only of getting well and following the doctor's orders. His thoughts went far beyond the confines of his adjustable hospital bed. That he would leave the hospital and return to Di An was a certainty known only to him, and what he would do when he got there was a constant thought in his mind.

This all-consuming desire was difficult for the doctors at the hospital to grasp. Their feelings were that he should be grateful just to be alive. And he was, but what they failed to understand was that he could not be grateful for living unless there was for him a purpose beyond merely being alive. And his only purpose was to return to Di An. Taking this one step further, his only purpose for returning to Di An was that the Viet Cong were there. So in the end, his strongest reason for being grateful for being alive was to destroy his enemy. After this was his natural concern for his wife and children.

The fact that he put his mission above everything else was only one reason he became the most successful and respected district chief in Vietnam. Because of this dedication, the Viet Cong would have been much better off had they killed him outright. If this couldn't have been done, there should have been no effort made at all, for it only served to crystallize his resolve to rid the district of every trace of the enemy.

The accelerated pacification campaign officially opened on the first of November, 1968, without Major Chau. We needed his guidance desperately during this period, for the campaign was an all-out nation-wide effort to put as many hamlets under government control as soon as possible. The Viet Cong violently opposed this action, since its primary purpose was to eliminate them and their control. It involved large military operations coupled with psychological operations, resulting in an increased emphasis on the pacification program.

This campaign meant an intensification of all programs, even mine. Pressure was placed on the Intelligence and Operations Coordination Center to provide more valid information about the enemy's locations. This required more of an effort from all of us, which meant an increase in the number of raids, ambushes, and operations. Captured Viet Cong provided the information necessary for more operations, resulting in more Viet Cong killed or captured, and on and on, setting off a chain reaction of events.

Still, the incident level remained high. Attacks on our outposts were a nightly occurrence. The Viet Cong continued to terrorize the district as the accelerated pacification program began to make its presence felt. Major Chau was informed daily of the situation and, whenever necessary, he would make a crucial decision concerning such matters as the deployment of his forces—from his hospital bed.

It was a trying time for all of us, Vietnamese and advisors alike, as the strain of the pressure often rubbed across raw nerves. Yet, in a strange sort of way, it seemed to pull us closer together than we'd ever been before. Now, with Major Chau gone and the campaign to push, we had to pull together, knowing that if we could survive this, we could accomplish anything.

Somewhere during the first two weeks of November, there was time for a promotion party for me. It was embarrasing for me, because the Vietnamese went to so much trouble. Tables, lined up end to end in the small courtyard of the compound, were loaded with cognac, beer, wine, French bread, duck, chicken, pork, and beef. After Major Allen pinned a silver first lieutenant's bar on my collar, the Vietnamese officers poured cognac on it. This was part of their tradition, though at the time I thought it was a waste of good cognac. At any rate, everyone thought it was great fun, and I was smelling like a distillery before the party even started. Then, according to more Vietnamese tradition, I was expected to drink a personal toast with anyone who desired to uphold the tradition. Within a very few minutes, I had consumed about 15 shots of cognac—an accomplishment I was proud of but was far from a record. It was a great party while it lasted, but unfortunately for me, it didn't last long. Somewhere around the twentieth "toast," I was "helped" to bed. This also had been predicted, since it was more of the tradition.

For those still standing, the party was still in full swing at three the next morning, or at least they told me it was. The next day, my first as a first lieutenant, was far worse than any I had spent as a second lieutenant. My head throbbed, my eyes felt as though someone had stepped on them, and my stomach wouldn't stop turning. I was beginning to wonder if promotions were worth the pain they caused.

114

Chapter Twelve

THE WOUNDING

The fifteenth of November was a Friday, a day I will never forget. We were still prosecuting the Accelerated Pacification Campaign, and on this day, we had planned a two-company operation in support of the effort.

This operation was to take place in Binh Tri Village, a favorite operating area for the Viet Cong because of its rugged terrain. We were going there because we had received reports of a recent enemy buildup in the area. This could not be allowed to happen, since Binh Tri, the center of the district, was a position that would allow the enemy to strike at any point he chose.

On this particular operation, we had asked the Scout-Dog Platoon at the base camp for a scout-dog team. According to the dog's handler, Sergeant Pine, the dog could do everything except walk on water, and he was working on that. He could sniff out Viet Cong tunnels, ambushes, booby traps, weapons caches, and even follow the enemy's trail. For months the "dog people" had been telling us how great their dogs were, so on this operation, Major Allen decided to give them a try. Lieutenant Vo, the district operations officer, was in charge. Captain Wentworth and I were to go with the PRUs, who were also a part of this operation. Sergeant Pine and his dog were with us.

I liked going with Wentworth, ever since the action at Hill 82. There was something about his easygoing manner that generated confidence, even though he had never been in combat before. With over eighteen years in the army, he was unusually aggressive for a man approaching forty. Yet his aggressiveness seemed to be directed toward himself—to prove that he had whatever it would take to get the job done. Korea had been a little too early for him, and when he got there, the war was over. Now he was determined that Vietnam would be different—he was determined to get a piece of this action, no matter how many operations it took. At 220 pounds, Wentworth was the heaviest man on the team, but he was far from being fat.

This weight was distributed evenly over his five-foot-ten-inch frame, with perhaps a little of it concentrated around the middle. A small, toothbrush moustache and a jungle hat pulled low over his eyes like Dalton's gave him the naturally rugged look of an experienced advisor. He knew it too, and actively cultivated this appearance. He always laughed when I told him this didn't seem fair because I'd been on the team much longer than he had, and that nothing would give me that seasoned look. Even his fatigues faded faster than mine.

It was a beautiful day, the sort of day I remembered so well from West Virginia; a day that was made rich early in the morning by a feeling of great expectations; a day that should have been reserved for very serious daydreaming. At seven-thirty in the morning the air was clean and crisp. It felt good to be walking through the thick grass with its dew-heavy blades striking my pants and making my boots shine with wetness. On this morning, death seemed to be a fantasy.

Our part of the operation started at the outpost of Binh Tri. We were to sweep south for about three kilometers and link up with Lieutenant Vo's force of one company, which was in a blocking position. The other company and the PRUs made up three elements. The idea was to flush the Viet Cong out of the thick, heavy brush and force them ahead of us, driving them into Vo's force. Then we would put on the "squeeze."

About one kilometer south of the outpost, we ran into heavy resistance from the foliage. Thick bushes with razor sharp thorns grew up about three feet, then curled around, creating a barbed-wire-like barrier. Slowly tracing our way through this maze was as painful as it was distracting, making a constant lookout for the enemy impossible. And when the sweat began to get in the cuts caused by the thorns, the distraction increased.

"No goddamn VC in his right mind would live in a place like this," Wentworth muttered as he took a long drink from his canteen. He purposely let a few drops run down his chin and then spread the cool water over his neck with his free hand. This seemed to refresh him, but his face still reflected a bit of agony. His fatigue shirt was already wet, and his pants were damp at the knees. I knew he'd never admit it, but he was tiring quickly, and we weren't half through the operation. And he seemed to resent the fact that I hadn't touched my canteen, while his was now half empty.

Sergeant Pine was in front of me and to the left with the scout-dog. The dog was unconcerned about the whole operation, stopping only occasionally to sniff at a bush or a tree.

"That son of a bitch ain't looking for VC. He's just trying to find out if another dog's been through here pissing on trees," Wentworth complained behind me. I was beginning to agree.

We had come to a particularly dense area, channelling us all through a tiny opening in the brush, when the dog suddenly stopped, and the hair on his back stood up. Sergeant Pine stopped too, and reached down and unleashed the big German Shepard. The dog took a few cautious steps forward and put his nose to the ground. Possibly another tunnel, I thought. I was about to tell Wentworth my analysis when I heard a sharp click.

Amazingly enough, I watched the ground under the dog explode. It appeared to happen in slow motion, the big black cloud of smoke expanding and rolling toward me, but I was powerless to react. And, for an instant, the dog became a part of the blackness, moving effortlessly upward with the cloud, until he ripped apart and disintegrated into a black and red mist. Then the cloud swept me up, slowly lifted me in the air, and dropped me in a clump of bushes some twenty feet from where I'd been standing. People around me were scattered about like bits of paper in a strong wind.

I lay on the ground for what seemed like a long time, trying to fit the pieces together in my mind, dimly aware of the confusion raging around me. There was no immediate pain—only a sharp, insistent ringing in my right ear. Even though I could see thorns deeply embedded in my right hand, it didn't hurt; it seemed like the hand belonged to someone else.

The closest man I could see was Nghia, the PRU who had been carrying my radio. Still dazed from the blast, I crawled over to see where he'd been hit. The radio had been blown off his back, and he was covered with greasy-looking blood. Nghia had been with me on that first ambush, and since then, we'd worked several operations together. Often, I had told him he was the ugliest man in the world—and he always laughed. IIe was ugly, too. IIis face resembled a dried coconut with two tiny black holes drilled in it for eyes, the left one considerably higher than the right. His nose—if you could call it that—was pushed flat against his face, exposing a pair of oversized nostrils that expanded when he smiled. Instinctively, I reached for his pulse. It was then that I noticed that his spinal cord was ripped out of his neck. The ugliest man in the world was dead.

Wentworth was sitting a few yards away, watching the blood run from a large hole in his leg.

"Looks like we really walked into one," he said trying to stop the blood with his hand. "The bastards knew this was a perfect place for a booby trap. Right here in this thick shit. What d'ya think it was?" He rocked back and forth on the ground in obvious pain.

"Had to be at least an artillery round. Probably a 105. Nghia's dead. They've killed Nghia." Wentworth didn't say anything.

"But the radio looks okay. I'll try to call the district," I continued. Before calling, I took the field dressing from my pistol belt and tied it tight around Wentworth's leg. The pressure almost stopped the bleeding.

Those who were only slightly wounded helped the others as best they could. I was trying to account for everybody, when I found Sergeant Pine lying face down with a hole in the calf of his left leg.

"How is it?" he asked anxiously.

"Not bad, but you'll be sore for a few days."

"How's . . . how's the dog?"

"He's gone," I told him, as painlessly as I could.

He started to cry and tried to turn away so I couldn't see the tears streaming down his dirty face.

Incredibly, the radio still worked. Wilson responded after my second call, and I quickly told him what had happened. I gave him our location, and he promised to get a dust-off immediately. He wanted to know the number of wounded, but I couldn't give him an exact count.

The next step was to get the wounded to a clearing big enough to handle the helicopter. We had just passed a small clearing about a hundred yards back that was just big enough; it was the only possible site. Those of us who were able began to carry the wounded back to the tiny clearing. I was well aware of the danger of other booby traps in the area, expecting any second to hear the same sickening sound, but there was no other way—the wounded had to get out. It took about ten minutes—carrying, pulling, and dragging the bloody, but still breathing men back to the clearing. There was very little Wentworth and I could do other than stop the bleeding. There was nothing for pain and very little water—most of the canteens had been riddled by the blast.

Sitting on the ground waiting for the helicopter, I noticed that the large blood stains on the front of my shirt were not drying. I had dismissed them before as blood from the wounded, but I now could see that they were spreading. Slowly I unbuttoned my shirt and looked inside. Blood was leaking from five different places, but there was no pain from the wounds. My right ear was throbbing, and I knew it was seriously damaged, but it didn't hurt either.

"What's keeping that goddamned chopper so long?" Wentworth muttered in impotent frustration, knowing as well as I that time was vital—not to us but to the Vietnamese.

"Tell them they are going to an American hospital," I told Phi, the only PRU that could speak English, "tell them they cannot die; we must come back and kill VC."

The PRUs took the pain well, without screaming or crying out. Knowing they were going to an American hospital boosted the morale of the conscious ones, and those who were unconscious needed no morale booster. As we waited there in the hot sun, paying for each passing moment with drops of blood, I felt fiercely proud of these little brown men. The fact that we had inflicted no casualties on the enemy made me want to scream out in frustration, but the frustration didn't take away the pride.

Finally, the helicopter was overhead, and I marked our position with smoke. In a few seconds he was on the ground, and the wounded were loaded in order of priority - serious first, then the walking wounded. With our twelve wounded, the pilot was concerned about being able to lift off. But we did, with the landing skids barely clearing the tree tops. On the way to Long Binh, Sergeant Pine asked me to look at his leg again.

"Still looks good," I said, "you're lucky."

The first stop was the 24th Evacuation Hospital where the seriously wounded Vietnamese were taken off, then we flew on to the 93rd which was a little less than a mile away. In the emergency room, Wentworth, Pine and I were placed on examining carts. A cute little nurse in starched jungle fatigues cut away the remainder of my shirt, along with my pants and boots.

I really didn't feel it was necessary to cut off my boots just when

119

they were beginning to feel comfortable. I was perfectly capable of removing them myself. When I asked her why she was doing this, she mumbled something about hospital policy and proceeded to give Pine and Wentworth the same treatment. Then a sheet was placed over each of us. My ear was aching now, and my right shoulder was beginning to stiffen. I looked over at Wentworth, and he flashed me a nervous, artificial smile.

"Guess we blew the hell out of that one," he said. I agreed.

"But you know what? This is Purple Heart Day for us, buddy, so it can't be all that bad."

He was right of course. We had more than met the requirements for a Purple Heart, but it didn't seem so important. In a few minutes we were rolled into the X-ray room where each little hole was photographed. The corpsman taking the X rays told me they would assist the surgeon in removing the fragments. This was a shock I hadn't counted on. For some reason, I had been thinking that I would be back in the district that night, and now this man was talking about surgery which would mean weeks in the hospital. I was still blissfully ignorant of the seriousness of my wounds.

After the X rays, we were rolled back into the emergency room and pushed to the side. It was a totally helpless feeling to be lying there, completely naked except for the sheet, watching people in the emergency room go about their business, drinking coffee, smoking, laughing, and talking. The same nurse that cut off my boots asked me several questions—name, age, rank, unit, etc. This information was typed on a card, and the card was placed under my head, like a shipping order. I asked for a cup of coffee, and she looked at me as if she had suddenly discovered I was a lunatic.

"Surgery patients aren't allowed to have coffee. You'd just throw up when they put you to sleep," she curtly replied, qualifying, with this single statement, as a first-class bitch.

They came for Pine first. As he was being rolled away, I told him I'd see him later, but he didn't respond. His left leg was now heavily bandaged. I was talking to Wentworth when Major Chau walked in. By a strange coincidence, he was being released this same day and Jackson had come for him. Our request for the dust-off had been monitored by Jackson, and he brought the district chief down to see us.

"I am very sorry for you," he told us, and I'm sure we looked

120

deserving of pity, lying there under the sheets.

"We'll be alright, sir," I said.

He wanted to see our wounds, so we pulled down the sheets and displayed the damage. Wentworth was proud of his because it was bigger than mine, but I had at least five smaller ones. Our conversation was cut short by the corpsman who came for me. Major Chau told me, as I was being rolled away, that they would take good care of me. This was reason enough to feel confidence—an American hospital being recommended to an American by a Vietnamese.

I was rolled into the operating room head first. Actually, it was one room with three operating tables. Bright lights hung from the ceiling, yet the room appeared dark except for the tables directly under the lights. Nurses scurried back and forth, looking coldly efficient in their light green smocks. The air-conditioning made the room cold; so cold, in fact, that I was shivering as they lifted me off the cart onto the table.

As my arms were strapped down, two masked men scrubbed the blood from my chest and shoulder. They found fragment wounds on my legs that I was unaware of. They were scrubbed too, and then shaved. I looked up at another masked man who told me he was my surgeon. His gown was blood-stained from previous operations, proof that he was indeed, a surgeon. All I could see of his face were his eyes and they looked tired. I told him who I was, but he already knew from the card under my head. He asked if I was afraid and I told him yes, a little. He then told me that in a very few seconds I would be asleep, because he was going to put a needle in my hand. The needle was attached to a rubber hose that led to a bottle over the table. He told me that the bottle was filled with sodium pentothal, which would put me in a deep sleep.

I was beginning to relax a little. It was easy to believe this man who sounded so sincere. I was told to count back from one hundred when the needle was in my hand. Just before the nurse inserted the needle, I looked over at the table nearest me. Pine was strapped down, asleep. With a stainless steel saw, another masked man was sawing off his left leg, just below the knee. I felt the needle go in, and I started to count backward. At ninety-six, the darkness closed over me.

The world returned slowly in the recovery room. When I opened my eyes, a sweet-looking nurse, one I'd never seen before, was standing over me, holding a piece of gauze pad against my shoulder. Her first question, which was how I felt, had little impact. I was hoping she could tell me how I felt. Time had been suspended since I was rolled into the operating room. That had seemed like only a few seconds ago, but the clock on the wall told me it was three-thirty. I realized six hours had passed since they had put me to sleep.

I awoke with the realization of Pine's amputation fresh in my mind. The sudden realization that it had happened touched off a mild panic. A lot of things could have happened to me or been taken from me during those hours, and everything I thought of was bad. I thought about my legs first, since their welfare was uppermost in my mind. If I still had them, everything would be alright, I told myself. Don't panic now.

By raising myself on both elbows, I could see the place at the end of the bed where they should be. There were two large mounds under the sheet where my feet normally were. I breathed easier, but I still wasn't convinced. I moved my left leg and the left mound moved, and when I moved my right leg, I got the same reaction from the right mound. This convinced me I had not suffered the same fate as Pine. The nurse told me to lie still, apparently puzzled at my sudden interest in my feet.

"I got both of them," I told her, "they're both here."

"Of course they are," she offered patronizingly, revealing her former experience with psychiatric patients, "now why don't you get a little more rest?"

As the effects of the drugs wore off, I was able to feel exactly where the surgeon had sliced me. I had four fairly large incisions on my right chest and shoulder and six smaller ones on my legs. I decided at this point that I was a poor judge of the seriousness of wounds. Pine's wound had appeared to be very minor—in fact, it appeared far less serious than Wentworth's. If anyone had to lose a leg, I was sure it would have been Wentworth, since his wound was the largest. But it didn't work that way. I was also surprised to discover that the wounds were left open after the surgeon removed the shrapnel. The nurse told me this was done in several cases to allow the wound to heal from the inside, thus reducing the chance of infection.

122

That night I was moved to Ward 3, a recovery ward. Wentworth was already there sitting up in bed watching a rerun of the "Tonight Show." Some young woman, in a sparkling, sequined dress, was telling Johnny Carson how rough it was to survive in show business. Her story, although convincing, produced little sympathy in Ward 3.

The first day following the operation was sheer agony, but on the second day I felt better; I was allowed to move around the ward and run short errands for the more seriously wounded. At meal times, I carried trays to those confined to their beds. Wentworth was a little slower getting out of bed, but he tried hard. I provided some good-natured incentive by accusing him of being an old man. On the third day he managed, with the aid of crutches, to go with me to visit Sergeant Pine. He was in Ward 2, the intensive care ward.

This was the first time we had seen Pine since the three of us had been together in the emergency room. I felt guilty about his leg. I had assured him, at least twice, that he was going to be alright, that there was really nothing to worry about. I felt that the doctor had, in some way, betrayed both of us. Now, with his leg gone, I didn't know what to say. When we hobbled in, Pine was sitting up in bed reading the latest issue of the "Stars and Stripes."

We asked him the routine, senseless questions about how he felt, and he gave the usual replies about being fine. I attempted to explain how I felt about his leg, and both Wentworth and I tried not to look at the flat place under the sheet where his lower left leg should have been. I was beginning to feel a bit awkward and guilty again, standing there before Pine on two, more or less, good legs.

"Don't worry about it, sir. It wasn't your fault," he told me. His positive attitude was staggering.

"I'm really lucky in a way, because I'm still alive. A lot of my buddies aren't as lucky. And I'm going home soon. But I do regret that I wasn't able to do any more. I really wanted to, you know."

I told him I knew. Then we discussed the nurses on our respective wards, trying to determine who had the most attractive one. We finally agreed that Pine did. He didn't say anything about his dog, and neither did we. A few minutes later we left.

The sense of betrayal and guilt I had felt earlier was replaced with admiration and pride. Pine's attitude was worth a place on the front page of every newspaper in the free world, but, unfortunately, it wasn't the story reporters were looking for. Somewhere along the way he had picked up more than he'd lost. He had done all he could—now the war was somebody else's burden.

Walking back to our ward, I asked myself how I would feel if I were in Ward 2. It was a difficult question, the type you rarely ask—it demands an honest answer. I felt I would have a different outlook—one that would feed on pity and self-hate. I knew I would feel cheated, not only because of the loss but by what the loss would mean. It would end my participation in the war, and I couldn't let that happen, not now. Somebody would have to make the Viet Cong pay for this, and I wanted to be part of it. It was no longer difficult to understand why Major Chau had felt as he did while lying flat on his back in this same hospital. He had felt outrage and hate. He had been insulted and humiliated. Such feelings were serious wounds in a war that feeds on violence, assault, fury and a personal hate for a soulless enemy. The damage to the flesh was only a side effect of the more serious damage.

After lunch, the administration sergeant came through our ward, handing out Purple Hearts. With the amount of dignity attached to the occasion, he could just as easily have been serving boiled cabbage. Just as Wentworth predicted, we both received one. And the impersonal attitude of the hospital was only fitting, since the booby trap that made it all possible had been impersonal. Nonetheless, it was an attractive heart-shaped medal suspended on a deep purple ribbon, with George Washington's likeness imprinted on the front and the words "For Military Merit" engraved on the back.

"This don't seem right," I told Wentworth.

"What do you mean?"

"This part about 'merit'. Did we do something meritorious out there?"

"Hell yes we did!"

"What? What's so damn meritorious about stumbling into a booby trap?"

"Well, for one thing, Charlie has one less now than he had before. We used up one, and that contributed to the war effort."

Wentworth refused to acknowledge any inappropriateness in the markings of his Purple Heart. While he may not have been looking forward to receiving it, now that he had it, he wasn't about to view it critically. It was all he had to offer as proof that his scars were received honorably, in the line of duty. And later, if his grandchildren wanted to know what he had done in the war, he could pull out his Purple Heart and explain, in whatever fashion he desired, exactly what "Military Merit" meant.

Our stay in the 93rd lasted exactly one week. On the morning of the eighth day, we were rolled back into the operating room and the surgeon closed our wounds. This time he was wearing a clean light green gown and he didn't look as tired as before. For the small wounds on my legs he used nylon sutures, but for the larger chest and shoulder wounds, he used stainless steel wire.

That same afternoon we were taken out to Bien Hoa Airbase for evacuation to the Sixth Convalescent Center at Cam Ranh Bay, some 200 miles north of Long Binh. Those of us chosen for the trip were loaded on a four-engine, propellor-driven plane called a C-130 by the air force, but before the flight was over, we had other names for it.

It was one of the hottest days of the year and, in keeping with the tradition of the air force, it was on this day that the air conditioning "was not working properly." As a matter of fact, it wasn't working at all. This, by itself, would have been sufficient to make the trip miserable, but as I started to sweat, the sweat penetrated the wounds, greatly increasing the misery factor. Wentworth was luckier than I. He was allowed to lie on a litter in the rear of the plane, since he had a wound of some magnitude. The ordeal seemed endless; with the plane so crowded, standing up or moving around was impossible. There was barely room on the canvas seats to sit down. But the air force did provide a fried chicken boxed lunch for those of us who felt like eating.

Three stops and some five hours later, we touched down at Cam Ranh Bay, completely drained of the normal anticipation that a new environment is supposed to bring. We were met at the air base by a fleet of ambulances that drove us down the sandy, windswept coast to a settlement of long, wooden buildings that appeared to be a movie site for a Nazi concentration camp.

This was a dramatic change from the scenery at Long Binh. There were no vast stores of supplies and equipment to clutter the landscape, or none of the hustle-and-bustle activity that characterized Long Binh as the largest supply depot in Vietnam. Instead, there were only the barren, lonely stretches of beach and white sand and sun which soon became a welcomed change from the place we had just left. Located right on the South China Sea, the sandy beaches were a favorite place to while away the hours.

Life was relaxed at the center, partly because of its location on the beach and because nothing more than recovery was expected of us. Wentworth and I were assigned to Ward Q, the Officer's Recovery Ward. Perhaps the Q was simply a coincidence of the numbering system, but I suspected it was deliberate, and I attributed it to the enlisted men in the administration division of the center. At any rate, it was good for a lot of laughs. The nurses were friendly and efficient. All major problems concerning appointments with doctors and therapists were handled by them, relieving us of nearly all responsibility for our own recuperation.

Time and the problems time usually brings slipped lazily by in this idyllic setting. My favorite pastime was to return from lunch and lie across my bunk, enjoying the slight breeze that was always blowing off the ocean. The wards were ideal for enjoying the breeze. Constructed of plywood and screen wire, they allowed the full effect of the breeze to penetrate. Unfortunately, they allowed the extra fine sand to come in also, making the wards impossible to keep clean.

On other days I would lie on the beach, watching the waves rolling in and the F4 Phantom jets that were constantly taking off from the air base a short distance away. This particular section of the beach was reserved for the exclusive use of the patients, and it was not unusual to find it deserted, especially in the evenings. This loneliness of the beach in the evening gave it an empty, forelorn atmosphere.

When I was feeling lonely or sad or depressed, I would walk along the deserted beach, burying my sense of desolation in the desolation of the beach, which occasionally, would help untangle the loose ends of my mind. The small dunes and scattered scrubs of trees, dwarfed early in life by too much salt spray and too little soil, made a very interesting and picturesque landscape. The peacefulness found on the beach was a sharp contrast to the violence and death I'd left behind in Di An. Walking alone, digging my toes in the sand made it very hard to imagine that a war could be raging anywhere in this country. I had experienced this same sensation before, and I had been tragically deceived by it. Yet it was even harder to forget my involvement in the war at such times; I soon realized this as I tried to separate myself from the events I'd been deeply involved in. The memory of the killings and bombings, and the hatred they generated in me followed me to Cam Ranh Bay and would not leave me alone. Now, far removed from the fighting, surrounded by a far less hostile environment and the possibility of going home because of wounds, my commitment to the war was placed to the test. Had it been anything short of total, it would have surfaced here. But it didn't.

In fact, during the weeks at the center, my original commitment was hardened. I knew I had to return to the district—there was still so much to do. Any other course of action was unthinkable. Major Chau had been right. There could be no rest until the last remnants of the enemy had been totally destroyed. This obsession scared me, but the thought of leaving before it was accomplished scared me even more. Realizing that there was no other acceptable course of action open to me, I considered each passing day as unproductive.

With recuperation our major objective, time soon became an enemy. Even the fascination of the sea became tiresome, and each wave that rolled in was disgustingly similar to its predecessor. Out of desperation, Wentworth and I discovered the craft shop. He became hooked on making a leather wallet that he finally loused up, and I made a model B52 bomber that never got off the beach.

There was only one bright spot in our otherwise monotonous days. Her name was Kathy, and she was with the Red Cross Office of the hospital. Kathy was the name on the plastic tag pinned to her blue uniform, but she was more commonly referred to as the "Blue Angel"—for reasons other than the color of her uniform. Her official duties included assisting the patients in passing messages to their families back home and in making emergency notifications in case of serious illness. Aside from this, and equally important, were her efforts to make life as comfortable as possible for us. Each new patient received a kit from Kathy that contained such necessities as soap, toothpaste, brush, razor, razor blades, etc. It could be considered a touch of home or at least representative of the things we had all left at home.

She seemed to care about us—a very simple, sincere caring. It seemed that she couldn't do enough for us. Her innocent efforts were an inspiration to those of us who had seen precious little innocence here. She would play cards and checkers with us, and bring us little bags of "goodies" like candy, cookies and chewing gum. It was a real delight when she stopped by, giving us another look at the beautiful form her uniform failed to completely hide—a body that matched her vibrant personality completely.

There were few things more important to discuss than women, and since Kathy was the best specimen in a fifty-mile radius, it was natural that she became the subject of many conversations. One lazy afternoon, Wentworth and I were discussing her assets, which were many, with nothing more serious in mind than passing away an unwelcomed afternoon.

"How'd you like to take her for a walk down the beach some night?" he asked offhandedly.

"What do you mean?" I replied, trying to match his casual reply. I failed.

"If you got sixty dollars, she'll go for a walk and stay in the bushes as long as it takes."

"Who told you this?" I demanded, feeling an obligation to defend the reputation of our Blue Angel.

"The helicopter pilot, down at the other end." He motioned toward the end of the ward facing the ocean.

Apparently nothing was sacred if Wentworth was telling the truth. The pilot was going "walking" with Kathy that evening, and since I didn't believe what everyone else apparently knew (and accepted), Wentworth suggested we follow and watch. At first it sounded like a plan worthy of a moron, but it had some merit, and Wentworth explained it to me. If nothing happened, then Kathy would be exonerated of suspicion. On the other hand, if something did happen, we would at least know the truth. The fact that it was none of our business either way had no bearing on our ultimate decision to follow and observe.

According to Wentworth, the meeting would occur outside our ward at about six o'clock. This was upsetting, both personally and professionally. As an intelligence officer, I should have known this tidbit of information long before Wentworth; it was the unkindest cut of all.

At any rate, just as predicted, she walked by our ward at six sharp. The pilot walked out and followed at a discreet distance, and Wentworth and I followed the pilot at a discreet distance. I had been taught the "Principles of Foot Surveillance" at Fort Holabird, Maryland, which qualified me to lead our stalking operation. If someone had been watching this whole affair, it would look like a rerun of a very bad Abbott and Costello movie.

At a point about a half a mile from the hospital, Kathy and the pilot met in a small valley between two sand dunes. Taking all the necessary precautions to avoid detection, Wentworth and I hid in a clump of bushes atop a small dune that commanded a view of the miniature valley. There was a conversation in progress, but we were unable to interpret it. Our pilot friend removed a number of bills from his wallet and handed them to her. This transaction apparently satisfied Kathy—she produced an army blanket that was hidden at the base of the dune and spread it on the sand—with the U.S. side up. Kathy then removed her blue Red Cross uniform, carefully folding it to avoid wrinkles, and made herself comfortable on the blanket. Our friend followed her lead, taking about five seconds to slip out of his hospital pajamas, clearly exposing his urgency. There were no preliminaries, no fondling, no hugging or kissing. Once positioned between her legs, he quickly went to work, and just as quickly, Kathy succeeded in earning his flight pay.

In less than five minutes it was over, and in another three they were both dressed. Kathy carefully placed the blanket back in its hiding place and walked toward the hospital, looking no worse for the wear. A couple of minutes later, the pilot followed. After waiting a decent length of time, we went back too. Wentworth was right, but it didn't justify his "holier than thou" smirk.

The fact that I had observed sweet, innocent little Kathy selling her body was not as upsetting as the business-like manner she chose to do it in. She could be had for $60, but not $55, and this was the real tragedy. By charging the higher amount, she wasn't cheap, hence she wasn't being had. Perhaps her rationalization went something like that, or maybe it was much simpler, relying solely on the old "all-the-traffic-can-bear" philosophy. Wentworth wrote it off simply as "the way things really are." Whatever reason or justification, I decided then and there to cease supporting the Red Cross in its worldwide mission of mercy, not from any sense of moral outrage but feeling, quite simply, that any organization as skilled as this in the subtle art of private enterprise, must be financially solvent.

After a month at the center, Wentworth and I were transferred to the main air force hospital at Cam Ranh. Only after arriving at the Twelfth Air Force Hospital did I realize how serious my ear damage was. The explosion had literally blown out my right ear drum, leaving a clear passage from my mouth to the outside world via my right ear. I should have realized how serious it was when I discovered I could blow smoke through my ear, but I didn't. I entertained my ward mates at the center with this little trick several times, and when the ear surgeon at the air force hospital discovered what I'd been doing, he nearly went berserk.

Both Wentworth and I had a hole in our right eardrums, but mine was larger. Seriousness in ear cases is determined by the size of the rupture in the drum (all sorts of valuable information can be picked up in hospitals). The surgeon explained to us that we would both have to undergo surgery to repair the damage. He went into great detail about the terrible things that could happen if the condition was not corrected immediately.

"Can it be done right here in Cam Ranh?" I asked.

"Well yes, but the usual practice is to evacuate these cases to Japan," he replied.

"Why do you want it done here?" he wanted to know. I told him that I was afraid if they sent me to Japan I would not be allowed to return to Vietnam. This stopped him cold, but he agreed to do the operations at Cam Ranh.

In both cases the operation was basically the same. A small piece of membrane was removed from the skull, just above the ear. This piece of membrane was used to patch the hole in the eardrum in the same manner a hot patch is used to cover a hole in a bicycle tube. In my case, the operation was complicated by the structure of that portion of the skull that protects the inner ear. Apparently, my head was malformed, a condition I had been accused of for many years, but this was the first time I had been presented with medical proof. I was told that a large portion of that bone would have to be drilled away before the operation could take place.

Lying in the bed next to me the night before the operations, Wentworth started laughing to himself.

"What's so funny? You think we're going to have fun tomorrow?" I asked.

130

"No, it won't be fun. But I think it's funny that your head is 'malformed.' Is that the word he used—'malformed'?" Wentworth asked.

"Go screw yourself," I told him and turned over and went to sleep. But before I did, I could still hear him chuckling to himself.

The operation was painful, even though I had been given several injections that were designed to keep me conscious below the threshold of pain. It didn't work out that way. I could feel the drill grinding away inside my ear, feel the shooting, searing spears of pain ripping into every nerve my head possessed, and above all this, I could hear the surgeon tell his aides, "I don't understand why he's experiencing so much pain. Give him another shot of local (anesthetic) above the ear."

I felt the pricks of the needle attempting to deaden the feeling in my ear, but they didn't succeed in reducing the pain—only deadened my ability to care, leaving me in a twilight zone of throbbing, outraged nerves and faraway voices.

The post-operative pain was tremendous. For five days following the operation, I was on a man-made miracle called Demerol. When the pain become more than I could bear, one shot of this stuff put me in a world far beyond the reaches of pain. But its side effects played hell with my nervous system, magnifying each sound and each sensation to unbearable dimensions. During these five days, I had some insight into the world of the drug addict, experiencing, on a limited scale, his pleasure and pain, frighteningly aware of why he is often compelled to steal and kill for this insatiable master who easily controls what is left of his life. On the fifth day, I asked to be taken off Demerol, deciding I would rather cope with the pain than the ups and downs of the pain reliever. And as bad as this pain was, I was consoled by the fact that it connected me to reality—something Demerol would never do.

The nurses at the air force hospital were very nice and friendly and much cuter than the army nurses we'd seen since being wounded. Wentworth told me my opinions were shaped this way because the air force nurses wore short, stateside uniforms, while the army nurses had to wear jungle fatigues. He told me I should be more loyal to the army.

We both got to watch the Bob Hope Show when it arrived at Cam Ranh. Ann-Margaret and the Gold Diggers were well received, along with "Miss World"—some heavy chested girl from Australia.

131

Being patients, we were allowed to sit up front and get a ringside view of the action. Even the rain at the end of the show took very little away from the performance of this extraordinary man who had freely given so many of his own Christmases so that Christmas wouldn't lose its meaning to America's fighting men. We celebrated Christmas, 1968, in the ward, drinking eggnog heavily spiked with smuggled rum, bourbon and scotch.

A couple of days after Christmas, Wentworth was released. This meant that I had to celebrate New Year's at the Officer's Club without him. I survived the flying corks and empty champagne bottles and the incredibly bad band from the Philippines. After that, I was ready to return to Di An.

The doctor was reluctant to release me. He kept saying that if I left too early, the patch would not take, and the operation would have to be done again. This argument kept me quiet for a couple of days, and then I began to restate my case for going home. I promised I would do everything he instructed me to do concerning the ear, and if any difficulty arose, I would return to the hospital immediately. On the eighth of January he had listened to enough of my reasons for leaving, and I was released. Outprocessing at the hospital consisted of paying "my bill," which was computed on the basis of one dollar a day. No one explained what it was for, but I assumed it was for use of the bed.

The trip back home aboard a lumbering, ancient old bird called a Caribu was uneventful, though I was fearful we were about to lose an engine on two occasions. At the landing strip at Di An, Sergeant Jackson was waiting for me. There was a small homecoming for Wentworth and me that night. It was good to be home. Major Chau was over, and we compared our wounds and discussed hospitals. After that, the discussion turned to the more serious business of destroying the enemy, and I was filled in on what had happened during the two months I'd been away. Yes, it was good to be home. There were a lot of things to do.

Chapter Thirteen

THE KILLING OF CHIN HIEN

Three days after my return a large operation was planned that would take us to the border of Lai Thieu District, our neighbor to the west. I was eager to get in the field again, even though I had promised the doctor at Cam Ranh that I would not do anything that could possibly result in more injury to my ear. The doctor had believed this was possible on an advisory team, he being so far removed from the real war that he believed everything he was told. He told me to keep it clean and dry and not to expose myself to any "loud noises"—as if I were in complete control of my environment. If, for example, a mortar round dropped through the roof of our compound, I was supposed to possess the power to direct it to explode quietly. A situation such as this would clearly do additional damage to my ear, among other things. I saw no need to tell Major Allen that the surgeon had placed me under severe restrictions. This would only cause confusion, since the Major thought in straight lines. If I was still in need of medical attention, why was I home? If I was home, I must be well. Facts would only confuse him.

The operation was a joint venture between Major Chau and the district chief of Lai Thieu. The idea was to attack the Viet Cong's sanctuary on the border separating the two districts. It had been known for some time that the enemy had been taking advantage of the area between the two districts, using the border as an operation base. It was standard practice for every district to leave a one-hundred-meter "buffer zone" between its operational area and the border of its neighbor. This prevented forces from one district stumbling into the forces of another district, resulting in needless casualties. But it gave the Viet Cong some two hundred meters of real estate, wherever two districts came together, that was rarely operated in. Hopefully, we could remedy this situation that allowed the Viet Cong to conduct raids in either district and being pursued by neither. If we were successful, the situation would come to an end; if we were extremely successful, we would kill or capture

133

the Secretary of the Lai Thieu District Party, a Mr. Chin Hien who was reportedly operating in the area.

A lot of time and effort had gone into planning this operation. Hau's information was solid, and he knew it. We would be aided in the operation by a skinny, sixteen-year-old guerilla who had been captured while I was still in the hospital. Under intense interrogation, he had admitted knowing the hiding place of Chin Hien and had agreed to take us there, providing we would change his status from "Prisoner of War" to that of "Defector." In a sense, he agreed to "turn state's evidence," a very common and often successful technique employed to lead us to the Big Fish. Life was made much easier in Vietnam if one was considered a defector instead of a prisoner. This bit of wisdom must have been passed to the original Vietnamese from the original American advisor. The only thing unusual about this operation was that we were after a party secretary in someone else's district.

The operation kicked off about seven o'clock. It was good to be back in the field again. My legs were stiff from the long, useless days in the hospital, and I was travelling about ten pounds lighter, but other than this, I was in fairly good shape. Sergeant Chi, the dependable one, was with me, along with our new radio operator, Tinh. (Phuc had been relieved for excessive drinking while I was in the hospital.) Hau was in charge which was only logical since the operation was being directed solely against a member of the infrastructure.

The first objective was to search an old pagoda. It was supposed to be the hiding place for the rest of our informant's group. We found the hiding place beneath the altar, but it was empty. Apparently it had just been evacuated. We weren't overly concerned about this because there were other places our informant had to take us—more important places that he promised would reveal Chin Hien.

Our operating force was quite small, making it possible to move rapidly from place to place. We had two platoons of Popular Force soldiers and the PRUs, which now numbered fifteen. This gave us a force almost equal to a company. We had planned no major engagements, and if we weren't pushed into any, this force would be adequate.

After the pagoda, the kid led us through several rice paddies to the edge of a small hamlet. The hamlet had all the appearances of being very poor. A few scrawny chickens pecked around in the dirt, apparently finding something to eat that I couldn't see. There were a couple of pigpens but no pigs and a little boy, with no clothes on, stared at us. In the back of the houses, near one of the empty pigpens, our informant pointed to a spot on the ground and said to Hau, "Hien hides there, in the ground."

It didn't look like much, just a spot on the ground. But I knew better than to dismiss it as a simple spot—the tunnel with the girl hadn't looked like much either. There was nothing about this particular place that would attract the attention of even the most suspicious among us. In fact, it would have been impossible to find without the services of our informer.

The procedure was basically the same one used at the tunnel with the tax collector. The troops quickly formed a circle around the area, anticipating and making preparations for, some kind of violence. And I began to feel the rising excitement, also. I was hoping Hien would be in the tunnel, and we would succeed in bringing him out. But my feeling went further than this. Secretly, I hoped he would resist, giving justification for violence. The long confinement in the hospital had given me time to brood and hate, and now that hatred was hungry for an outlet.

As an advisor, however, I knew it was my duty to tactfully remind Hau of the importance of capture, but it was a listless, unconvincing reminder, offered more from routine than conviction.

Hau told me of Hien's reputation for performing all sorts of terrorists acts against the people of Lai Thieu. He had once forced a rice farmer to witness the murder of his three young children, and while two of Hien's henchmen held her, the farmer's wife was raped several times before her throat was cut. The farmer's crime? He had refused to give Hien half of his rice crops. This alone was more than enough justification for killing Hien. The fact that he was the most powerful Viet Cong in the district would only make his death more desirable.

There were several options we could use to flush the enemy out of the tunnel providing, of course, there was a tunnel and they were in it. One technique, the most common, would be to have one of the soldiers rip the cover away. But a more logical approach would be to let our informer do it since he seemed to know so much about the tunnel's layout. This would serve two purposes: first, we would uncover the tunnel, and secondly, we could determine the loyalty of our young friend. If the lid happened to be booby trapped, we would lose only the kid, who was more dispensible than anyone else. My trip to the hospital had made me touchy about the possibility of booby traps, and I urged Hau to take the more pragmatic course of action.

"Okay, Troung Uy. We let him do it," Hau said.

Then Hau told the kid what he wanted, and the kid was all for it. It worked out well for everyone, even our young friend. He unceremoniously ripped out the dirt-covered wooded covering and threw it in the weeds. Once it was removed, Hau ran over and shouted into the opening.

"What is he saying?" I asked Chi.

"He tells them to surrender," Chi replied.

There was no reply. Hau and the kid talked for a few seconds, with the kid insisting someone was in the tunnel. His insistence was understandable, since his status as a defector depended on it. It was obvious from the construction of the lid and the fact that the tunnel was so near the houses that the Viet Cong who had dug the tunnel had collaborators on the outside. Otherwise the opening would not have been so well disguised; and it could only have been disguised from the outside, making it blend perfectly with the undisturbed surroundings. Yet it gave all the appearances of being empty. Again Hau shouted into the tunnel; again no reply.

"What now, Troung Uy?" I asked.

"Maybe I send soldier inside to see if VC hide here," he told me.

Our young informer was vigorously protesting this possibility, but Hau had waited long enough. A soldier was about to be sent in when gunshots started coming from the tunnel. As the rest of us dashed for cover, the soldier who had prepared to enter the tunnel tossed a grenade into the opening. The ground gave a slight shudder, and the inevitable cloud of smoke drifted slowly upward from the hole, followed by silence. In less than five seconds it had happened, as automatically as a reflex. No more difficult decisions would have to be made about the tunnel and its inhabitants—it was now a near certainty that anyone inside was dead.

Even before the smoke had cleared, preparations were made for the dirty work of dragging out the dead. Two volunteers slipped through the tiny opening and immediately reported finding three bodies. One by one they were dragged out into the sunlight. The kid, standing at the tunnel entrance, identified each blood-smeared body as it was removed. The last one was Chin Hien. Both his legs were mangled and there were large, gaping holes in his stomach and chest, but he was still alive. He turned his head from side to side, looking around him with a dazed and frightened expression frozen on his bloody face. He mumbled something softly, almost under his breath.

"What's he trying to say?" I asked Chi. Chi and Hau bent over the form of Hien and listened. Hau told Hien something, and a few seconds later Hien replied. This conversation continued as the soldiers forgot their looting for a minute and gathered around, attracted by this unusual scene.

"He ask Hau if he will live and Hau say no. Hau tell him he is hurt very bad. Too bad to live. When he hear this, Hien ask Hau to kill him," Chi told me, dispassionately.

"How about a dust-off? Will it help?" I asked Hau. We both knew the answer, but the question had to be asked.

"No Troung Uy, he does not need a helicopter. He does not need anything. The hurt is very bad and he will die soon. He wants to die." Hau said something to Sergeant Minh, the chief interrogator. Minh was commonly referred to by the advisors as "Sad Eyes" because of the constant expression of sadness mirrored there. Sad Eyes, who was standing over Hien, unholstered his .45 and pulled back the hammer. There was more conversation between Hau and Hien, as Sergeant Minh made final preparations for the job he had to do. Then Hien said no more and closed his eyes. Hau stood up and backed away and, as if this signal had been preconceived, Sad Eyes blew the top of Hien's head away with a single blast from his .45. A violent tremor shook Hien's body, then he lay still.

"We will report three VC die in tunnel," Hau told me.

"Yes, Hau. Three VC die in tunnel. It is easier for us this way."

The tunnel contained a wide assortment of weapons and documents. The documents were of more importance to the Lai Thieu Intelligence Officer, but the weapons were ours. Hau gave me Hien's personal weapon, a new K-54 automatic pistol.

"For you, Troung Uy. This is—what you say—souvenir. You can take it to your country," he told me.

I was shocked because the weapon was extremely rare, and now that we had captured one in perfect condition, Hau was giving it to me. Its value on the war souvenir market was at least $300, and Hau was fully aware of this. Also, there could be some difficulty for Hau if it were discovered at Bien Hoa that he did not report all weapons found. But we were both familiar with this routine; I would give him an old .45 when we returned to the district and he could report the .45 as the personal weapon of Hien.

As we walked back across the dry paddies, I asked Chi what Hien's last words were. For some reason, at the time, I felt this was important. Perhaps it would make the justification of what I'd just seen easier.

"He tell Hau he must do this one last thing for him. He tell Hau he is not asking for much, only death. And then he say to Hau, 'I know the end would be like this.' Then Hau say he will do it and Hien say 'Thank you, Troung Uy.' His last words were 'goodbye,'" Chi told me.

The operation had been a success, of this there could be no doubt. Our primary objective, the elimination of Chin Hien, had been accomplished. His death had diminished the effectiveness of his Party's operation and, in a smaller degree had enhanced our position as the eliminators of the infrastructure. This had to be considered on the plus side of the ledger. The fact that his life was terminated at his own wish was only an extension of a truth we already knew—war is hell. If tears were to be shed that day, then they would have to be shed by his followers. Had this scene occurred when I had first arrived, I would have drawn a quick and wrong conclusion whose impact would have been greater. I would have immediately labeled Hau and those who responded to his orders as savages. But now—countless killings and murders and assassinations later—I had no compassion for those like Hien.

Yet, in spite of this, I was still aware that he had been a human being, whether he deserved the title or not. And as a human being, he was accorded the dignity of dying as quickly and painlessly as he could. There seemed to have been a brief, common bond between Hau and Hien at the end, as if there was some unwritten code that demanded certain things be done under certain conditions. It was more than I cared to probe—more than I was capable of probing; going beyond the normal rules of war that were supposed to guide our actions. And yet I hoped that under the same conditions, the Viet Cong would grant me the same consideration—and mercy. Nothing would have been accomplished by allowing him to die a slow and painful death in the sun, and even less would be accomplished by moralizing about the end he received. Perhaps a fate equal to Hien's was in store for all of us—the reminders were everywhere. And then I realized the meaning of a truth I had heard long ago, a truth that had been written long before Vietnam, but could very easily have been penned for this conflict. Plato had been right: "Only the dead have seen the end of the war."

Chapter Fourteen

BINH TRI OUTPOST

A week after the operation against Chin Hien, I was ordered to report to General Kerwin, Commander for all U.S. Forces in Three Corps. I didn't know until I arrived that the purpose of my trip to Bien Hoa was to receive a Silver Star. General Kerwin presented the award for my participation in the operation at Chau Toi Mountain four months earlier. It was impressive ceremony, but I was somewhat disappointed that the some decoration was not given to Wentworth—he had earned a Silver Star that day if anyone had.

Back in the district, life was continuing as usual. Operations at day, ambushes at night. We were winning—at least I thought we were, but each setback was a serious one. There were no more small defeats or small losses, as both sides intensified the action.

Somehow, during the busy month of January, there was time for me to take a week's leave and go to Hong Kong. It was a wonderful place, but most of that week was spent trying to find items on a ten-foot-long shopping list the team gave me. The list took me into Hong Kong's darkest streets and narrowest alleys, forcing me to barter for everything from human hair wigs to belt buckles that glowed in the dark. The seven days I started with quickly melted away to nothing, and long before I was ready to leave Hong Kong, I found myself at the airport on my way back to Saigon.

There had been changes in the seven days I'd been away. New outposts were being built and old ones beefed up. There would be more attacks—we all knew this. The new outposts were not designed to eliminate attacks but rather to keep the number of casualties as low as possible, and hopefully, to prevent an enemy takeover. This was the sort of thing the enemy wanted to accomplish more than anything else—the complete and total destruction of a government outpost. If he could accomplish this, it would seriously strain the people's faith in the government's forces. On the other hand if he tried and failed, it would be the enemy who lost face in the eyes of the people.

During the last week of January we were subjected to a rash of outpost attacks by Viet Cong, motivated by their destructive objective. Most of the activity seemed to be centered around the Binh Tri area where we were concentrating our efforts at outpost building. The severest attack of the month was launched against the newly fortified outpost there.

I was on radio watch when the attack occurred. The Vietnamese messenger on duty in the operations center came running in the radio room, shouting for Chi. I knew only too well what this meant and wasted no time rushing back to Chi's room. It took a few seconds to shake some awareness into the sleeping, shorts-clad interpreter, but when I did he was ready to listen to the messenger's story.

"What is it?" I asked when the messenger was finished.

"VC attack Binh Tri with heavy mortar and small arms fire about twenty minutes ago. He say we have two dead and three wounded."

At this point, Major Chau, who had been notified by his radio man as the attack started, hobbled in.

"Can we get dust-off for Binh Tri, Troung Uy?" he asked.

"Yes sir, we'll get on it. Chi, get everybody up."

While I was requesting the dust-off from Long Binh Dust-Off Control, Jackson started working on artillery support from the base camp with one of the other radios. By this time the whole team was up. I knew it would be impossible to direct the helicopter directly to the outpost, and I also knew that advisors were required to be on the ground when the evacuation was made. This left no option other than directing the dust-off into our pad, putting a couple of advisors aboard and then proceeding to the outpost for evacuation. The only decision left, which would have to be made by Major Allen, was deciding which two would go.

Wentworth had long since decided he was going, and he was fully dressed and armed to the teeth. I wanted to go also, but the Major was reluctant to let "Batman and Robin"—as we were called—go together since we had been wounded. This time, however, he agreed to it. I was dressed and ready by the time the dust-off was on the pad. Chi had started back to bed before I suddenly remembered that no one at the outpost spoke English, and his presence was necessary.

Once in the air, the district took on a whole new appearance. I had never seen it from the air at night, but I knew we had to fly due north to reach Binh Tri. We knew before we left that the outpost had lit their directional arrow—a series of oil-filled cans arranged in the shape of an arrow that could be pointed in the direction of the attack—but every light and fire in the district was clearly visible from the air, creating confusion. This forced the pilot to fly dangerously low, as Chi and I searched for and finally found the outpost. The pilot was concerned about the situation on the ground, hoping to avoid ground fire if possible, but I could only tell him what I knew, which wasn't much. Hunching directly behind the pilot, I directed him into the tiny landing pad just outside the perimeter of the outpost, expecting any second to be ripped by a VC machine gunner. We were as vulnerable as we would ever be, hanging there in the air, slowly lowering to the brightly illuminated landing pad.

Even before we were on the ground, I could see the wounded lying by the pad. As the skids touched, Chi, Wentworth, and I raced for the opening in the perimeter, avoiding the craters that had been blown by the incoming mortar rounds. There was firing in the distance, but I couldn't tell if it was directed at us. The wounded were quickly loaded aboard, and the helicopter lifted off immediately.

Lieutenant Viet, Outpost Commander, met us inside. He explained the situation to Chi, while Wentworth and I looked for a suitable place to set up our radio. We were planning on spending the night, our purpose now being to direct artillery fire in the event the attack was escalated. I established communication with the artillery unit and not the district, since the district couldn't help us now.

Lieutenant Viet showed us the damage of the outpost. One bunker was completely destroyed, and another was heavily damaged. Debris from pieces of support beams and exploded sand bags littered the small triangle-shaped fort. Craters had been battered into the hard-packed ground by the mortars. One mortar had missed the flag pole by less than five feet, but the flag was still flying. A dud—one that had failed to explode—was imbedded in the side of a bunker, with only its tail fin visible. Viet said it would be removed in the morning; he wasn't overly concerned about it at the time.

The two dead soldiers had been moved inside the undamaged bunker. The oil light fixed to the wall gave the bunker the eerie appearance of a funeral parlor. They had been caught in the open during the attack, trying unsuccessfully to make it to their fighting positions on the perimeter. One was fully dressed, having been on duty in the radio bunker. The other one had been asleep. He was wearing only a pair of green shorts and a Seiko wristwatch. I knelt down beside them for a closer look to see if the faces were familiar. The arms of the one wearing the watch had been folded across his chest, and the watch was still working, faithfully ticking away the seconds that were now meaningless to its dead owner. Both were young, about eighteen or nineteen. I recognized the one with the watch. He had been the messenger for the outpost.

Later that night, we received rifle fire, but no more mortars. The base camp fired illumination rounds over the outpost periodically, and occasionally they would drop an artillery round a few hundred feet from the outpost, just to keep the VC honest. Aside from this the night was quiet.

Lieutenant Viet made coffee for us, which helped fight off the early morning cold. A couple of hours before dawn, Chi slipped in one of the bunkers for a little sleep, and Wentworth and I waited for the dawn alone. When it finally came, we surveyed the damage of the outpost more closely than was possible the night before.

Shortly after sunup, Jackson arrived with two squads of Popular Forces in "Claymore" to take us home. There was nothing left to do at Binh Tri Outpost, but I didn't want to leave. The same old familiar feelings of frustration and bitterness caused by inflicting no damage on the enemy flooded over me, filling me with useless outrage. Yet it was incidents like this that would keep the hate alive, giving us more victims that had to be avenged. But this thought gave me precious little consolation. Perhaps after breakfast and a few hours sleep, I'd feel better, but I knew the uncompromising hatred would remain.

Chapter Fifteen

WENTWORTH'S PIGS

With the coming of Tet, we all relaxed a bit. Everyone seemed to be in a festive mood, though the shadow of war was hanging low over us. Those who survived the previous Tet in 1968 had vivid memories of the viciousness and savagery of the enemy's attacks in Di An. So it was not a complete relaxing or forgetting one's self, but there was a noticeable change in the daily routine of the people, and the change was good.

Technically, Tet was the celebration of the Lunar New Year, celebrated each year by a week of feasts and merriment. The time of the year fluctuates between the end of January and the middle of February, depending on the moon's cycle. But Tet is much more than this—it's much more than can ever be explained. It was as if something strong and powerful in the history and culture of these people was appealing to them and had to be satisfied.

The coming of Tet and what it meant generated an electricity and excitement that was nearly uncontrollable. Tet *would* be celebrated —there was no alternative. Tradition, which was far more important than the present threat of the Viet Cong had to be observed. The Viet Cong would come and go, but Tet would always come—otherwise, why go on living? Such an attitude was everywhere, expressed by everyone as they decorated their homes with bright, beautiful paper ornaments. It was a time of friends visiting friends, lots of food and drink, and the wearing of beautiful clothes. It mattered not at all what one wore for the rest of the year, but during Tet new clothes were a necessity. For a few days, the anesthesia of happiness and parties and feasts dulled the harsh realities of living with the war, and no one needed the realities dulled more than these people.

And, of course, there was the dragon. The soldiers played the part of the traditional Tet dragon that visited everyone's home accepting gifts and offerings. In return, the dragon insured a happy new year to those he visited. The "dragon" was a three man affair;

144

one supported the huge paper head and another gave life to the long, trailing cloth-covered tail. The third man kept the dragon's belly from dragging on the ground; his position was midway between the head and tail. A drummer accompanied the dragon, providing the rhythm to which it danced and swayed. Occasionally the dragon would attempt to leap into the air, but rarely would the leap be coordinated. The belly would go up, but the tail and head would remain firmly on the ground. These spasmodic movements were more entertaining to the following crowd than any graceful leap could ever have been.

It was an uneasy time for the advisors, since we were more than expecting a repeat of the year before. We would have been much happier had the District Chief ordered a full alert as protection against a surprise attack, but he didn't and none of us really expected him to. Caution finally and grudgingly gave way to resignation, and we all had a good time, settling for a fifty percent alert and hoping it would be enough.

Fortunately, no disasters occurred, although a week prior to Tet we had uncovered a cache of rockets in Tan Dong Hiep Village. The defector who led us to them stated that they were earmarked for an attack against the District Headquarters during the Tet period. Finding them gave me considerable relief but also made me apprehensive about more rockets, hidden somewhere, that could come crashing down on our little world at any time. This wasn't an acceptable risk but there was nothing to be done about it.

After Tet, Di An returned to normal, more or less; however, "normal" was becoming increasingly difficult to define. In areas where the infrastructure had been destroyed, we were experimenting with pig-raising projects. The idea was to get the hamlet residents interested in community projects like this that would ultimately be moneymaking business endeavors, if successful. It was an old American trick known as private enterprise.

Captain Wentworth was greatly excited about the possibility, feeling that if economic growth could be stimulated, the whole pacification effort would be accelerated. In fact, economic growth was at the heart of our present pacification plan, making all real success dependent on it. It was concerned, also, but not as intensely as Wentworth; my concern was generated by a natural curiosity. This was the reason I would occasionally go with Wentworth and

Major Chau when they visited the experimental projects.

The week after Tet we made our rounds. Tet had taken a heavy toll among the fledgling pig population, with little regard shown for those pigs earmarked to be the vanguard for the revolutionary revival of the district's economy; they were treated the same as those pigs with a less important purpose in life. Hamlets that had gone into Tet with eight or nine pigs emerged with barely half that number. When asked why his pigs were missing, the hamlet chief usually gave the standard deadpan answer his pigs had "died," and he really didn't know the cause of death.

This mysterious "epidemic" was explained in one hamlet where Chi and Major Chau questioned a small boy who lived near one of the experimental pig pens. The boy confirmed what we had suspected—the pigs had been sacrificed for the Tet feasts. The "hamleters" saw no damage in this; there were still pigs left in the pen, and they would raise these. The experiments would continue.

The hamlet chief at Tan Hiep admitted that two of the eight pigs in his hamlet had been killed and roasted, but he quickly added that the rest would be raised in accordance with the pacification guidelines. Major Chau reprimanded his hamlet and village chiefs, warning them that he would not tolerate such acts any longer. Wentworth was shattered, feeling that the people had betrayed him. He asked me why they had done this. Didn't they realize the pigs were the means for a better way of life for them? That it was for their benefit?

It was somewhat amusing, watching Wentworth ranting and raving because his pigs had met an untimely end. But I could also sympathize with him. A lot of hard work had gone into this project, mainly because Wentworth believed in it. What he said was true; it was for their own benefit, not his. Their actions during Tet were difficult to understand, and although I had been there longer than he, I didn't really understand them either.

The next day, after Wentworth had cooled down, we discussed it with Mr. Quy, our civilian deputy. He was a little man, with a round face as expressionless as a grapefruit. His jet black hair was always slicked back over his head to conceal a large bald spot. Mr. Quy counseled the advisors on matters such as the pacification program, village self-help projects which included our pig project and everything else of a non-military nature. As an administrator,

Mr. Quy had few equals. His suggestions and recommendations were highly respected by all of us. He was well versed in the interworkings of the American agencies such as USAID (United States Agency for International Development) and JUSPAO (Joint United States Public Affairs Office)—the people who could offer us special assistance in special situations. In short, Quy was the advisor's expert on what was available to us through the various assistance channels.

Not only did he tell us what we could and could not do, but vastly more important, he told us what we should and should not do. Quy was the ultimate in an advisor, for his advice was never given unless it was solicited. Whenever we were up against a problem that seemed to be insoluble or incomprehensible, Quy's analysis was sought.

Nguyen Van Quy was no newcomer to the war in Vietnam. During the Japanese occupation he had been a member of the Viet Minh, Ho Chi Minh's Communist Party that gained a lot of support under the guise of working for "nationalism." Discovering later the true nature of the Viet Minh, Quy assisted the French against this same organization. He had gone to school in Hanoi with Vo Nguyen Giap, long before Giap had turned his talents for destruction against the South as the Commander of all North Vietnamese and Viet Cong forces. Because of his onetime association with the Viet Minh, Quy was destined to go no higher in the Vietnamese administrative system than civilian deputy, but for our purpose on the pig issue, he was the final authority. The fact that the Vietnamese government held his past against him was their loss, yet it was another one of the complexities of the war that made it complex. Perhaps, at another time this, too, would be discussed with Quy, but not today.

At first Quy was reluctant to discuss the pigs, thinking that we would perhaps hold him responsible for the partial failure of the venture. After convincing him this was not the case, he began to open up. After listening patiently to our problem, he kindly and very diplomatically informed us that we did not fully understand the situation, a fact we had long since conceded. Our lack of knowledge, he informed us, was a condition beyond our control, caused by *our* being Americans instead of Vietnamese. Only Vietnamese could understand, he continued.

147

Quy displayed absolutely no emotion, the black eyes betraying nothing; yet the polite little apologetic smile was ever-present. He told us he was glad that we wanted to improve the lives of his people.

"But you insist on doing it as if my people were not Vietnamese but Americans. All the things that are good for you are not good for them" he explained. "You talk of marketplaces and economy and income. It is all difficult to understand. Why must a rice farmer make much money? Why must people have houses with wooded floors and running water? Why should he make more than he can use? He can only eat so much and sleep in one bed. A good life here is not the same as the good life in America. You must first ask yourself what the Vietnamese need and want. We must answer these questions. If you offer them much in the beginning, they do not understand."

I asked if there were answers to these questions. We talked about how much the program offered by the Americans meant to the average Vietnamese. Why was it so difficult for them to understand that that which was offered today would mean a better tomorrow? Patiently, Quy tried to fit it all together.

"It is difficult because they cannot understand why you come. You come to fight and die for them and for no other reason, and they cannot understand this. It has never been done before. Always before when foreigners come they took from the people. The French took, the Japanese took, the Viet Minh took and now the Viet Cong take. So it is hard for them to understand why the Americans, who fight so well, come to help them and ask for nothing. Now can you see why they have trouble understanding?" he asked.

"Yes I understand how they can feel this way. But the Viet Cong have promised to do the same things for your people," I reminded him. Mr. Quy laughed at this.

"The VC do not plan on doing these things for my people, they only promise them. That is not the real difference anyway, even if the VC did do the things they promise," he went on.

"But what is the real difference if it is not these things?" I asked. He paused for a moment to collect the exact words, then continued.

"The real difference is this: right now my people can do what they want. This is good, but it is not - what you say - the true test of freedom. Right now, if they do not want to do something, they do not have to. Right now, they can decide. If the VC win, this will change. We will lose our freedom, this is true. But more important, we will no longer be able to do nothing."

I was beginning to piece together the loose ends of Quy's thoughts. He saw this reflected in my face and hurried on.

"If the VC win, we cannot quit. Now we can, if we like. Now we have true freedom. And this is what we must protect, sir. We must protect this choice to do nothing if we like. This is why we cannot make pig project work if people are not ready for it. And they are not ready for project that makes much money; they only want enough to use today. They only want the war to end and the VC to go away. Then they would be happy. Some want to do nothing. Each hamlet is different, and all cannot be treated the same. The old ways die slowly. But more than anything else, they only want to be left alone."

Quy said much more, all of it spoken carefully but candidly. When there was nothing left of the conversation, Wentworth and I knew how one Vietnamese felt about the two competing ideologies that were producing the war. Quy had seen both sides. His views were worth listening to, if nothing else. And he made more sense than anyone else I had listened to. Assuming what he said was true, it all boiled down to a very negative philosophy. The ultimate freedom in South Vietnam was not the chance to do what one wanted to do or achieve great success. No, the ultimate was the freedom to fail—to do absolutely nothing—to be able to take a siesta from noon until three in the afternoon—to be able to get drunk on bacsi dai everyday if you wanted. This was what the communists, if they were victorious, could never afford to give. This, in the end was the real difference. Quy had realized this all along, perhaps picking it up somewhere along with the shattered hopes he once had for the Viet Minh before realizing these hopes would always be shattered. He knew much more than his brothers in the paddies, but he knew how they felt and what they wanted, even if they could not articulate their desires and hopes and dreams.

So this was why I was here, and Wentworth, and everybody else in the whole American effort. Not to see great economic and "social" success take place while destroying the North Vietnamese and Viet Cong. This was part of it, of course, and it would have to happen before our primary objective was achieved, but our primary objective was not nearly this complicated. All we had to do was protect Nguyen Van Rice Farmer if he decided to say "the hell with raising rice." It was another view of the vicious, tragic cycle that still added up to war.

If Quy asked me right then to name the most important freedom I had, I would probably have said something different from the "freedom to say the hell with it," but he had touched a very sensitive nerve in an area I had never probed before. I tried to reject his analysis, not because he was wrong, but because I found it difficult to accept the possibility that I might die defending the inherent right of a rice farmer to become a failure.

Chapter Sixteen

THE SYSTEMATIC ELIMINATION OF TO VAN PHOUNG

The projects and activities of other advisors greatly interested me, for they shed light on some of my own problems. The pig project would reappear a year later, under different circumstances and when it did, I would forget the gentle wisdom expressed by Mr. Quy. But during March 1969, I had to turn my full attention to my primary purpose for being in Di An, which was assisting in the destruction of the Viet Cong's political structure.

I knew that no pacification program would ever work unless security became a reality in the outlying hamlets and villages. To achieve this, control had to be taken away from the infrastructure which meant they had to be eliminated. I likened the whole operation to a construction project where the ground must be cleared, leveled and smoothed before the foundation of the building is poured. My job was at the ground level, preparing the ground for the foundation.

With almost a year's experience in this business, I knew most of the techniques in use, both official and unofficial, but there was still much to learn. A rule of thumb that I relied heavily on went something like this: if it works, it's a great technique; if it doesn't work, it's lousy. During March we were using a lot of techniques in our attempt to apprehend the district party secretary, To Van Phoung. And all of them were proving to be lousy.

We knew that Phoung was the key man in the district. Every attack, ambush, assassination, raid and bombing incident conducted against the district was carried out with Phoung's guiding hand. He was extremely successful in avoiding our ambushes set up in his honor, and he also avoided the raids we planned. If he could be eliminated, it was just possible that his whole empire would crumble.

The dossier on him was growing like cancer, but it produced no results. Every bit and piece of information concerning Phoung was handled as carefully as if it were the crown jewels. With the help of agent reports and defectors, we often charted his movement in the district to a particular area in a particular hamlet. A carefully planned raid would follow, only to find that Phoung had slipped away once again, vanishing into thin air. Appropriately enough, he became known as the "elusive one."

Phoung had a twin brother who lived in Ap Tay Hamlet. The brother, who was an upstanding, law abiding citizen was well known to Hau and me. This was simply another irony in a war riddled with ironies. His help was solicited in trying to persuade Phoung to give himself up. The brother was willing to assist us, for he knew that Phoung's activities would eventually get him killed. We had hoped that the influence of the brother might be enough to persuade Phoung to defect and take advantage of the liberal "Chieu Hoi" Program, a program designed to increase defection among the enemy by offering the defector a new life. But this proved to be wishful thinking; Phoung was truly hardcore, dedicated completely to the Viet Cong's bloody cause.

There was only one course of action left open to us; one that I had hoped would not be necessary. Hau and I both knew what it was, but I brought it out in the open.

"Troung Uy, there is only one solution to our problem with Phoung," I said. "We must offer a reward for information that will lead us to Phoung. There is nothing else to do."

There was nothing unusual about paying for information offered secretly—if proved to be valid. But this was the first time that a public appeal for information was seriously considered. Hau was completely agreeable to the idea, since it would be American money that would be spent. After a lengthy discussion we both agreed that an extremely large amount would be necessary in this case. But beyond this point, Hau had his own ideas.

His plan involved plastering the district with WANTED DEAD OR ALIVE posters, offering a reward of 100,000 piasters for information leading us to To Van Phoung. This amount was roughly equivalent to $1,000 in U.S. currency, enough money to tempt the average man to turn his mother in, even in Vietnam. I agreed completely with the amount of the reward money and even the concept in general, but I tried tactfully to point out to my counterpart that the Geneva Convention prohibited WANTED DEAD OR ALIVE posters. This came as a shock to Hau, not the wording of the convention, but that I actually considered it an

152

obstacle to his scheme. Hau looked as if I had betrayed him; as if I were choosing a lifeless, written document over his vibrant and imaginative plan.

"Troung Uy, we cannot always do as the convention says," he pleaded. "Sometimes we must do what we know is the best thing. We must do what will work."

I agreed completely, telling him he was perfectly right. Phoung did not deserve protection from any source, but we had to be certain that we stayed out of trouble. This was the important thing—not what happened to Phoung, but what happened to us. Phoung was not worth over getting in trouble over.

When Hau understood that this was my only reason for mentioning the convention, his mood changed quickly. Now, it was simply a matter of conveying the message to the people in language that would not violate the letter of the Geneva Convention; the spirit of that document was not my concern. Hau and his staff at the coordination center drew up their proposal of the poster. All the vital information concerning Phoung was listed—height, weight, color of eyes, hair, etc.—even a photograph. The amount of 100,000 piasters was listed as the reward that would be paid "for information leading to the arrest or capture of To Van Phoung, alias Bay Phoung." It looked good to me. Now all I had to do was get Hau's posters reproduced by the Psychological Operations people at Bien Hoa, and we were in business.

The next day I drove to Bien Hoa with this as my sole purpose. It was my first trip to the PSYOPS compound, and I was hoping it would be productive. When I presented my proposal to the two captains and major there, they damn near went through the ceiling.

"Are you serious about getting this poster printed, Lieutenant?" asked the bald-headed major, who resembled a cross between a Southern Baptist minister and a very nervous Wally Cox.

"Yes sir. I'll need about 10,000 of them to completely cover the district and have enough for an airdrop," I told him.

I was about to ask for an aircraft when the bald one hastily informed me that it was illegal to state the amount of the reward on a wanted poster.

"In fact, Lieutenant, I would rather have no part of your plan at all," he stammered, trying not to lose his rapidly declining composure.

I thanked him very much and walked out, noticing as I did that he was firmly clutching a copy of "Do's and Don'ts of the Geneva Convention." In spite of my disappointment, I had to laugh at this funny little man who was so totally unaware of the nature of the real war.

It was obvious from my encounter with the PSYOPS boys that they were afraid to give us any assistance on this one, and I still didn't know where the reward money was coming from. A discussion with the Phoenix Advisor at Bien Hoa was just as unproductive. Apparently, this was too much money for any one "personality." His suggestion was to reduce the reward, but Hau and I had no intentions of doing this. We were determined to offer 100,000 piasters and we were just as determined to find somebody to put up the money.

After striking out at Bien Hoa, I presented my plan to the intelligence officers at First Division, fully prepared for them to turn it down also. But here I was pleasantly surprised, finding them more than willing to support me when my own official advisory channels had refused. We reached a "gentlemen's agreement" on the issue. If To Van Phoung was either killed or captured, the full reward would be paid to the person or persons who provided the necessary information.

Certain conditions would have to be met, however. The district would have to present conclusive proof that the man we claimed to be To Van Phoung was, in fact, To Van Phoung. We further agreed that no mention of this deal would be made at Bien Hoa or anywhere else due to its questionable legal status. Hau and I were more than willing to agree to these conditions since it made absolutely no difference to us where the reward money originated. And the First Division would be happy to have Phoung eliminated, for Phoung's guerrilla band was keeping a considerable U.S. force tied up in the base camp at Di An, a force that could be used more effectively further north.

As for the posters and leaflets, we did the best we could. A few hundred were run off on our mimeograph machine and distributed throughout the district. They were placed in strategic places such as hamlet offices, schools, health stations, and marketplaces. Underlying the distribution of the poster was the district chief's personal guarantee that a 100,000-piaster reward would be paid. This bit of very vital information had been discreetly spread through the district as the posters were being displayed.

This was a classic example of Vietnamese pragmatism. When it became obvious that the American system of doing things would not provide us with the kind of posters we wanted, the Vietnamese turned to methods that were time-tested. There was no anger or emotion displayed by Hau because I could not deliver what we needed through my channels. He understood perfectly the American way of doing things—the bald-headed major who was afraid to help and the Phoenix Advisor who was afraid to set a precedent—a way that appeared utterly ridiculous at times. Did these people surely believe that success would not be accomplished without their support? Were they naive enough to believe that we could afford to follow only established guidelines when our district was being threatened?

When I was frustrated and disgusted with the system, Hau would only smile. I had already convinced him that I liked his plan, and somehow we'd make it work. This was enough for him, so the posters were created and plastered over the district. They violated nothing. It was the words that were spread with the posters that gave them meaning, but they were not written down, therefore they could never serve as an indictment against anyone. Once again I was awed by the "little people" who had given me a firsthand view at the inter workings of one segment of their society. And I knew it was a rare privilege.

With the spreading of the leaflets, we had done about all we could do about Phoung. We continued our operations against lesser members of the infrastructure, and they were successful, but it was Phoung we were waiting for. Reports continued to flow into the center concerning him, and each was carefully checked out: but it wasn't until the first week of May that we received the kind of report we'd been waiting for.

One day during that first week, a young lady walked into the center. She had been directed to the center by the hamlet chief of Binh An Hamlet where she lived. She was obviously nervous, looking quickly about the small room, avoiding direct eye contact with us. She was a tall, frail-looking girl with long black hair drawn back in a tight bun. Sergeant "Sad Eyes" Minh asked if he could help her.

"No," she replied. "I have come to see the district chief; he is the only person I can tell my story to. It is very important and I have very little time. Please let me see him."

Hau informed Major Chau of the young lady's presence, and she was immediately shown into his office, which was adjacent to the center.

For more than a half hour the major talked with the woman. When their conversation was over, the district chief asked for Hau and me.

"I would like for you to meet Le Thi Hoa," he said after the door had been closed behind us. "She has brought us some very good information." She was very attractive and very young—about eighteen or nineteen. After a brief introduction, Major Chau told us her story.

She had been the girl friend of To Van Phoung for over a year. During this period, she and Phoung had spent a lot of time together, hiding in tunnels or safe houses, rarely spending two nights in the same place. She had hoped, before, that some day they would be married. But that was all in the past now. Phoung had a new girl friend and he no longer had any need or desire for her. I would glance at her occasionally as Major Chau told her story, and although he spoke in English, she knew what he was talking about, and it caused her to blush. Because of Phoung, she had left her home in Bien Hoa. Her actions had brought disgrace to her family; her father had disowned her, but at the same time she could think only of Phoung. Now she was going to have Phoung's baby, in about seven months. When she told Phoung this, he laughed, saying he had more important things to worry about than a pregnant girl. She could no longer stay with him, now that he had a new girl friend; and going back to her family in Bien Hoa was out of the question. Things had been bad for some time between her and Phoung. He was really concerned with only one thing—the war. Everything else was secondary and unimportant. As Major Chau talked, Hoa twisted and untwisted a small, embroidered handkerchief, staring constantly at the floor.

When Major Chau was finished, Hau asked her some questions. She would look up long enough to reply then quickly return her eyes to the floor, trying to hide the embarassment Hau and I were causing her, an embarrassment she had not felt with Major Chau. A truck stopped in front of Headquarters, releasing soldiers from the

156

day's operation. The sounds of laughter and shouting could be heard above the noise of the truck. A good sign—we had suffered no casualties. A moment later the tailgate slammed shut, and the truck drove away. Once again I was aware of the sound of Hau's voice.

Hoa knew where Phoung would be the next day, and she was willing to take us there, provided we would promise her certain things. She wanted no harm to come to him. Major Chau explained to her that this condition could not be guaranteed and that he would do the best he could. Next, she wanted us to know that she wasn't doing this for the money, but "for Phoung's own good." Sooner or later he would be found, and she believed his chances were better this way. We all agreed with her.

She said nothing of the outrage and jealousy I knew she felt; not one word implying she was seeking revenge was spoken. Yet it was all there, as obvious as if it had been written across her face in English. It was her game I kept telling myself. It was not necessary for me to know why she was doing this—the fact that she had agreed to do it was enough. But I couldn't help believing she wanted to see the son of a bitch dead.

Phoung would be hiding in a tunnel the next day—a tunnel located in Binh An Village. The tunnel was in a public works yard where road building equipment was stored. Hau asked her if Phoung would be worried about her absence and assume she had turned him in to the district. If this were the case, then Phoung would not be at Binh An the next day. But she told Hau that Phoung thought she had gone to Saigon to live with her sister, a course of action she had planned to follow, before changing her mind.

She went over Phoung's timetable with us, explaining that he was having a meeting with the Viet Cong village secretary of Binh An. From Binh An he would go to Dong Hoa, but she did not know exactly where he would meet with the Dong Hoa village secretary. He would arrive in the public works yard in the afternoon, around three o'clock. This way he would avoid district's operations that usually kicked off at seven or eight in the morning and were over before one in the afternoon. This statement caused no noticeable reaction from Major Chau, but I knew there would be a change in the district's operational routine.

Just to make sure she knew what she was talking about, Hau asked her if Phoung had any brothers. She told us about Phoung's

157

twin in Ap Tay, and she knew of our efforts to use his brother to get Phoung. Major Chau asked her to draw a map of the area, including the tunnel where Phoung would be hiding. She had a talent for sketching, and when it was finished, I recognized the area. We had been there several times on operations. I even recognized the pile of rusty drain pipes located near the tunnel. Suddenly I remembered that I had sat on those same pipes during a break on an operation.

She knew Phoung by his other name—Bay. And she was able to pick his photograph from a stack of other photographs. It was a different photograph than the one used on the posters, but she had no difficulty at all in picking the right one. She passed every test we could think of, and at the end of our interrogation, we were convinced she was real. She knew what she was talking about.

Hau told her she would have to spend the night in the district headquarters, partly for her own safety, but mostly for the safety of the operation we were launching the next day. She understood. After the operation she would be processed as a defector, if all went well. However, if she was setting us up for an ambush, she would be dealt with in a far different manner. This was made perfectly clear to her, and she was also told that she would be going with us the next day. With that, we called it a day. The final plans for the operation would be worked out the next morning. We had time— Phoung wouldn't be in the tunnel until the next afternoon.

That night sleep was impossible. The very idea of ridding the district of Phoung caused so much nervousness and anticipation that I couldn't sleep. Yet I was afraid to expect too much, to hope for too much for fear that he would slip through our fingers again. I told myself this was just another operation that just might succeed, but I knew better. This was shaping up to be our best shot so far, and if we blew it, there was no guarantee we would have another one.

The next morning, I was out of bed long before daybreak. Captain Wentworth got up as I was making coffee. He was aware of our plans for the day and I knew, without asking, that he would be going. Long before this operation I had promised Wentworth I'd let him know when Hau and I had "hot" information. This was part of the bond we shared. Often, Wentworth was told of an upcoming operation before Major Allen. This way, he could plan on being one of the advisors that would go along. The fact that Wentworth and I accompanied most of the operations was no accident—it was a conspiracy, even though Major Allen often objected to it.

While waiting for the coffee to brew, we discussed the possible events that could occur on this operation. We agreed that if it worked as we planned, it would be unbelievably simple. It seemed ironic that a man like Phoung would be had by a woman; a woman who was blowing the whistle on him because he had another girl friend. It didn't seem right for some reason.

"Does it seem right to you that his girl friend would turn him in?" I asked Wentworth, who had far more experience with women than I did.

"Hell yes," he replied. "You can't trust any of them. Why do you think the VC would have less trouble with their women than Americans do?" He had a point, and I dropped it.

After coffee and breakfast, we went over to the operations center. Major Chau and Hau were there, planning the minor details required of the operation. It was decided that the National Police and the Province Reconnaissance Unit would be best suited for this one. This decision was not completely free of politics. The National Police had been complaining that they were not getting their share of the action which, when interpreted, meant that they weren't getting their share of the glory. After all the operational decisions had been made to the satisfaction of all concerned, the interrogation of Hoa resumed.

She knew the location of two other tunnels in the district. They would be checked later, after our business with Phoung was complete. She knew absolutely nothing about the Viet Cong military strength in the district. Like a good communist leader, Phoung had managed to keep mostly everything about his activities from her; they had not interested her anyway. It was obvious that she had cared only for Phoung, the man, not Phoung, the District Party Secretary.

Our plan was to leave at two in the afternoon. By 1:45 the PRUs started boarding Claymore. A few minutes later the National Policemen ambled up from the Police Station, still drowsy from their midday siesta and crawled in the truck behind the PRUs. The late comers, who couldn't find room in the back, straddled the headlights, sat on the hood, and hung from the sides, dangerously obscuring the driver's view. Lieutenant Hau, Le Thi Hoa, Captain

159

Wentworth and Tinh—the faithful, toothless radio bearer—rode with me in my jeep. Tinh was wildly excited about the prospect for the day.

"Today we will kill VC, Troung Uy. Okay? Okay, Troung Uy?" He asked the question as if I could control the outcome of the operation.

"Maybe Tinh, maybe we kill VC today," I replied, trying to put him off with something less than absolute certainty. But this was as good as a positive commitment to Tinh.

"Okay, Troung Uy, you number one. VC number ten. We shoot beaucoup VC today."

On the way to Binh An, Wentworth called the district to make certain we had communication. A very meticulous man, this call was in keeping with his character. I liked that. It was good to know I could depend on him to see that the small, though important things, were taken care of. It reflected a detached coolness that would get the big things done also in the same efficient manner. Hoa sat very quietly in the back of the jeep, displaying no emotion I could detect.

Wentworth carried a unique weapon on operations such as this one. Basically, it was an M-16 rifle that had been modified to receive a grenade launcher, attached under the barrel. This gave him actually two weapons—an automatic rifle and an M-79 grenade launcher. The only disadvantage was its weight, but he claimed the extra weight was more than offset by the advantage of having two weapons. Just like Dalton with his shotgun, I thought, but I never voiced my opinion. He thought it was worth it, and that's all that counted.

At the public works yard, the troops unloaded and formed a circle around Lieutenant Hau. With all the pose of a professional quarterback, Hau explained to his team the deployment he wanted. The National Policemen and PRUs had been briefed earlier in the day, but Hau was now giving them specifics. As he was doing this, I looked at the pile of rusted pipes in the corner of the yard, about a hundred yards away. Hoa, who was in the jeep still displayed no emotion.

When Hau had finished, the PRUs deployed around the pile of pipes. Only when this had been done did the police lead Hoa from the jeep. Her job now was to discover the tunnel entrance for us. I had long since ceased being surprised at the places the Viet Cong choose to dig their tunnels. They had a talent for picking the most unlikely, innocent-looking spot to dig holes in the ground. This was one exception. The area around the pipes was covered with tall, thick grass. Only by looking closely at the grass was I able to detect slight disturbances in the blades; a condition that would normally go unnoticed. Hoa carefully parted the grass and exposed a wire handle. Extremely clever, I thought. It was easy to imagine a complete underground tunnel complex reaching from Hanoi to Saigon, with all the small tunnels we discovered being only branches or diversions. Maybe they were only letting us find the small ones in order to keep the big ones hidden.

A rope was quickly attached to the handle by one of the PRUs. The rope was long enough to allow him to take cover behind the pile of pipes with the rest of us. When everyone was clear of the entrance, he jerked the rope, and the grass-covered, wooden cover flew into the air. I could feel the excitement rising, anticipating the end of To Van Phoung. I tried to fight it, but my palms were sweaty, and my hands started shaking. From a purely professional viewpoint, I was hoping for more luck than we had at Lai Thieu. It would be nice to capture Phoung and take advantage of his knowledge, using what he knew to set off a chain reaction of elimination against his organization. But aside from all this, I personally wanted to see him dead.

With the entrance removed, the troops slowly advanced on the opening. This operation was shaping up like a number of previous ones—ones that had ended in disaster for the Viet Cong. The same demands to surrender were repeated this time by a soldier who had pulled the lid away. Routinely, I reminded Hau that we should make every effort to take Phoung alive, and just as routinely, Hau said he would. There was no real need for martyrs this day, but if martyrs were made, it would be the decision of those inside.

Once again the demand to surrender was shouted, and again it was unanswered. For just an instant I considered the demoralizing possibility of the tunnel being empty, of being faced with just another hollow disappointment in a long line of disappointments. This had to be it, I told myself over and over. This time we had to win one. The awful depression another setback would bring was more than I could think about. By allowing myself to believe this

161

was it—the big payoff—I had allowed my hopes to soar. I wished that hadn't happened.

"Looks empty to me," Wentworth speculated. "Another dry run. The bastard's probably in Bien Hoa, eating Chinese soup, laughing at us."

Hau thought this was funny and he took it one step further. "Maybe he with girl friend in Bien Hoa," he said.

"What now?" I asked with resignation.

"Now we throw smoke grenade inside. If Phoung inside, he must come out for air, then we grab him," Hau explained. "Do you think that a good idea?" he asked.

"Very good, Troung Uy. Let's do it," I replied.

A smoke grenade was tossed in the opening, and almost immediately a large cloud of yellow smoke bellowed out of the hole. We stood watching the smoke for a few seconds, not really knowing what to expect. At first I thought I had imagined it, that my mind was playing tricks on me. But the second time I heard it, I was convinced someone inside the tunnel was coughing. The sound was faint but unmistakable. Hau and Wentworth had heard it, too. As the grenade continued spewing out smoke, the coughing grew louder and more frequent.

"Tell him to come out, Troung Uy," I demanded, getting a renewed hope from the coughing.

Hau personally renewed the surrender demands. The smoke grenade had exhausted itself, with only a thin wisp of yellow smoke ascending from the hole. This time there was an answer. Tinh pushed his way to the tunnel entrance where the soldiers had gathered and peered inside.

"Now we kill VC, Troung Uy? Now we do?" he asked with unignorable urgency. He pointed to a hand grenade on one of the soldier's belts and made a gesture of dropping it in the hole. Then he flung his arms skyward, simulating explosion.

"Okay, Troung Uy?" he insisted. "Now we do?"

"No, Tinh, not now. Maybe VC *Chieu Hoi*"—I held my arms over my head in the indicated *Chieu Hoi* or surrender fashion—"and if they do, we cannot kill."

This caused a noticeable let down in Tinh, and he mumbled something about a *Chieu Hoi* being a "number ten."

The conversation between Hau and the tunnel occupants continued.

162

"Why don't they come out, Chi?" I asked. "How many do we have in there?" Chi listened a minute before he answered.

"I think maybe two are inside. One is Phoung. They say the smoke make them very sick, and they cannot come out. They ask for somebody to come inside and help them." More waiting and discussion, then a decision.

"I send policeman inside for Phoung," Hau announced. This was an unusual procedure to follow. The fact that hand grenades had not been dropped inside was even more unusual.

"Why Hau?" I asked.

"Because we must be very careful with Phoung. As you say, Troung Uy, he is valuable to us."

The implication was obvious. The policeman was going in only because of my presence; otherwise his life would never have been placed in jeopardy. There was a very real possibility that Phoung and his companion were faking their sickness, waiting for someone to enter the tunnel. But Hau was willing to make that risk, and I was commited to my official position of "making every effort possible to capture alive"—a position I was totally opposed to.

There was a volunteer for this dangerous mission, and his comrades quickly prepared him for going inside the tunnel. A rope was tied firmly around his chest in the event something went wrong and he had to be extracted. If nothing went wrong, and Phoung and his friend really needed help, then the rope would be used to haul them out.

Armed with a flashlight and a .45-caliber pistol, our man disappeared into the tunnel. A running commentary was maintained between the policeman and Hau. After a few seconds, he reported that there were two men in the tunnel. This report was followed immediately by gunshots and a frantic request to be pulled up. The PRUs quickly pulled the policeman from the tunnel, shattering forever our chance of taking Phoung alive.

His blood-covered shirt was ripped away by fellow policemen and revealed a bullet wound in the right shoulder. Fortunately, it was only a flesh wound. The bullet had caught the top of his right shoulder where it joins the arm—the place where the "good guys" get shot in the John Wayne westerns. Wentworth placed a pressure bandage on it to stop the bleeding, and I called for a dust-off, even though it wasn't critical. He was perfectly conscious as he related what happened.

163

There was very little to tell. When he had shined the light on the men in the tunnel, one was armed with a pistol which he promptly used to shoot the policeman. Our man fired three or four shots—he wasn't sure—but he was positive he had hit the one with the gun. Perhaps the other one had been wounded also; again he wasn't sure. Having done all we could for our wounded hero, we left him to bask in his newly earned glory and returned our attention to the tunnel.

It was pointless to plead the case of Phoung any longer, even from a professional position. His fate was never seriously in doubt after the shooting. There would be no other attempts to capture Phoung and his friend; no one else would be sent in the tunnel. Hau did make one half-hearted attempt to convince them it was in their best interest to crawl out, but there was no reply. Hau removed a hand grenade from the belt of one of the soldiers, (the one Tinh had pointed eagerly to earlier), pulled the pin and tossed it inside. Three seconds later the ground trembled ever so slightly, coinciding with the dull thud, as a dirty white cloud of smoke belched from the hole.

There was little to hope for now, other than a positive identification of Phoung. With the ever-present smile firmly in place, Hau told me there had been no other way—he had really wanted to take Phoung alive, but I had witnessed the failure of that attempt. Phoung had taken away all the options.

There was no use pointing out that we could have kept trying, perhaps using tear gas grenades that would force him out, or simply wait—wait for them to crawl out when they were hungry or thirsty. None of these things were necessary because we had taken a casualty; therefore, we had "made every effort." There could be no criticism from Bien Hoa or anywhere else on the way we handled To Van Phoung. I could have intervened one more time with one more suggestion. Perhaps it would have made the big difference, perhaps not. At any rate, it was too late for any of that now. It was over, and Hau and I were equally responsible for the outcome. Hau had wanted this outcome from the beginning; of this I was certain. And we had both played our roles. He had done as I had asked; no more could be expected from him. If the plan had succeeded, I would have been correct. Since it had not, Hau's actions were justified.

Tinh was pleased over the outcome, also. "VC finished, Troung Uy," he shouted. This phrase was repeated over and over until Tinh

164

was thoroughly satisfied. Hoa, who had been standing quietly near the pipes during the whole procedure, walked over to observe the "recovery" operation. Two soldiers went inside with a rope and flashlight. A moment later, the remains of To Van Phoung, late District Party Secretary for Di An District, was hauled unceremoniously into public view. Making certain it was no one else, Hoa took a close look at the fragment-riddled body. She paid particular attention to the face which was, for the most part, intact.

"It is Phoung," she stated simply.

The same procedure was repeated for the Village Secretary, who was identified as Ho Van Long. Documents concerning the Viet Cong's plans for Di An were found, along with a listing of the more important members of the infrastructure in the district. This incredible find would serve as the basis for many operations that would virtually destroy the infrastructure in Di An. But this would come later in the year. For now, To Van Phoung was dead, and that was enough.

This was cause for merriment among the troops. Tinh was still elated, repeating his "VC finished" phrase for my benefit, while taking time to poke fun at Phoung's body. Hau and Wentworth were obviously pleased, and they had a right to be. For me, it was mostly a feeling of relief—the kind of relief that comes with the warm feeling of accomplishment. It had been a valuable lesson, this tracking-down business of Phoung. It had taught me a great deal, and for this I had my Vietnamese friends to thank. But even more important, our idea of tracking Phoung down systematically had worked—the Phoenix Concept was far more than theory (we had proved that over and over again)—and the Vietnamese had accepted advise. I could ask for nothing more.

Hau ordered the soldiers to place the body of Phoung on the hood of my jeep. It would be taken back to the District Headquarters and placed on display at the landing zone.

"Many people will not believe Phoung is dead unless we show them," he explained. "Tonight we have party and tell everyone they can see Phoung. Is this a good idea, Troung Uy?" he asked. I told him it was one of his best ever. With that, we drove away from Binh An Village with Phoung strapped securely on the hood of the jeep in much the same fashion as a prize, buck deer.

Chapter Seventeen

DECIDING TO STAY

I gave Hoa her reward when we returned—the whole 100,000 piasters. Afterwards, the report on the operation was prepared and sent to Bien Hoa. Then we got on with the party that Hau had promised. It was to celebrate the death of Phoung, to celebrate the long hours of hard work spent to make the party possible. It was only fitting that the party last a long time, and it did.

The next day Major Chau allowed Phoung's family to claim the body. It was picked up at the landing zone in a small truck by Phoung's brother, the one who lived at Ap Tay Village and had predicted such an end for his twin. Hau and I were on hand when he arrived, and Hau told the brother how sorry he was that Phoung had been killed. It was the same tone and same smile he had used the day before. Always so polite, I thought, even when he's lying. This day was the happiest day for Hau in years, and the reason was Phoung's death.

There could be no denying that both Hau and I greatly enhanced our image through this operation. It had pleased everyone—Major Chau, Major Allen, the advisors at Bien Hoa, the First Division, our troops and most of all Tinh. After taking time to consider Phoung's death in all its aspects, I was convinced Hau had done the right thing. There was always the possibility that, had we simply captured Phoung, he could have been released at a future date by the Vietnamese further up the line. It was a remote possibility, but it had been known to happen before. And there was always the possibility that he could have escaped, putting us right back where we had started. By taking no such chances, Hau had protected us in the only way he knew how. But we had sacrificed the chance to interrogate Phoung, which could have proved very interesting. This misgiving, the only one I had about the way we conducted the operation, was purely on a professional plane.

With my year rapidly drawing to a close, I had to make a decision concerning Vietnam. Was I really going to stay longer than I had to,

166

or was I going home? The first year had evaporated, passing almost overnight into nothingness. We had accomplished a great deal, but there was still so much more to be accomplished. I resented the popular philosophy among advisors that "everything would be alright once it was left behind." This was too simple, too easily explained. The cost of success had been high, far too high to leave now, at this stage of the game. As the time for deciding grew nearer, I became more convinced that I had to stay; going home was not the answer, at least not for me. I could not accept the familiar argument that "I had done my duty, now let somebody else do their's." I didn't feel that way, and I knew I never could until the job I had set out to do was done.

At this point, I began to honestly question my motives for wanting to stay. Was I doing it because of an abnormal hatred (could there be any other kind) for the enemy, or was I doing it for my own personal satisfaction? There was no denying that I was attracted to the work I was engaged in. We were riding high, feeling almost indestructible. The morale and aggressiveness in the district was extremely high, causing us to pursue the enemy with almost reckless abandonment. The awesome Phoenix Program machine Hau and I had put together needed eliminations such as Phoung's to fuel it, and fueling this destructive machine gave me great pleasure. And I knew if I stayed it would be a direct result of the way the war had affected me personally. My staying would be not only because of the nameless, faceless people who had been sacrificed by a warped, political ideology, but because of the ideology itself, an ideology I took pleasure in destroying. These two reasons for wanting to stay were inseparable.

In the end, after the options were considered in depth, I discovered there was no choice for me. There were really no options to consider—there never had been. Since that first ambush with Colonel Andersen—the options had been taken away. Since the first morning when I looked down into the stark and staring eyes of those two men who had died as an example of the Viet Cong's power, there had been no choice. The crying window who told Hau the Viet Cong had been killed too late had taken away my options— that had been a long time ago, countless operations and ambushes ago, but the impact of that scene was still fresh. Objectivity and rational thought were no longer considered, because they had been

167

proven ineffective long ago. If we were to succeed, it would not be because of objectivity or rational thought. To leave would be admitting a personal defeat, and that would be the ultimate outrage. And if by staying, I could prevent just one more murder, if I could assist in saving just one more life by taking life from the Viet Cong, then it would be worthwhile. Our work had to go on to its logical conclusion; otherwise, it would all be a wasted effort. The fact that staying longer could bring my life to an early end was not even considered—which probably explained better than anything else the intensity of my feelings.

As I mentally sifted through my experiences in Di An, the discussion with Lieutenant Nam long ago came readily to mind. Now, with a year behind me, I knew that he had been right, and I understood his anger. Before, when I'd been young, green and naive the issues hadn't been nearly so clear-cut. Then, I'd only wanted the war to end, like most other Americans. But now I realized that a simple ending was no solution; "peace at all costs" would be no peace at all. Appeasement had failed with England's Prime Minister thirty years before, and I saw no reason for it to succeed now. Nam knew that there was really nothing to negotiate in Paris as long as Hanoi's divisions were in the south—an obvious truth the North Vietnamese had never admitted in Paris. Yet this shocking, glaring fact failed to generate the kind of outrage necessary to insure a victory for South Vietnam. From the States, news of peace demonstrations and student riots seemed to hopelessly blur the real issues. In the confusion, Americans had grown weary of the war and, in their weariness, seemed willing to accept any solution that would lead to an end. But for me, the issues were too real for blurring or rationalization; I couldn't forget.

Nor could I forget the discussion with Quy concerning our objectives in the war. He had shot holes in my idealism with his negative analysis. Was there really nothing more meaningful to fight for than a rice farmer's right to say "no" or "screw you"? Yet wasn't this the ultimate expression of freedom? If, after the shooting stopped and the smoke cleared away, this right was not secure, what else really mattered? I was willing to settle for a little less than I had hoped for if this right could be granted. Perhaps I had reached a compromise with my idealism in exchange for Quy's reality. I was learning—the hard way.

168

The question was quickly settled in my mind. I had to stay longer. And, until a better reason presented itself, I would be staying to help Quy's rice farmer exercise the ultimate in freedom. Two days after the death of To Van Phoung, I went to Bien Hoa to formally initiate a six-month extension of my one-year tour.

Hau quickly spread the news of my latest decision. When I returned from Bien Hoa, I discovered that a party had been planned for me at a restaurant in Thuc Duc, the district to the south of us. This was a pleasant surprise, since I had not expected any fuss over my decision to stay, but I should have known better. Hau wasn't about to let an excellent excuse for us to take the afternoon off pass quietly. After the dinner was over, we sat around the restaurant laughing and talking and drinking beer for at least two hours. We recounted most of the important events of the past year in those hours and made solemn promises to do even better in the coming months. Wentworth was along, adding his bulk and humor to the occasion. Near the end of the party, Hau told me he was glad I had decided to stay.

"Maybe you will be sorry I do not go home, Troung Uy," I told him.

"Why do you say this?"

"If I leave, you will get a different advisor—maybe one who is better at this work than I am."

"Yes, this is true. But he may be worse, and already I have spent a year with you, showing you what must be done in Di An. With a new advisor I would have to start over. And what would I do if I did not like him?"

This drew a laugh from those remaining. Of all the things accomplished during the year, not the least was the fact that Hau and I knew each other well enough to joke openly. He could call me the "ugly American" if the situation warranted it, just as easily as I could ridicule his "oriental mystique." On these occasions we both played our assigned role with expertise. It had been a long, happy day. When the restaurant owner regretfully informed us there was no more ice for beer, we knew it was time to go home.

Part of the package offered by the Army to induce extending one's stay was a thirty-day leave, anywhere in the world. For awhile I thought about going to Australia or some other equally strange land, but I finally decided to go home to West Virginia. Just like my decision to extend, there was really no other choice. There was an invisible and unexplainable force that pulled me back to the mountains, a force more powerful than a normal longing to go home. I needed time away from Di An to try to recapture the things I'd lost, to try to become, once again, the person I had once been. Although I didn't really understand what it was, I knew the year in Di An had changed me. I'd grown harder and more pragmatic during the past year, partly because I had to in order to survive, and partly because I wanted to. Maybe I would lose some of the hatred I carried for the Viet Cong among the familiar surroundings of my youth and regain some long-lost objectivity. Perhaps back home, in the mountains, I could fit it all together and place it in perspective.

A week after I signed the extension papers, I was on my way back home. The 707 that took me from Saigon to San Francisco looked a lot like the one that had brought me to the war zone, although I couldn't be certain. From San Francisco I managed to get a non-stop flight to Chicago, and after an hour's wait, I was winging toward Cincinnati, where the good luck ran out. I killed four boring hours leafing through magazines in the airport bookstand before Piedmont Airlines was ready to fly me to Charleston. And after taking a look at the plane, I understood the delay. It wasn't the kind of aircraft to inspire confidence—large, suspicious looking oil streaks marred both wings behind the ancient propellor engines, and I wondered if four hours had been long enough to make it airworthy. The left engine belched blue smoke when the pilot fired it up, ran for about five seconds, and then quit.

On the second attempt, it caught but threatened to vibrate the wing off. The right engine started without hesitation, but produced a horrendous, high pitched whine—the kind of sound an amplified window fan would make. As the plane taxied away from the terminal, I had serious misgivings about what would soon take place. There was a sudden sinking feeling in my stomach that made me wish I'd taken a bus or a train. I was looking out the window at the left engine, determined to be the first one to see it quit when the little old lady next to me spoke. It took me a few seconds to realize she was speaking to me, and when I turned to face her, she was smiling.

"I said it's like this everytime," she nearly shouted as the pilot revved up both engines for the takeoff. She was about sixty-five or

170

older with a soft, pink, grandmotherly face; much too old to be subjected to this. Her dress was a simple flowery blue print that looked like it had been made from feed sacks, and her plump, short body slightly resembled a sack of feed. I smiled when I thought of this, and she thought I was smiling at what she'd said.

"But don't worry none, sonny. We always make it. I take this here old bird to Charleston about once a month. That's where my girl and her husband live. Been doing it for over a year now."

I turned away from her and looked out the window as we roared down the runway. The terminal building rushed into view and quickly disappeared as the engines strained to lift us off the ground. More speed, more runway, more vibrations and then we were in the air, wobbly at first, but flying. The broad Ohio River was under us when I turned back to my companion who was still talking about her daughter in Charleston.

"So you do this once a month?" I asked, feeling somewhat better, but not compeletely relaxed.

"Shor do. And it used to scare the dickens outa me. But not anymore. I done figgered this flying business out, and it ain't nothing to it."

"You mean you don't worry about the danger of this plane crashing in the mountains?" I asked.

"Oh no, sonny. Ain't no use in 'that. When your time comes to go you have to go. Don't matter who you are or where you are. Now I could spend all day on a bus for this trip to West Virginia, but if I fly it takes about two hours. When you get my age, you don't have any time to waste. Where are you going?"

"I'm going to a little town about a hundred miles south of Charleston. I don't guess you've ever heard of it, but it's home to me," I told her.

"What's the name?" she wanted to know.

"Matoaka."

"Oh yeah. I been there, sonny. Long time before you were born, too. What's your name?" Her eyes narrowed as she peered over the top of her pinchnose glasses, seeming to question if I was really from Matoaka.

"Cook, John Cook," I told her, and was about to ask her name but didn't because it seemed rude, somehow.

"Nope. Don't know any Cooks but I know some Johnsons. You

know Louis Johnson?" she asked.

"There's a Louis Johnson that used to live out on the road to Lashmeet. Is that the one?"

"By golly you are from Matoaka! That's the one alright. He's my baby brother. If you get a chance, stop out and tell him you met his sister Bertha on a airplane. That'll just tickle him to death." The fact that I knew her brother tickled her to death, and I promised I'd tell him. She asked where I was coming from, and I told her. She didn't say anything for a few minutes, and then she told me that the war had killed her only grandson. But that had been two years before, and she really wasn't blaming anyone for it. It was just something that happened, she said, and it couldn't have been prevented.

"He was a sergeant," she told me proudly and she looked at the shoulder of my khakis to see if I had any stripes. "But he was older than you and worked real hard." I saw no need to tell her that officers wear their rank on the collar.

We talked about her family and her dead husband and the high cost of living, but we didn't touch on the war anymore. When the plane landed in Charleston, I helped her gather up her bags and boxes.

"Be sure and go see Louis," she reminded me as she wiggled up the narrow isle, and then she was gone. From Charleston to Bluefield, I wasn't concerned about the plane. I kept thinking about an old lady who had lost her only grandson in a war she didn't understand, yet carried no bitterness about the loss. And I thought about her brother in Matoaka and realized that the world wasn't so big, after all.

A light, mid-May rain was falling at Mercer County Airport in Bluefield when the plane taxied up to the terminal. Through the window I could see my mother and father huddled under the tin roofed baggage area. My mother rushed out in the rain to hug me as I stepped off the plane, and I could see that she'd been crying.

"We been waiting over an hour, and I was getting worried. Did you have any trouble?" she asked, still hugging me. I told her about the delay in Cincinnati as I shook hands with my father. They both looked older than I'd remembered. He'd lost a little more hair, and she seemed to have a few more wrinkles around her eyes. I wondered how much of this aging I was responsible for.

"Where's Edie?" I asked. But before anyone could answer, my sixteen-year old baby sister rushed out of the terminal with a paper Coke cup in her hand and gave me a welcome hug.

"Boy, you've grown," was all I could think of to say. And she had. When I had left for Vietnam a year before, she had been a girl, but now she was almost a woman and much prettier than I'd remembered.

"And you've lost weight," she replied. "But we'll fix that, won't we Mommy?" Mommy only smiled at this and gave me another hug.

On the way home from the airport, I was filled in on the local news—marriages, deaths, births, and scandals. And I felt good to be the recipient of this information, listening to my mother and sister rattle on about the friends and neighbors. As familiar names and places were mentioned, I became more relaxed, realizing that now I really was home. I imagined, after awhile, that I really hadn't gone anywhere; hadn't really left; hadn't gone to war. And it almost worked too, until my mother told me what a tragedy it was that Helen Mayes was going to have a baby and wasn't married. Then I realized how small the tragedies were here in southern West Virginia against the really tragic backdrop of South Vietnam. And I knew then that it would never be the same. I could never consider Helen Mayes' plight a tragedy after seeing the death and destruction that was a way of life in Di An.

"Do you really have to go back?" my mother asked as we neared Matoaka.

"Alice, don't you remember? He volunteered to go back," my father answered.

"I know, but it all seems so awful. Do you really want to go back to that place?"

I knew this part would be incomprehensible, and I had prepared for it. I told them about the impact the people in Di An had had on me, and why I felt I had to go back. And I told them a lot of things that could never be explained in letters, for letters are only words, but now, face to face, I could come close to making it understandable.

I was still talking when we got home. The old two-story brick house looked just the way it had always looked—slightly faded around the window, but still homey.

Before I got a chance to go inside, my father insisted that I see his garden. And like always, it was perfect. His tomatoes and cucumbers were behind the barn that now served as a chicken house, since he'd sold the old milk cow, and the flat out from the house was in corn and potatoes.

"Nobody else around here had potatoes out of the ground yet," he told me with pride as we looked down on the three-inch high potato plants, "but I took a chance by planting them in March. If we'd-a had a late freeze, I'd-a lost every one of them."

After the tour, we went inside and had a lunch of cold fried chicken that Edie had cooked that morning, and then I went upstairs and took a nap. I wasn't really sleepy, but Mommy insisted on it, and I didn't feel like arguing.

"This evening we have to go down to your grandmother's," she announced as I was climbing the stairs. "She made me promise I'd bring you down when you got home. And she wants you to wear your uniform, too."

The days at home passed much more quickly than I had expected. But they were good days, filled with doing familiar things and seeing familiar places. I hoed the weeds out of the potatoes and fed the chickens and went barefoot. And I gained weight, too, just as Edie had predicted. In the evenings, friends and relatives would stop by, and we would spend many peaceful hours out on the porch talking and listening to the crickets. Invariably, the conversations would turn to Vietnam and the fact that I was returning. On more than one occasion, I was sorely tempted to explain Quy's negative theory, but always decided against it. It was a fragile theory, far too fragile to be entrusted to people who had no frame of reference; people who thought only in straight lines. Because their world was twelve thousand miles from Vietnam, they would demand far more concrete, explainable reasons than this. And I had nothing better to offer.

"What about them there Vietnamese women, John?" my mother's oldest sister asked one evening. Aunt Elizabeth, now fully settled into the middle-aged spread, had made a lifelong vocation of henpecking her spineless spouse, Uncle Ralph.

"What do you mean, Aunt Liz?" I asked innocently.

"Well, you know. Are they good looking, nice to talk to. That sort of thing," she explained, using her hands to supplement her words

174

and causing her double chin to quiver like jello in the process.

"Oh, I got you. Yes, they're beautiful women. Probably the most beautiful women in the world."

"Surely you don't mean they're prettier than the girls right here in West Virginia?" she stammered excitedly. "You can't mean that."

"That's exactly what I mean, Aunt Liz. You should see how graceful they are when they walk down the street with their long dresses almost touching the sidewalk, and their little waists are so small you can reach around and touch your fingers." I shot a quick glance at her bulging midsection that was putting a lot of pressure on the seams of her generously sized dress. I could see my father grinning out of the corner of my eyes, and I had to fight to keep from laughing.

"Well, as long as you don't get any silly ideas about bringing one of them back with you," she said nervously. "After all, John they are foreigners, you know."

"But that's the best part, Aunt Liz. These women make the best wives a man can have. They never argue with their husbands and never tell him what he can or can't do. Why if a Vietnamese man decides he want to go to town with a few of the boys and have a few drinks or whatever, he just goes on. And his wife knows better than to open her mouth. Now, that's the kind of marriage to have. And you know what? There are no divorces in Vietnam because the woman don't cause any problems like they do here. I'd marry a Vietnamese girl anyday before I'd marry a girl from West Virginia."

She didn't say anything after that, but I could tell by her beet red face that I'd raised her blood pressure considerably. As soon as she'd regained enough composure to walk, she huffed into the house to tell my mother that I'd surely lost my mind. After she left, my father and I couldn't keep from laughing. And even Ralph, who'd sat through the whole thing managed a weak laugh, but the certainty that he was going to catch hell when he got home kept him from really enjoying it.

Before I was ready, it was time to go back. On the morning I had to leave, there was a light rain falling that made the day overcast and dreary. It had rained the day I arrived, but the sun had been shining then. Somehow, it seemed only fitting that I should leave on such a day. My father and Edie drove me to the airport, and we said our goodbyes over the noise of the plane's engine.

"Write to us often," Edie said as she gave me a final hug. "Be careful," Daddy commanded simply and shook my hand. They were still standing at the gate as the plane sped down the runway. Then we lifted off and banked to the left and they disappeared from view. And as they did I felt more than a slight twinge of homesickness.

Chapter Eighteen

CHI AND THE LIMITED WAR

"What does this mean Troung Uy, this talk about 'limited war'?" Sergeant Chi asked as he folded the newspaper that had prompted the question.

It was late at night, and I was on radio watch. Chi had decided to keep me company. For the past week, since returning from the United States, I had been explaining the changes that were taking place there to Chi. I had covered these changes in the order of their priority, starting with the mini-skirts that had transformed San Francisco into a beautiful paradise, and ending with my own analysis of people's attitudes toward the war.

"The people really don't understand what's going on here," I reported. "They think we should leave and let the Vietnamese fight their own battle. The American newspapers and television reporters have convinced the people that the Viet Cong and the North Vietnamese are really not such bad people. They are saying that our war is really a civil war. All the Americans have to do is leave and everything will be alright."

He asked what the American people thought about the good things that were happening because of our presence; such things as Dalton's MEDCAPS and Wentworth's pig project. What about the schools and hospitals and roads that were being built? What about the improvements made in crop production and public health facilities? These questions I tried honestly to answer, yet the answers were as harsh as the conditions that produced them.

"Oh, the people back there never hear about these things. There is only enough space in the newspapers to cover our mistakes and losses. And besides, things like MEDCAPS and pig projects are not nearly as dramatic as the reporting of outposts being overrun and corruption in the South Vietnamese government. Bad news sells newspapers, not good news."

"Why is it this way, Troung Uy?"

"Because the people have been convinced that the war is wrong.

177

They think the American government and the South Vietnamese government are responsible for the war."

"But do they know it is North Vietnam and the Viet Cong that make the war?"

"Some of them do, others don't care. There are other things Americans want more than a victory here. Such things as unemployment and education and welfare occupy their minds."

"What is this 'welfare', Troung Uy?"

"Many people argue if there was no war, we would have billions more dollars to give the people who do not work."

This baffled Chi. At first he thought I was joking, but I finally managed to convince him that there was a welfare system in the United States, and it did cost billions of dollars a year. After this was as clear as I could make it for him, we returned to the war.

"What about the many Americans and South Vietnamese dead? Does this mean nothing?"

I told him Americans have short memories, that most people will forget that aspect of the war quickly. Those that will remember are those who have suffered the personal loss. They will remember when they look at the photographs of their dead son or husband, but the others will soon let the memories slip away.

The complexity of this war, devoid of front lines and an easily recognizable enemy, was more than the people were capable of understanding. The fact that a highly efficient political infrastructure was controlling every action taken by the enemy was completely unknown.

It was difficult to explain to the faithful taxpayers that the enemy was using terror as a policy to realize his political objectives. That terrorist attacks were initiated in a business-like manner was an alien concept to the God-fearing American public. This aspect of the war had not been exploited by the news media for obvious reasons; it would destroy the spontaneous, independent flavor of "nationalism" they were trying so hard to ascribe to the Viet Cong. The news media was always eager to disclaim the government's optimistic reports of success in winning back the population under the enemy's control, while faithfully reporting the enemy's exaggerated claims of controlled areas.

Suddenly, I realized that it was as difficult for Chi to understand the feelings of the Americans, as it was for the Americans to understand why I had to return. There was a communication gap of enormous proportions here—a deliberate gap perpetuated for self-serving purposes. Chi was unable to understand why it was so difficult to grasp the situation we were faced with; the Americans were unable to understand why victory was so difficult to attain. Now he was questioning a concept that had plagued me as long as I had been involved in the war. At face value, the idea of a 'limited war' closely resembles a logical absurdity. Deeper investigation does nothing to make it more acceptable.

"Limited war means that we want to achieve something here that is less than defeat of the North Vietnamese. If we could stop their attempt to take over South Vietnam, we would be very happy," I answered.

"You mean we are not supposed to make him surrender. We are only supposed to make him quit? This would make the Americans happy?" Chi asked.

"Something like that, Chi. You see, Americans must not appear too aggressive; otherwise, the world will think we are terrible people. We call this "world opinion." It is very important to the United States."

"But the North Vietnamese do not worry about this. They do not care what the people think."

"Yes, and this is the difference between us, Chi. We must care; otherwise, there would be no difference between us and the North Vietnamese. If we did not care what people think, then people would say we are as bad as the Viet Cong and the North Vietnamese. It is really very simple."

"If you say so, Troung Uy, but I still think we should care more about winning the war and defeating the enemy than what the people think about us," he said.

"There you go again, Chi. Talking about winning. We only want the enemy to quit. If we were trying to defeat him, it wouldn't be a limited war. It would be a regular war. Surely you understand now."

"But is it possible for us to win such a war, when you are not supposed to defeat you enemy? How is this possible?"

"Oh, it's not possible to win such a war. But if winning is never one of your stated objectives, then it is also impossible to lose. This is the kind of war the politicians like. Nobody wins and nobody loses.

You must understand this is the way politicians in Washington think."

Chi stared at me for one horrible instant, as if this incredible dialogue could somehow be true, as if it were possible for me to believe what I had just told him. I tried not to smile, but it was more than I could bear. Then we both laughed.

"Ah, you put me on, Troung Uy. Why you do Chi like this? Now you must tell me what 'limited war' means," he insisted.

"Okay, Chi, I will tell you. It means that the war must be kept small. That we must be careful not to make the Chinese angry. There is much fear in American that the Chinese will enter the war on the side of the North Vietnamese. This means that we cannot invade the North. This is why the war must be fought in the South. Now you understand?" I asked.

"Oh yes, Troung Uy, I hear this many times but I do not believe it. Do you believe this?"

"No, Chi, I do not believe it either."

"Then we will win, Troung Uy?"

"Yes, Chi, we will win. We must because there will be no tomorrow if we fail. It is important that you know the Americans will never allow North Vietnam to win the war. We have fought too long and lost too many men for that. And now we are very close."

This pleased Chi, but he still wasn't sure he understood about welfare.

"How many Americans do not work, Troung Uy?"

"Many, Chi. Millions of Americans do not work. The government supports them."

"And these are the people who say it is more important to give money to people who do not work than defend South Vietnam?"

"Something like that, Chi. You see, if the United States stopped spending money here, there would be more money to give away at home."

"Do many people think like this?"

"Yes, many Americans believe this. It is a very popular belief in America now."

"I cannot believe that anything like this could be popular in America. Americans are too smart for this."

"Most of them are. But politicians who want to get elected say things like this, and they hope the Americans will vote for them. If they get enough votes, then they win, and they give more money to the people on welfare. But by then, there will be many more Americans on welfare."

"But then there will be no money to fight the communists if this happens. Is this not true?"

"If that happens, then you are right, Chi. But it will not happen."

"Then the war is a political war in America. Is this true, Troung Uy? It depends on who the people vote for?"

"Yes, Chi, it is a political war."

"Then you are putting Chi on, Troung Uy. You are putting Chi on again," he charged.

"No, Chi, not really. Because these things will not happen."

"How can you be so certain, Troung Uy? How can you say for certain the people who get this—what you say—welfare do not elect man who believes giving money away to those who do not work is more important than a free Vietnam."

"I cannot say for certain, Chi. But I cannot believe such a man as this will ever be in a position to decide anything."

He accepted this, but he was far from satisfied. The welfare concept I discussed was totally unacceptable to Chi. Such an easy life was beyond his realm of comprehension in a country such as Vietnam, where simply living was a daily struggle. He had not completely forgiven me for teasing him about my first definition of 'limited war.' He would wait until the next night I was on radio watch and try to get even. We did this quite often—"putting each other on," as Chi called it.

These discussions made the long nights go faster. It was very easy for both of us to believe that South Vietnam would win, regardless of the other possibilities that were only theories to us—dirty, ugly theories conceived in the minds of dim-witted men with political ambitions. No, these possibilities were not seriously considered. Now, we thought, it was simply a matter of time before the North would realize this obvious fact. With the bliss that ignorance often brings, we had assumed that winning was as important to everyone on our side as it was to us. We had no way of knowing that very shortly, as if by some tragic coincidence, an offer would be made by our side at the peace talks in Paris, to sell out South Vietnam.

Chapter Nineteen
SATURDAY NIGHT AT THE MOVIES

Throughout the summer of 1969, we continued to press ahead with our efforts to strengthen the control of the government in our hamlets. We used the Hamlet Evaluation System to reflect the growing influence of the government's efforts. Often this was dull and routine work, but it had to be done. Fighting for this control was at the heart of our efforts to make life better for the more than forty thousand people who lived in Di An District. Any technique or device that could help us was pressed into service. This search for new and better methods to win the population to the government's side was responsible for our use of movies in the hamlets at night. Showing movies was technically the function of the Psychological Operations section at Bien Hoa, but they never seemed to get around to it. Designed to "win the hearts and minds," the concept was simple; in practice it was suicidal.

The program got off to a slow start, because everyone was more concerned with combat operations, and also because there was very little hope for the success of such a venture. But it proved to be successful, at least in Di An. Sergeant Davis, our psychological operations advisor, made it succeed. Davis had been sent down to replace Sergeant Mason who went home, and he was given the job of Psychological Operations Advisor as an additional duty. Major Allen liked the idea of showing movies at night, and he instructed Davis to see what could be done about it.

We had none of the equipment necessary for this mission, but the base camp had everything we needed. Since Psychological Operations was the responsibility of the S5 staff officer, Davis contacted the S5 section at the base camp. They liked the idea right away and wanted to participate. After Davis assured them that security would be provided by the district, the program was launched.

The first hamlet chosen to see a movie was in the northern part of the district, Tan Hiep II. I wanted to be present for this historic occasion, and so did Wentworth. When David heard of our plan to

182

go with him he appeared pleased, but a bit apprehensive. We had been discussing the possibility of using these trips to the hamlets as a means of flushing out the Viet Cong by letting them think that the small, unarmed Psychological Operations team would make a tempting target. Then, if the enemy did attack, we would be lying in wait—with a strong reaction force.

"What do you think of this plan, Sergeant Davis?" I asked in mock seriousness, "do you think it has a chance?"

"Sir, I know you got your job to do and I got mine, but—"

"Good, then we can work together, right?" I persuaded.

"Well, not exactly sir. You see, I don't like being used for bait like this."

"What do you mean 'bait?' Don't you want to help Lieutenant Cook kill the VC? You want them little bastards taking over?" Wentworth said, putting the needle in a little deeper, when he realized I was needling Davis.

"Captain Wentworth's right, Davis. If we don't use everything we got, every trick in the book, we won't make it. I know you want to help all you can," I added.

"Yes sir, I sure do want to help. But do you really think this is the way?" he asked.

I looked at Wentworth and winked. Wentworth grinned, and Davis saw it. We told him we were only joking and had no intentions of doing such a thing, but he wasn't completely convinced—he knew us too well.

"Look Davis, this is your baby. You know what I mean? You run it anyway you want. You've done the work and the coordination and all the other stuff that had to be done to get this thing moving, so you deserve to call the shots. Me and Lieutenant Cook are just going to watch. Okay?" Wentworth explained. This satisfied Davis and convinced him the program was truly his.

On the night chosen, which was a Saturday, Wentworth, Davis, Chi, and I met the team from the base camp at the District Headquarters as planned. The team from the base camp consisted of one lieutenant, a sergeant, and a specialist fourth class projector operator. Two squads of Popular Force soldiers were chosen to go with us.

We headed to Tan Hiep II in convoy fashion—"Claymore" in front with the soldiers, the team from the base camp in their jeep, and my little party bringing up the rear. Earlier in the day, a representative from the Vietnamese Information Service had visited the hamlet as the advance party, passing the word of our coming. Hopefully this would guarantee an audience.

Our arrival was greeted by barefoot children who watched in shyful awe as the Psychological Operations team unloaded the small generator that would be used to power the projector. A site was chosen near the hamlet office, for convenience more than any other reason. By tacking a bed sheet to the side of the building, we created an instant screen. The projector was set up about thirty feet from the wall and connected to the generator. That was about all that could be done until darkness came.

While we waited, the hamlet chief brought beer for all of us. It was the first time the Americans from the base camp had been given the opportunity to try Vietnamese beer. The young specialist four looked suspiciously at the bottle with the number "33" printed on the label.

"You'll get used to this if you stay in the movie business," I told them. "In fact, you'll get so used to it, you'll never drink another Schlitz." They liked it immediately, and the lieutenant offered to pay.

"You're about to make your first mistake if you try paying, Lieutenant," I told him. "This is the old hamlet chief's way of saying you're welcome. And if he sees your money, he's going to be insulted." The lieutenant was grateful for having successfully avoided a social blunder.

As the last rays of light faded away a crowd began to materialize from the shadows. The people clustered into the space between the makeshift screen and the projector, compelled by a combination of curiosity and anticipation. They moved slowly in the thickening darkness, identical forms quietly seeking a place on the ground. The latecomers jockeyed for the remaining room on either side of the projector. Some, knowing what to expect, came equipped with low stools. When it was fully dark, the Sergeant started the generator, and our newest effort to strengthen the ties of these people with their government was underway.

And it was fun. The film selected for the first night was a Walt Disney nature film. The crowd that had seemed so lifeless in its forming was soon roaring to the antics of a beaver building a dam.

A jackrabbit that narrowly escaped the murderous attempts of a bald eagle emerged as the film's reluctant hero, while the black snake that devoured a couple of field mice played the villain's role. Through the magic of Disney photography, violets and water lilies were allowed to blossom in seconds, performing as ballet dancers, turning and swaying in perfect time to the film's music. Before it was over, our audience was laughing openly, applauding wildly. We had successfully bridged the communication gap—the universality of the movie had taken care of that. Unconsciously I was caught up in the excitement. It was easy to forget that the purpose of this venture was to "win" these people for the government. It was much more appealing to think of it as only an attempt to destroy the monotony of their lives—if we could just make them laugh and forget the daily struggle of existing, then this would be enough. And we had succeeded in this latter objective. We had made them laugh, and our movie would not be forgotten.

When it was all over, our collective audience became individuals again and faded into the night, but their leaving was far different than their arrival had been. The sound of laughter and loud talking could be heard long after they had disappeared. The soldiers, who had been deployed around the hamlet office, emerged from the darkness and boarded the truck. In a few minutes, the projector, generator, and screen were packed away and we were ready to depart, leaving no tangible evidence of our visit.

On the way home, I asked Chi what the people thought about it. He told me the people had enjoyed it, yet I was able to detect just a trace of reservation in his voice. I had grown to know Chi quite well during the time I'd been in Di An. We had walked through the long, hot days and the endless rice paddies together. We had shared the same canteen, the same box of C-rations, the same risks. When we suffered losses, they had been mutual losses, a phenomenon Chi was not able to understand at first ("how can an American care about the death of a Vietnamese or pretend to be sorry when a Vietnamese dies?"), but was forced to accept as being true ("why else would an American risk his life to save a Vietnamese unless he cared?"). All of these things had been vital in building a relationship that was free of deception and dishonesty. We had reached the point where Chi no longer told me only the things he thought I wanted to hear—a common condition that plagues most advisor-interpreter relation-

185

ships—but everything he thought I should hear. However, on very rare occasions, he would attempt to soften some particularly bad news, but if I asked, he would tell me. Now, on the way home, I could see through Chi's poorly disguised effort to conceal something.

"What do you really think about the movies at night, Chi?" I asked directly, giving him nowhere to hide.

"I think the people like very much, Troung Uy. I think that everywhere we go in district, we will find many people waiting to see movies. Our movies will make the people happy, and if the people are happy, the VC are mad. When the VC know the people are enjoying our movies, they will tell the people not to go. And if they go anyway, the VC will kill them," he said.

"Do you think this will happen, Chi?" I asked.

"I am very much afraid it will. It causes what you call the difficult situation. Is this not true?"

"Yes, Chi, we call it the difficult situation."

I could not discount Chi's bleak prediction, yet we had to face facts. If the Viet Cong did kill people because they were attending the movies, did we advisors have any cause to be shocked? Was this not the policy of our enemy—discrediting any attempt by the government to assist the people? And if people were killed watching the movies, did we not have to accept the moral responsibility for this? Chi had placed it in the proper perspective with his "difficult situation" label.

The optimism and spontaneous happiness I had felt watching the movie began to fade. Would this always be the case, I asked myself. Did there have to be a price or a condition for everything we did? And if there always had to be a price, could we always afford to pay it? How much was the entertainment really worth? How much should we pay to make these people laugh? Was it worth the life of a villager, chosen at random, to die because he insisted on watching a nature film? But if this point was conceded, what other points would we concede? How much was their right to say "no" worth? Was it worth dying for? Could we put off the sacrifices today and take responsibility for the larger ones that would follow tomorrow?

Only here, where logic gave way to uncompromising terror, could anything as innocent as a movie projector be responsible for murder. This was what had to be prevented, with whatever means we had. If this was the price, then we had to pay it. It was not the

186

best of all possible choices—it was the only choice. And in the end, I knew it would come down to a test of wills. Just like everything else, I thought.

It would not be easy to continue the program when Chi's prediction came true, but the program would continue. We had to win this one, just like all the others. There could be no compromise because compromise would never end. Perhaps with the program we would find out exactly where we stood. If the people would come willingly at night and laugh at what we offered, there could be no question of who controlled what. Maybe, just maybe. . . .

It was a lot to hope for, almost too much, and at this point there were a lot of questions that had to be answered; the "wait and see" kind. But one thing was certain: Saturday Night at the Movies had been a big hit.

Chapter Twenty

THE DEPARTURES

Major Allen left us in July. It seemed to me that his year had passed incredibly fast, but he didn't share my opinion. During his tour, his wife had given birth to their third child, making him naturally anxious to get home and meet his new son.

As the date for his departure drew near, the parties given in his honor became more frequent; gifts were given to him by the Vietnamese—some for him, others for his wife. He was gracious during this period, hiding his impatience to leave extremely well, accepting all gifts and honors diplomatically. In a word, he played the "role" very well.

He had served the team well as senior advisor. We had this to be thankful for. Understandably, he had taken no great risks or made no great sacrifices; he had left this to the idealists. As a career officer, he considered Vietnam just another assignment in a long list of assignments. He had accomplished his mission, he had served his tour, and now he was going home. It had been a business to him, and he had approached it in a business-like manner. Such men would live a long time and go far in the army, for they were objective men. His relationship with the war had been impersonal, much like the relationship between dentist and patient. I understood this. The war was not the most important thing to him, and I didn't blame him for feeling as he did.

On the morning of his departure, we were all up early, ready to assist him in any last minute details. He spent most of the morning saying goodbye. The last goodbye was for Major Chau, and then he was ready to go.

He left us in much the same way Colonel Andersen had left— quickly, almost apologetically. That had been a year earlier and a lot had happened during that year. It had been marked by setbacks and success, and a large part of the credit for the success belonged to Major Allen. Yet, no matter how much things changed, the departures remained the same, as if it wasn't quite finished, always a bit awkward. Something else should have been said during that last goodbye with Major Chau, I thought. These two men had worked together closely during that year. They seemed to know each other extremely well, yet there at the end it was embarrassing. I wondered if it would be that way when I left. Would I know what to say when I shook the partially paralyzed hand of Major Chau for the last time? What would I say to Hau—see you later? And Chi. How would I tell this man goodbye? Or Quy? Could I tell Quy that I had accepted his "negative theory" as the gospel truth?

I had never thought about it seriously before. Leaving had always seemed so far away—and there had always been so much to do before I could go. This was why I could never be a career officer, I thought. My involvement couldn't be measured away with a calendar until there were no more days left. I lacked Major Allen's protective coating of detachment. Because he possessed this asset, he had known full well from the beginning that this day—the day of his departure—would come.

I finally reconciled myself to the fact that if I left at all, it would be in the dead of night with no attempts at the goodbyes. I would leave goodbying to the more rational men.

With the departure of Major Allen, a vacancy was created at the top of the Advisory Team. The next senior advisor was not due to arrive for another month, so it was decided at Bien Hoa that Captain Wentworth should have this position during the interim. Even though it was virtually impossible for a captain to command a district Advisory Team, even temporarily, no one deserved this honor more than Wentworth.

This turn of events pleased everyone, especially Wentworth. It was only fitting that this last month with the team should be spent in the number one position. And he shouldered this enormous responsibility very well, retaining his natural, easygoing personality. Because of this, he got along well with the other advisors, sharing their stories and experiences at the bar, after the day was done. Because there was no pretentiousness about him, he could tread safely on the thin line that separated overfamiliarity from an honest concern for his men. The camaraderie that held the team together was shared by all of us, and the nights we spent at the bar only strengthened this sense of comradeship. Lesser men have been unable to achieve this, but Wentworth possessed the special gift of charisma that infected us all.

There was never any question as to who was in charge of our little group. As the only other officer on the team, I was elevated to the status of deputy senior advisor. It had been almost a year since I had held this position under Colonel Andersen, but it was more fun the second time around. Everything seemed to be more fun with Wentworth, a bit more relaxed. He demanded only what was necessary, and because this was all he asked for, we gave him everything we had. Based on "The Principles of Leadership" I had been taught at Fort Benning, Georgia, Wentworth should have been a miserable failure since he invariably violated those principles. Yet the opposite was true.

I found that I was unconsciously comparing Wentworth to the other senior advisors I had served. All were professional officers, yet Wentworth was a special breed. He was from another era when wars were fought to be won. He was not as polished as the others, and perhaps he didn't know as much about foreign policy. But he did know about war. He had "studied" it first hand in Korea, though most of the action was over when he arrived there. Sometimes he would talk about how it had been in Korea. He spoke of the weather, placing special emphasis on the bitter cold and how the only way he could keep his weapon from freezing was to "piss on it." That war had been a bitter disappointment to him. Yet he was still idealistic about Vietnam, about our coming victory, and his idealism could not be discounted because of his age—he was too old for that.

To Wentworth there was very little difference between the little brown men in Korea and the little brown men we were fighting now. This war would be his last chance to get at them, and he knew it. In a way his motivation was negative, for more than anything else he was opposed to the enemy's presence. If the destruction of the enemy gave the people a better life, then this was even better, but the destruction of the enemy was a justifiable end in itself. In this respect, his thought process was vastly different from Quy's, yet both were negative in nature. To achieve the enemy's end, he was prepared to sacrifice his life, and this disregard for his own safety made him an excellent advisor. Senior advisor was the ideal position for him in the Army's Complex Structure; he certainly didn't belong in some mundane staff position.

Perhaps he realized that he would never be a success as a staff officer, anyway. Somehow, he didn't fit into that world of the spit-and-polish officer. He was an individual, and the price he paid for being an individual had been high—extremely high. He refused to be a "yes man," and because of this he was a captain while other officers his age were lieutenant colonels.

The new action Army—with the bright, young, two-year captains so bitterly detested by Wentworth—was passing them by. Since I would soon be a two-year captain, I was about to fall in this category. Yet for some reason known only to Wentworth, he considered me an exception, and some nights when we were alone at the bar, he would tell me so. Perhaps his reasons were based on the countless days we had slushed through the swamps and rice paddies together and the firefights we had been involved in. Perhaps the day we were wounded had something to do with it, also. Or perhaps it was because I had been in Di An when he arrived, and I would be there to watch him depart. There is always a certain, inseparable bond between men who have shared a great danger or have entrusted their lives to each other. There was such a bond between us. It was never spoken of or referred to, but it was there.

The fact that he would be leaving shortly caused him much frustration. He was leaving while the rest of us were staying, and to him this constituted betrayal—a running out. I told him this was not the case, that he had to return, that he had no choice. His tour was up, and his family was waiting for him. He took exception to this, telling me that he really did have a choice, but he was afraid to exercise it, not knowing what to tell his family if he extended. I told him I understood, but he denied this, reminding me that I voluntarily decided to stay longer. My case was different, I replied; the two were incomparable. Then I realized why he considered me different from the other young officers—I was staying, and to Wentworth this made the big difference. I told him that I had nothing to return to anyway, staying another six months was really no big deal. But he didn't buy this any more than I did.

As the time he had remaining was running out, he pushed for more aggressive operations, hoping for one more big contact before he left. In some way he felt this would make everything worthwhile, meaningful. If he could not win the big war, which he had reluctantly agreed to leave to someone else, then perhaps he could win the smaller war, the more personal conflict, that was raging around him. This was more important than the "other war"

191

anyway, he thought. Perhaps there really was no big war, only a whole series of little ones that had to be brought to an end, one at a time. Perhaps, if he had just one more chance, he might be able to win the war that he was fighting with himself, and then be allowed to leave with a good, clean conscience.

But this chance never came for Wentworth, and when the time for his departure arrived, he made it as simple and painless as he could. His goodbyes, the ones he had to say, were taken care of in advance. This allowed him to simply slip away when the day arrived, drawing little attention to himself or the fact that he was going. Yet his going was different from the rest.

It carried with it an undeniable implication that he had not had enough, had not done enough, to be satisfied. Unlike the others, Wentworth was unable to consider his tour in Vietnam as "just another assignment" in his career development. And because of this, there was no doubt that he would be coming back.

Chapter Twenty-One

THE QUOTA

With the departure of Wentworth our new senior advisor, Major White, assumed command of the team. He was the fourth senior advisor I had worked for in fourteen months. During this period I discovered there were only two types of advisors: those who honestly and sincerely tried to do their job to the best of their ability, and those who were only marking time, waiting for the year to end.

Major White fell into the latter category. This was a disappointment to me personally, but it was no real surprise. One of the first things he told us was that he knew all there was to know about being an advisor, so if we had any doubts as to his ability, "we could forget them." From that point, I began to have doubts—deep, serious, dark doubts.

He had a reason for being such a highly qualified advisor, or at least what he considered to be a reason—Major White had just graduated from a new course in Washington taught by the Foreign Service Institute and, by his own admission, this was the ultimate in Advisor Prep Schools. For a whole year he had studied the solutions to the problems facing the Vietnamese, and now he was determined to put them into practice. He didn't tell us how much time he had spent studying the problems.

The first meeting between Major White and Major Chau was somewhat strained. Major White insisted on using the Vietnamese he had been taught in Washington, and Major Chau tried very hard to understand him. After this initial disaster, Major White made no other attempt to converse in Vietnamese. From that very first day, I knew this would be a rough one. I wanted to tell the new Major that Di An was not the personification of that mythical Vietnamese district that he had studied in Washington. Our problems and the solutions to our problems were not hypothetical, subject to the treatment of some mystical, universal panacea, but I decided to wait before I said anything. There was always the possibility that he would see these things for himself.

193

For the time being, I wasn't particularly concerned about the new senior advisor. There were too many things that had to be done for me to worry about this man. In August the most pressing matter I was faced with was the latest requirement levied on the district by the Phoenix Program. This requirement came in the form of a quota—each district was now responsible for the elimination of a certain number of infrastructure members a month.

It seemed that the people in Saigon had decided that the best and fairest method of ridding the country of this structure was to systematically distribute the burden among the districts. By making it a requirement, the logic continued, we would have no alternative other than satisfying it. In essence, we were now being ordered—by a specific number—to do what we had been doing for over a year. Apparently the other districts had not been nearly as successful in their elimination program as Di An, and now the powers in Saigon wanted to insure success everywhere. I found myself in complete agreement with their motives, but I was immediately opposed to their means. The problem was obviously not going to be solved simply by demanding it be solved.

I was notified of this new "policy" before Hau; he would be notified through Vietnamese channels at a later date. The purpose of this procedure was to give the Americans advance notice; it was always done this way if a policy change was involved. The document was stamped "NO FOREIGN," which meant it was not to be disseminated to anyone other than Americans, who had a legitimate "need to know," and certainly not to the Vietnamese. At levels higher than Hau's and mine the Americans and Vietnamese played this game of cat and mouse with one another, but we couldn't afford to. We were both familiar with this game and paid only lip service to its rules. To us, the one unpardonable sin was withholding information. As soon as I read this document, I gave it to Hau.

"What do you think, Troung Uy?" I asked after he had read the document.

"I can think nothing because I am not suppose to know yet. This is only for you," he replied, smiling as the document was returned to me, "but I think it is an American idea."

"You are wrong, Troung Uy; only the Vietnamese care this much about numbers. And besides, if it were an American idea, you would have received it before me. You know this is the way things are done."

"Yes, but you can see that the document is more concerned with results than anything else. Only the Americans care this much about results."

It was worth a laugh at least. In the end we compromised, agreeing that both the Americans and the Vietnamese had taken part in this idiotic statement of policy.

But it was far from being funny. Some of the obvious shortcomings of such a plan were immediately visible. For starters, it would now be a tremendous temptation to claim that regular Viet Cong guerrillas, killed in combat, were actually members of the infrastructure. This was sure to happen if the powers above us insisted on a certain number of eliminations. The actual status of such people could be easily falsified by switching their identity with that of a known member of the infrastructure. Such action would set off a vicious chain reaction, forcing those who falsified reports to become victims of those same reports. If, at a later date, the real member was captured or killed, this action could not be reported, for you can only eliminate a man once—hence you can only report it once.

Hau and I discussed such possibilities, knowing full well that the spirit of this newest directive was sure to be violated. It would give many of our peers a chance to "clear up" a lot of dossiers that were still active.

We were somewhat fortunate, since we were only required to make five eliminations the first month. We really didn't foresee any immediate difficulties since we had been averaging about ten a month. But if the quota remained in effect, and there were no more members of the political structure left, then it could get sticky.

A few days later there was a meeting at Bien Hoa for the Phoenix district advisors. At this meeting an attempt was made to explain the reasoning behind this latest change. It was explained to us by a representative from the Phoenix Program in Saigon that this was a means of exerting pressure on the Vietnamese to force them to do their job. The representative took great pains to make sure we understood that it was not a method of placing pressure on the American advisors. Too bad, I thought. Too bad it wasn't designed to make the Americans do their job. All too often I had seen advisors spend their whole year in Vietnam, screaming and shouting that their Vietnamese counterpart could not listen to him, would not follow his advice. There is nothing I can do, the same advisor would continue. And that is exactly what would happened—nothing. Now here was another excuse we were offering the advisor, another chance for him to say that his counterpart was not abiding by the latest directive, another chance for the advisor to excuse his lack of success with the well-worn story that he had received no cooperation from his counterpart.

The meeting proceeded as I knew it would. Some of the advisors complained bitterly about the lack of enthusiasm displayed by the Vietnamese. Invariably, these advisors were the least enthusiastic in the field. Then the Phoenix representative asked what we honestly thought of the idea. For the most part it was accepted, but it was accepted only because the burden was on the Vietnamese.

I opposed it as strongly as I could, offering the same arguments that Hau and I had talked about and other arguments that we had not discussed. I knew that the weaknesses in this system had to be obvious to other people if they were obvious to me, yet this didn't appear to be the case. The Phoenix representative insisted that the policy would be strongly enforced, and that identifications would have to be verified. I asked how this would be accomplished, and he began talking about another requirement, in the form of a report, that required the Vietnamese and the American advisor to state exactly how the identification was made in each case.

"The important thing is the number we get," he told us over and over again.

"Yes, but isn't one district party secretary worth at least three village party secretaries?" I asked.

Wouldn't we be far better off if we had the party secretary for Bien Hoa Province than a whole sackful of hamlet-level cadres? This business about numbers would be acceptable if we were dealing with apples or automobiles, but people were different. Some are simply worth more than others. If they insisted on concentrating only on numbers, then no one would have time to go after the higher-ranking members of the political structure. All of our time would be spent on satisfying this silly-ass requirement, which could be done quite simply by eliminating the lower-ranking, relatively unimportant members of this organization.

Of course, I realized that this man was simply doing as he was

196

told, the same as the rest of us, and he was in no position to decide policy. Yet, if he didn't know these things someone should point them out to him. Only someone who had been in the field would know how things really were, not how they should work. But the people in the field were never consulted before a policy change; they were only informed after the change had taken place. The meeting finally ended with only one thing clear to us—the quota system was now in effect, and we would support it.

Back in Di An later that evening, I gave Hau a description of the meeting. He told me that there was a meeting for him in Bien Hoa later in the week, when all the Vietnamese S2's in the Province would be formally informed.

"I will pretend that I do not already know, Troung Uy. I will try to be surprised. And if I get the chance, I will speak as you did about what is wrong with this plan. But it will not change anything. This is why they tell us now, because there is no more changes to be made."

I agreed with him. Now all that was left was to wait and see how soon this latest venture would come apart. I suggested to Hau that we go over in the market for a bowl of soup and some beer. It had been a long time since we had done this. He agreed to go only on the condition that he be allowed to buy.

"Okay Troung Uy, you buy," I said. And we left for the market.

Chapter Twenty-Two

THE CRANES

During August we managed to satisfy the requirements of our quota; in fact, we exceeded it. One area we had been concentrating on was the place where To Van Phoung had been killed, which had yielded several of his followers, and we planned on milking it for all we could get. I had suggested to Hau that we pay particular attention to the Binh Au Public Works, and he was in complete agreement. I had no way of knowing that part of Hau's motivation—the biggest part—was generated by something other than the infrastructure.

Partially hidden in the thick, heavy grass of the public works yard were five very old, rust-covered cranes. The vintage was at least pre-1954, which placed them in the French period of influence. During the many times we had been through this place, I had scarcely noticed these towering, silent giants. They were there, and they did not bother me, so I had extended the same courtesy. I felt sure they had been used during the earliest attempts to carve roads through the jungle. Now, their usefulness gone, they had been dragged here to rust away; replaced by the more modern, efficient machines of the American period. They were forgotten relics from another time. Well, almost forgotten, anyway. Once again, I had let my American mentality make a decision for me, and this decision was wrong. As far as Lieutenant Hau was concerned, these cranes represented a fortune.

One day, late in August, he asked me if I had ever noticed the cranes in the public works yard. I told him that I was vaguely aware of them but had really paid little attention to them due to their obvious unimportance to us. I knew from the innocent sound of the question that it was far from being innocent. Hau was taking more than a passing interest in these rust piles, and this interested me.

"Why do you ask me this, Troung Uy? Are we now going to build roads?" I asked assuming an air of mock seriousness.

"No, Troung Uy, we do not build roads with them but maybe we,

198

what you say, 'win hearts and minds' with them," he told me.

"What do you mean?" I asked, now fully interested in whatever plan Hau had in mind.

Whatever it was might prove to be a diversion from our routine of eliminating the enemy infrastructure. It proved to be just that.

"I have a plan that I will tell you about," he stated, "then you tell me what you think."

"Okay, Troung Uy, tell me about this plan," I said.

"It is very simple. I know of a place in Saigon where we can sell the cranes. There is a Chinese man there who will buy them. He sells them to Japan. The money we get from the cranes will go to the soldiers. This will help their spirit very much when they fight the VC," he told me.

"Is that all there is to your plan, Troung Uy?" I asked.

"That is all."

He had told the truth—it *was* a simple plan.

"Who do they belong to?" I asked.

"The Americans who are now in charge of the yard. The ones you call 'engineers'," he answered.

"These are the people who must say we can take them, is this right?" I asked, knowing full well that it was.

"That is right. Perhaps if you ask for the cranes they will give them to you. They are very old and are of no use to the Americans," Hau explained.

"Then you want me to go to the Americans and ask if we can have the cranes?" I asked.

"I would like that very much."

This seemed simple enough; in fact it seemed too simple.

"Is there anything else I must do besides asking the Americans for the cranes? Is that all there is to it?"

"Only one thing more. We must have paper signed from the engineers that say they give the cranes to us. If we do not have paper, the Chinese man will not buy the cranes. If we have the paper, then he knows we do not steal them. He must be certain that they belong to us," he explained.

This was a fantastic idea, and I liked it immediately. It promised to help the people who needed the help the most—the soldiers. The poor little bastards needed all the help they could get—from any source.

I didn't ask Hau why he came to me with this plan instead of the senior advisor. I knew the answer without asking. Any deal such as this, which would result in money changing hands along the line, would be rejected. Somewhere, buried deep in the mountains of regulations that controlled American advisors, I was certain there was one that prohibited what Hau and I were planning, and I was just as certain that Major White would say "no dice." I was about to ask how much Hau would get for those cranes in Saigon, but thought twice about it, deciding the less I knew, the better.

The more we discussed this, the more obvious it became that Hau had researched his objective very well. I attempted to discourage his usage of the pronoun "we" and replace it with "you," emphasizing my desire to consider this whole operation as Hau's idea and eliminate me from the picture.

"How do you plan on delivering these cranes to Saigon?" I asked.

"I will take care of that, Troung Uy, You do not have to worry about it," he said. I was most grateful for this reply.

The next day, Hau and I visited the public works at Binh An. I talked to the man who was in charge of the works, a Mr. Burke, explaining in detail exactly why I wanted the cranes. He listened patiently to my story, which admittedly was a little sadder than facts warranted. Hau sat silently beside me during the conversation, prominently displaying his most pious expression. I could tell, from the way his eyes narrowed when I explained how much the cranes would mean to the soldiers, that we were impressive.

When I finished, I was sure he would say yes, but he surprised me. Mr. Burke said he would have to think about it and let me know. I realized that if I failed to get a commitment from him at this time, the chances of Hau and I getting those cranes were almost nonexistent. I was hoping that I wouldn't be forced to play our hole card, that Mr. Burke would cooperate with us. But he was being difficult and left me no choice. I reminded Mr. Burke that we had a platoon of Popular Force soldiers committed to providing security for his yard. If they were removed due to operational necessity, then we could not be responsible for the protection of his operation. Now, if Lieutenant Hau were to recommend to the district chief that they be removed and the intelligence advisor concurred, then.
. . . Mr. Burke got the drift of the conversation immediately.

"I don't think there is any problem, Lieutenant Cook. As a matter

200

of fact, I have been trying to get rid of those cranes for some time, and if you can use them, then you are certainly welcome to them," he told me nervously.

Hau beamed at this. The suggestion that the Popular Force platoon just might be withdrawn had been enough incentive to convince Burke that he could live without the cranes. The only other matter left to settle was the slip of paper, stating that the cranes had been given to Hau. Mr. Burke quickly took care of this, and Hau and I thanked him for his "cooperation" and left.

Hau had made arrangements with a friend of his who had a wrecker to haul the cranes to Saigon. These arrangements had been made long before Hau had approached me, asking for my assistance. His cunning never ceased to amaze me. There was never any doubt in his mind that I would help him in his venture, or any other venture, that would benefit the troops. We were both a little surprised that it had gone as smoothly as it had, but I was grateful nonetheless.

A couple of days after our visit with Mr. Burke, Hau initiated the removal operation. In three days all the cranes had been delivered. I felt much better after the cranes were gone, as if their removal had been final, and the case was closed. I had no real desire to know the details of the deal Hau had worked out, and I was perfectly content to let the whole matter be forgotten. The whole operation had been a diversion from our more serious task, but now these tasks had to be resumed. As I once again became engrossed in the endless numbers of reports that had to be sent to Province, I rarely thought of our little conspiracy. It was over, I kept telling myself, yet somehow I knew it wasn't.

For one thing, the morale of the troops had improved about five hundred percent. There was much laughing and talking around the compound and on operations they performed their duties with obvious aggressiveness. And although I tried to ignore it, there was an undeniable increase in the number of soldiers riding Honda motorbikes—bright, new, shiny motorbikes. Several times during the day, I would be interrupted by soldiers who walked into the center, saluted sharply, shook my hand heartily, and showered me with profuse and obvious praise. At lunchtime, there was always at least a squad of soldiers waiting for me at the door. They would proudly escort me to the marketplace and treat me to whatever delicacies I desired, plying me with Vietnamese beer and green tea. Hau was usually present, serving as the head of this spontaneous delegation, nodding approvingly with his ever-present, saintly smile firmly in place.

I wasn't quite sure why these honors were bestowed on me, but I had an idea, and I was afraid my idea was correct. Soon, the daily luncheons in the marketplace were no longer adequate for displaying the soldiers' fondness of me. They escalated their devotion to the point of throwing a party nearly every night, and invariably I was the guest of honor. It seemed that no expense was spared, on these occasions. There was roast pig and duck, French bread, cognac, beer and fresh fruit. It was a bit embarrassing, yet, I really enjoyed all of it.

Major White found it hard to understand why all this attention was being paid to me. I explained it was due to my interest in the soldiers' welfare, which was an understatement in light of the situation. I felt it was more prudent not to explain, in detail, exactly why these things were happening to me. It would all end shortly, I kept telling myself, and then things would return to normal.

One night shortly after it all started, Hau, Chi, a platoon of soldiers, and I were having dinner in the market. The soldiers were particularly happy this night, and I was happy also. A thin soldier stood up and made an announcement that brought immediate, wild approval from his comrades. Everyone present picked up his glass and drank, as if to confirm the thin soldier's proclamation. I asked Chi, who was sitting beside me, what this was all about. I could tell from the slight hesitation that he was choosing the exact words for his explanation.

"The soldier make a toast for you, and he also make a suggestion. He say we should make you next village chief of Binh An Village. Everyone agree with him," Chi explained.

Before Chi had finished, another soldier was on his feet making an emphatic statement. His speech was followed with thunderous applause.

"What does he say Chi?" I demanded. This was neither the time nor place for subtleties.

"This soldier," Chi began, "say we should tell everyone how good you are to the soldiers in Di An. He say we should tell everyone about the cranes, and how you make all the soldiers happy." This had gone too far.

With a sad, cold, sinking feeling in the pit of my stomach, I suddenly realized that this whole affair had gone far beyond what was acceptable. I had visions of a court martial convened for my benefit, and charges of "money manipulation" leveled against me. By this time the restaurant was in an uproar. Someone had proposed another toast, and Chi was standing with glass in hand doing honors to the originator of the toast. Frantically, I pulled at his sleeve, at the same time shouting, "Tell them they can't do this. Tell them it must be our little secret. Tell them anything, but for God's sake, don't let them leave here with the idea this is what I want. Tell them it will cause much trouble for me."

"Okay, Troung Uy," he said, "I will try to make them understand."

It was several minutes before Chi had an opportunity to speak. When he did get a chance, he spoke to them, and they listened. Chi was very insistent about something, for he waved his hands up and down and changed the inflection of his voice. When he was finished there was a silence in the restaurant, a sudden, embarrassing silence.

"What did you tell them, Chi?" I asked in anticipation.

"I tell them that they must forget about the cranes. I say that in America there is an old custom about such things as cranes. Once they are sold, they must be forgotten. I say that you will be insulted if they do not stop. Do you think I say the right thing, Troung Uy?" he asked.

"Yes, Chi, I think you say the right thing."

Then we had one more drink with the soldiers and went home. The cranes ceased to be an embarrassing subject. In fact, I never heard of them again.

Chapter Twenty-Three
THE TROUBLE WITH MAJOR WHITE

With the coming of October there was a noticeable change in the relationship between the advisors and the Vietnamese. A small, invisible wedge had been driven between us, slowly forcing us apart. At first, it was a difficult thing to track down, but the cause of this division could not remain a mystery forever.

The small things were the first to change. The spontaneous, open greetings of the soldiers, a thing that was taken for granted since I had been an advisor, began to chill. They became more reserved, more dignified and formal in their dealings with us. There was less laughter around the compound, less contact with the troops after the day was over. A cloud was hanging over us, and I knew we, the advisors, were responsible for it.

Before the arrival of Major White, nothing like this had ever happened. Complete and open honesty had been the trademark of our relationship, even when there had been a disagreement. Now, that was slipping slowly away, only to be replaced with caution and more than a hint of mistrust. What I had hoped for when Major White arrived did not happen. The understanding I had hoped he would acquire with time didn't pan out; he continued to view what both the advisors and Vietnamese did in an extremely critical manner.

No matter how hard we tried, we just weren't up to the standards he had been taught in Washington. Nor would he be confused by the facts—facts that should have convinced anyone that Di An was not a typical district. The fact that the Viet Cong infrastructure was being systematically destroyed did not impress him. The fact that the number of hamlets under government control had more than doubled in the preceding year was not impressive. Neither was the program that Dalton had given so much to; the fact that each hamlet now had a Public Health Station was considered trivial. And so on.

Each success that had come so hard and that we treasured

because we knew its price, meant very little to this strange man. He should have been proud of the efforts and the achievements that had preceded his arrival. Major Allen had been proud of us, so had Colonel Andersen, and of course, Captain Wentworth. These men had contributed, and now they were a part of the legacy. Their imprint was on the district—each had left his own mark and his passing had been duly noted. Now, with so much already accomplished, what was there for Major White to do?

He had two courses of action open to him. He could acknowledge the success that had been achieved and try to add to it, or he could discredit what had happened before his time as being insignificant and declare himself responsible for getting us "on the right track." The latter action, if successful, would enhance the major's position and guarantee him a "successful" tour as the senior advisor. The former action would require him to accept the truth and give credit to those responsible for the present situation in Di An, and he was reluctant to do this.

It was obvious by the middle of October that if there had ever been a "honeymoon" between Major White and the district chief, it was over. No longer was the senior advisor invited to the district chief's house two or three times a week, as was the policy before. In turn, Major White intensified his criticism of the district's progress and the things that needed to be done. He had christened himself the ultimate advisor, far above any suggestion that perhaps he wasn't as perfect as he thought himself to be. And, due to this self-oriented, self-serving philosophy, the relationship between our team and the Vietnamese slowly began to erode. The sweat and blood and countless days and weeks spent on gaining such intangible goals as trust, understanding, sacrifice, and a purpose for going on, were crumbling before me.

This was felt more than observed. There was really nothing I could point to and say "this is proof of my feelings, and it justifies what I think is happening," yet what I felt was far more concrete than anything I could touch. In the shadowy, emotion-oriented world of the advisor, it is soon realized that the flowing, cloudy sensations are far more accurate than anything that is written or said.

The Vietnamese, true to their tradition, were far too polite to state the problem, yet they had realized it, in all its ugly ramifications, long before I did. It was such an elusive thing to pin down that I really didn't know where to start to solve the problem. Yet I knew, since I was the only other officer on the team and had been there nearly eighteen months, it was my responsibility to try to close this growing rift. It couldn't be tolerated much longer; this was obvious.

When I brought the threatening, brooding atmosphere to the attention of Major White, he refused to accept responsibility for it. He refused to consider that he could be insulting the Vietnamese in any way, yet that same day he ordered Sergeant Jackson out to Binh Tri II Hamlet to personally count the residents in that hamlet, after refusing to accept the figures given to him by Major Chau. Even more serious than sending Jackson out was the fact that he told the district chief what he was doing and why.

The time had come for me to make an appeal to my thickheaded commander. It was a quiet, lazy Sunday afternoon with little activity to compete with. We were alone in the radio room, which appeared to be an ideal location for presenting my case. Perhaps, I kept telling myself, I just might be able to get through to this man and make him understand that his view of things in the district was not shared by the Vietnamese, or the other members of the team for that matter.

"Sir, I think it's about time we had a little talk about a problem we have here," I began.

"What is it Cook?" he replied without looking up from his *Time* magazine.

"Well, it's about you and the way you feel about the district. I don't think anyone here is particularly happy about your attitude. It seems that things really aren't as bad as—"

"That's about enough of that shit, Cook. I don't need you to tell me how to run this goddamned district. And don't ever forget who's in charge here. *I'm* the Senior Advisor!"

"I know that, Major, It's just that—" Again I was cut off.

"When I want your opinion on running this team, I'll tell you. Until then, I suggest you keep your thoughts and ideas on your own job, and let me handle mine."

He had expressed his views in no uncertain terms. The approach I had hoped would be successful was now closed forever. The matter would not be resolved easily, but one thing was certain—it would be solved.

206

Chapter Twenty-Four

CA MAU

A week after the disastrous encounter with Major White, I received orders to attend the Vietnamese Intelligence School at Ca Mau. This was to be a three-day affair. Hau was also ordered to go, and we were planning on having a short vacation while we were there, since Ca Mau was on the outskirts of Saigon. Officially, the purpose of our going there was to "discover new methods of making our operations more successful, and to learn the latest technique in eliminating the infrastucture."

There was another subject scheduled to be discussed in Ca Mau also. It concerned the use of certain terms. During this period of 1969, the term "eliminate" had been replaced with the less harsh, less concrete, "neutralize." The reason for this change was the unfavorable publicity being given the Phoenix Program. The newspapers were saying that this program was responsible for "counter-terror" operations against the Viet Cong infrastructure, and had promptly concluded this was wrong. The army had reacted to this in a perfectly predictable fashion by overreacting. It was obvious that the term "eliminate" left very little to the imagination, therefore, it had to be replaced with something just a little nicer and considerably more vague. The perfect solution was "neutralize"—no one would take violent exception to it, and it was still broad enough to cover our operations.

This and related matters would occupy most of the three days in Ca Mau. Of course Hau and I considered the term applied to our operations a secondary matter. Far more important than this were the treats Saigon could offer. We would have a steam bath every night, eat in the best restaurants, visit the massage parlors, and maybe even have fun with some of the girls that Hau knew there. It was shaping up to be an interesting three days away from the increasing stress and strain of the district.

When we arrived at Ca Mau, I discovered that the American advisors there had made plans for the advisors attending the course to stay in the North Pole Bachelor Officer Quarters in Saigon, but I would have none of that. I explained that it was important that Hau and I stay together, and we did. Hau, the lone bodyguard that accompanied us, and I took two rooms at the Diplomat Hotel. It was far from being in the same class with one of Hilton's, but it was adequate for our purposes.

There were forty of us in the class; half American and half Vietnamese. The first day at the school was devoted to lectures by American experts in the insurgency business. Using a smooth, slick delivery, they reviewed all the popular theories concerning communist-oriented revolutions. Their neatly tailored, tropical suits were a sharp contrast to the way we were dressed, in our faded, worn, jungle greens. How strange, I thought, that none of these people are down in the districts to take a firsthand look. Like so many machines programmed to perform at a higher level than necessary, they dealt with platitudes and theories far above our dirty little war. They spoke in impersonal tones about what had to be done and how we should do it, as if we were in the business of selling life insurance, with a bonus going to the man who sold the most policies. Those districts that were performing well with the quota system were praised; the poor performers were admonished. And it all fitted together nicely with all the charts and figures they offered as support of their ideas.

One of these self-appointed experts told us more emphasis should be placed on arresting members of the infrastructure and, that only as a last resort, should they be killed. He explained how adverse publicity in the States was resulting from our operations, and that we should "make every effort to see that the news media was not given any fuel for their fires."

It seemed incredible that they could expect us to do the jobs we were doing without feeling an intense hatred for our enemy, yet not a word concerning motivation was spoken. It seemed that they had assumed far in advance that the Phoenix Program could be initiated without the benefit of this vital ingredient, as if we could find some way of remaining indifferent about what we were doing. How vastly different was the view from the top, I thought, that allowed these men to feel this way.

I bitterly resented this "pre-packaging" of our problems—this lumping together of the factors that were making the war possible, as if one general solution could be applied everywhere. But most of all, I resented the term "problem areas" which implied that these areas had been identified, and now all that was required was applying the solution. Didn't they read the reports from the districts? Weren't they aware that each district was different, that each had different problems, some fighting merely to survive?

No wonder the war is still going on, I thought, with such pretentious men in high positions, men who failed to grasp the significance and scope of what was happening, yet they were expected to tell us what was taking place and why.

Finally the first day was over, and Hau and I returned to our hotel. After a shower and a short nap, we were ready for dinner. Hau knew all the good places, so it was just a matter of making a decision. He chose an Indian restaurant around the corner from the USO. Their specialty was chicken curry—unbelievably hot but delicious. Great quantities of Ba Muoi Ba were consumed to put out the fire, along with long loaves of French bread, and salad.

After dinner, which took over an hour, we decided to have a steam bath. Actually, the idea was Hau's, and I didn't feel like arguing with him. The day had been difficult to endure, leaving me depressed and tired. Perhaps a steam bath would be just the thing to make me forget. At its very worst, it could do no harm.

We located an attractive looking establishment on Tran Hung Dau Street on which Hau was willing to stake his reputation as a connoisseur of steam baths. After a long, hot twenty minutes in the steam, we surrendered our bodies to the masseuses' experienced, waiting hands. It was a pleasure to lie face down on the table and enjoy what was happening.

As the young Chinese girl slowly traced the curves of my back with her soft, strong fingers, I could feel the agony of the day gradually disappearing. She rubbed the long, tiring hours in the classroom away, and the trivial dribble about facts and figures from the well-groomed men in their tropical suits began to fade from my mind. How easy it was to forget, to let it drift away, rejected and valueless—as limited in duration as the sweet-smelling balm used by the Chinese girl. I closed my eyes and relaxed, allowing the smooth, liquid softness of her hands to put me at ease with the world, as my tired mind fought off the strong desire to sleep.

The next day was like the first in many respects. The wooden seats were just as hard and the hours were just as long, but now there was a significant difference. The briefings were given by the Vietnamese this time, and they were briefings, not lectures.

There was a representative from each of the Vietnamese agencies involved in the Phoung Hoang Program (their designation for Operation Phoenix), and they were allowed to give a brief explanation of what their agency was responsible for and what they hoped to accomplish. I was surprised by the candor of these men. They were extremely forthright and honest in what they told us, explaining their weaknesses in the same tone they told of their strengths. Perhaps they, unlike the Americans, realized that it was pointless to attempt a "snow job" on us, since we represented practical experience. There was no attempt to convince us of anything, nor did they offer any shabby excuse or justification for their existence.

Small, business-like, appearing almost humble before us, they were vastly different from the Americans who had preceded them the day before. The god-awful enthusiasm of the Americans was not present. These little men had seen too much of war to present that image; there was very little emotion they had left to show.

I suddenly remembered how enthusiastic I had been when I first arrived and how long ago that had been. But now, I could identify more with these Vietnamese than the Americans for, like them, I was tired also, yet painfully aware that we had to go on, had to struggle, had to fight. Unlike the Americans, these men knew that destruction of the enemy was not enough; he had to be defeated. To do this, we had to destroy his will to continue. And this factor could not be computed on the impressive-looking charts the Americans had shown us. It could not be measured in percentage of the population we controlled, nor would it be reflected in any of the "trends" the Americans were so fond of referring to. Like cancer, it could never be reduced to "an acceptable level," for there was no acceptable level. And the only real effective weapon against a strong will is a stronger will.

Here was where the real conflict was to be found between the Vietnamese and their allies; where it had always been. Because it was invisible and immeasureable, it was discounted as unimportant by the logical Americans who became impatient with things that aren't clearcut and tangible. The Vietnamese knew it was there, understood it, and hated it for what it was.

The second night was much like the first, except for the steam bath and massage. After dinner, Hau and I discussed in his room what had happened that day. Nothing was new to us. We had heard it all several times before, yet we had never been exposed to briefings quite like this. After months in the district, it was hard to visualize a joint command at the top controlling everything. Now that we were reminded once again that it did exist, it was disappointing to discover that they were not operating on the same frequency. The Americans had been a disappointment. I had at least expected them to be more realistic and less smug. I asked Hau why it was this way.

"You ask because it is not supposed to happen this way. Usually it is the Vietnamese who paint—what you call—the rosy picture. But this time they are honest, and the Americans are happy. And so you know you can ask "why." But you ask much, Troung Uy. If the Vietnamese had talked of much progress and numbers, then you would not ask me this question," he said.

"Yes, you are right," I told him. There was no point in lying to Hau.

Hau smiled. "You do not tell a lie very well, Troung Uy. You believe too much in what you do. And for this, it will be difficult for you to change. You expect too much from the Americans in Saigon. They cannot know about the things in Di An as we do, yet we do not see all they see. You cannot expect them to understand our problems completely."

"Why can I not expect this from them? They are supposed to be experts."

"Yes, but they search for only those things that agree with what they already think. And if a program does not work as they want it to, they make a new program that will give them the right figures and numbers they want. I have seen it many times. To defeat our enemy, we do not need the charts that tell us how many we have killed and are supposed to kill. We must fight true, but more important, we must be patient and last longer than the enemy. But the Americans here cannot wait. They must do everything quickly, or they lose interest. But this cannot be done quickly. This is understood by the Vietnamese, and because it is understood, there is no need for them to paint the rosy picture."

That night it was a little easier to sleep, thinking about some future success we would achieve because we had resolution and hope and patience and practical experience. Yes, I thought, we will win because we have earned a victory, and now it is within our grasp. There could be no doubt that at this time in 1969, the enemy's main force units were in bloody shreds all over South Vietnam. There was reason to be optimistic in spite of the plastic front displayed by the unconvincing Americans at Ca Mau. Hau had been overdramatic, I rationalized, just as I had been with Chi that night on radio watch. We had to win and the Americans had to be patient, because there was simply no other acceptable solution. This was the last conscious thought I had that night. And it was a peaceful sleep, undisturbed by the unknown truth: that already plans were being made to withdraw American units from South Vietnam—unilaterally. The Americans at home were waiting no longer for a victory they did not believe would come. If Vietnam was going to be saved, it would have to be a Vietnamese salvation. The sellout was underway.

The next day, which was the last one in Ca Mau, was more pleasant than the first two. There was a joint effort by the Americans and the Vietnamese to salvage this last day. They talked of "going forward together" and the things that could be accomplished by a "united effort." After the summing up was over, we all posed for a group photograph in front of the school, said goodbye to the people we had met there, and left.

The drive back to Di An was peaceful. It was good to lean back and let the sun burn the smell of Saigon away, to feel the cool breeze in the open jeep. The air was sweet and heavy with the coming of the rainy season. It would be good to have the rain again. It would be good to be home, leaving the rush and noise of Saigon behind where it belonged.

But the anticipation of returning to Di An was spoiled by what I knew was waiting there. I tried to visualize all the disasters that Major White could have generated during our absence. I pictured the compound burning down, the advisors under arrest, the Viet Cong in full control, and Major White strung up on the flagpole, just beneath the flag. And then I had a vision, for one horrible, split-second of an enraged Major Chau. All the other imagined disasters paled in comparison to an enraged Major Chau, for I had never seen him enraged. And I knew that somehow, we could survive anything but this.

212

I was afraid to let my mind run wild any longer, afraid of what it would reveal. I tried to think of the endless rice paddies we were passing and how much sweat had gone into the countless dikes that hold the water when the rains came. For some reason, the sight of rice paddies always seemed to soothe me, but they couldn't quite erase the apprehension I had about returning.

In Thuc Duc, we stopped at the "chicken restaurant," and had a beer. The last time we had been in this restaurant was for the party Hau had given me. It hadn't changed much since then. The old man still remembered us. Without speaking, Hau held up three fingers and he brought three bottles of beer. Once certain that he could be of no further assistance, the old man shuffled off to a table in the back, his sandals softly slapping the concrete floor. As we drank the beer, we joked about our trip. I asked Hau if he had learned anything.

"Sure," he exaggerated, "I learned all I need to know to be the best S2 in Vietnam."

"And can I now be the best advisor in Vietnam?" I asked.

"Sure, Troung Uy," he replied, "and the next time we must invite the VC."

We were all laughing as we crawled in the jeep for the short ride home.

Chapter Twenty-Five
MORE TROUBLE WITH MAJOR WHITE

The district was in much the same condition as when we left. My worst fear was immediately eliminated as we drove in; Major Chau was in the doorway of his office, smiling. He welcomed Hau and me back with a sincere display of enthusiasm, pulling us in his office and sitting us down, all at the same time. As soon as he sent one of his messengers for tea, Major Chau settled back in his chair behind his large, wooden desk. We discussed the things that had occurred during our absence.

Nothing of an earthshaking nature had happened. A new bridge had been installed in Binh An, three AK-47s had been found in a tunnel at Ap Toi Moui, and two defectors had given themselves up to the Popular Force platoon at Dong Hoa. This was all routine, and Major Chau related it in a routine manner, though there was some intelligence value in the things he said. The defectors would be interrogated in greater detail later, but the initial interrogation conducted by "Sad Eyes" had revealed nothing of tactical value.

The tea arrived, and we sipped the warm, green liquid as Major Chau continued. He had visited several outposts and found them in satisfactory condition. I wanted to ask if Major White had gone along, but I didn't. I would know soon enough anyway, and I had no desire to experience the embarrassing silence if the answer was "no." It was important that the senior advisor accompany the district chief on such visits. It presented a unified front to the soldiers and boosted their morale when they knew the Americans cared about them. And I knew how important this was to Major Chau. When the tea was gone, I thanked the district chief and left. I felt better after talking to Major Chau, even though the conversation had been light.

I found Sergeant Jackson in the radio room, cleaning his rifle. Jackson and Dalton had both extended their tours in Di An for much the same reasons I had stayed. We discussed Saigon for a few minutes, and then the conversation turned to the team. It was safe to ask Jackson if Major White had gone with the district chief to visit the outposts; advisors were below embarrassment. Major White was in Bien Hoa, which allowed Jackson and me to discuss the situation without fear of being interrupted. He told me that Major White had not gone for the simple reason he had not been invited. We both knew the seriousness of this situation; the damage had been done. It wasn't necessary to ask why or pretend it was simply an oversight on Major Chau's part. He was much too careful for that. Major Chau's not inviting Major White had been an obvious affront, and I could only hope that Major White realized this.

"Sir, it ain't none of my business, but I feel you should know what happened while you were in Saigon," he said.

"Tell me, Sergeant Jackson. And don't feel it's none of your business. Everything here is your business as long as you're part of the team," I told him.

"Well, sir, it's about Major Chau's old truck, you know the one that used to be out there in the back of the yard."

I knew the truck, and remembered I hadn't seen it since returning from Saigon. Since I had been on the team, the truck had quietly occupied an empty corner in the compound waiting patiently for growing sploches of rust to consume it. It was beaten and battered, of an earlier vintage than Claymore, and no longer able to perform any function other than serve as a hiding place for introverted snakes. During the rainy season, it was almost hidden by the tall grass and vines, and even when it wasn't partially hidden, it was completely forgotten by almost everyone. Yet it belonged to Major Chau, and only he could determine its ultimate fate. That's why I didn't want to hear what Jackson was determined to tell me.

"Two days ago, Major White told me to drag that old truck away and get rid of it. At first I didn't think I heard him right, but that's what he said. "Get rid of it," he said. Yes sir, them is his exact words. I tried to explain to him that the truck belonged to Major Chau, but it didn't do no good."

He held up both palms, indicating by this gesture his helpless position.

"He said it was an eyesore, and that Major Chau really didn't want to keep it around."

"Where was Major Chau when this was going on?" I asked bewilderdly.

"He was in Binh Hoa seeing the Province Chief, and that didn't help matters none. When I told him we ought to wait for the district

215

chief to come back, he told me he didn't need to listen to none of my shit, and that he was the boss and I'd better not forget it."

Jackson paused to light a cigarette. A district to the south of us, Long Thanh, was asking for a dust-off for two wounded Vietnamese. Long Binh dust-off control was busy and told the advisor he would have to wait thirty minutes. This pissed the advisor off; he said he couldn't wait that long. Jackson turned the radio down and continued.

"I didn't want to do it, but I had no choice. Nobody ever told me to do anything like that before, and I knowed it would cause trouble, but he's the boss. So I pulled the old truck down to the bridge that goes over the Dong Nai River and pushed it off. Just one big splash and that was the end of it. Then I come back here. I hadn't been back long when Major Chau got back from Bien Hoa. I was sitting right here in this chair, when he walked in and looked at me straight in the eye and asked me about his truck."

"What happened then?" I asked.

"Well sir, I thought it would be better if Major White told him about it, so I went in the back and told him Major Chau wanted to see him. Then they had a long talk in Major Chau's office, and when it was over, Major White told me I had to get the truck back because the district chief wanted it back. I reminded him that he told me to get rid of it, and that's what I done. He nearly fainted when I told him the truck was in the bottom of the Dong Nai. And now all the Vietnamese know the story, and you know how bad this makes Major Chau look, losing face and all. And this is why Major Chau ain't asking our boss to go with him—anywhere. I just thought you ought to know, sir."

Of all the possible things Major White could have screwed up, something like this had never occurred to me. As if we didn't have enough problems, he seemed to be dreaming up new ways of producing them. This one would be hard to cover, no doubt about it.

"Thanks," I said, "it's nice to know what we're up against."

As I walked out, Jackson turned the radio up. Long Thanh was just getting their dust-off.

At dinner that night, the atmosphere was strained. A few snide remarks were made about my trip to Saigon indicating that my story of the spartan night life there was not credible. Yet the thing that wasn't spoken of was hanging there, like a cloud. Major White barely spoke during the meal. It was obvious he was concerned with something more than Tom's beef stew. There wasn't enough interest generated in the movie that night to justify threading the projector.

After dinner, I was sitting in front of the Operations Center enjoying the night air, when Chi told me that Lieutenant Hau was going to the marketplace for coffee, and I was invited. I had seen a lot of Hau during the past few days and really didn't care about seeing him that night, but there was nothing better to do so I went. I had a feeling Hau had something other than drinking coffee in mind. Usually when we went to the marketplace, he would stop by and ask if I wanted to go; now he had told Chi to tell me. Or perhaps I was more suspicious than I should have been.

We cut through the back alley to save time and avoid the mud puddles at the end of the street. Following Chi through the dark, familiar alley, I thought of the day the Viet Cong had blown up the market, and I could see once again the woman with her arm hanging in shreds, looking so pitifully at me for help. Although that had happened a year before, it seemed as recent as yesterday, as if there had been a timelessness to that horror. At any second, I expected to hear that same sickening muffled explosion and see once again the broken bodies scattered around the street.

Hau was seated at the back table with "Sad Eyes" and one of the body guards known affectionately as the "Hoodlum." We received the usual reception that required hand shakes all around. This display of formality was exaggerated deliberately and Hau loved it; I think his one frustrated ambition in life was to have been an actor.

After the first cup of coffee, Hau told me he had talked with Major Chau earlier in the evening. Now I knew he had something to talk about other than drinking coffee. Politely, I waited for him to begin.

"Do you hear what happens to Major Chau's truck?" he asked, the question flowing into the room like water from a ruptured dam. I nodded that I had. Hau chuckled and said he thought it was funny. We all laughed, but it wasn't funny. This was not the time for the funny laugh; this was the tragic laugh. The Vietnamese were angry, but anger could not be displayed while we were having coffee; it would have been in poor taste. Now the stage was set for ridiculing the recent actions initiated by the senior advisor.

Sergeant Jackson's attempt to conduct a census in Binh Tri II Hamlet was brought to our attention. The idea of an American trying to count the residents in a Vietnamese hamlet without knowing who was supposed to live there or who had moved away or moved in—when this very task was enough to make a professional Vietnamese census taker become a full-time alcoholic—was truly hilarious. Or maybe tragic. A week after this fiasco, Major White had order Dalton to survey every well in the district to determine if the water was safe to drink. This task had been performed many times before by Vietnamese and American health officials, people far more qualified than Dalton. Dalton had tried to explain, to no avail, that this task would take one man, working alone, several weeks to accomplish, and that there was no possible way for him to analyze the water even if he had time—time that would have to be taken from his other projects. Major White accused Dalton of making excuses and defending the "lazy Vietnamese health officials"—a charge that was more than a little unjust.

"Has Sergeant Dalton completed this task?" Hau asked. No reply was necessary, only a smile.

"Major White is a very smart man, Troung Uy, because he can see clearly that the Vietnamese are stupid people. If we were not so stupid, he would not have come so far to give us advice. We are very fortunate to have such a man. But, because he knows so much more than we do, perhaps we do not deserve him."

His flippant tone did little to conceal the bitterness lying just beneath the surface, yet he was careful not to let it show.

The second cup of coffee arrived, and I watched as it slowly seeped from the minature dripalator into the small glasses. It was a painfully slow process, and I always grew impatient watching this happen, but when it was over, the wait was rewarded with a cup of coffee far superior to anything produced in our electric perculators.

"What do you think, Troung Uy?" Hau was asking, "Do you think we deserve such a man?"

He was really asking if I was willing to let Major White make light of the things we had worked so hard to achieve. He wanted to know if I was willing to let this man destroy everything we had bought at a price we couldn't afford to pay, but had paid anyway. It had been slow, unproductive, and frustrating in the beginning, and now the success we claimed was being threatened from a quarter that had never before produced a threat. The intangible, fragile bond that had bound the destiny of the advisors and the Vietnamese into one was about to be ripped apart, and what this meant to us was beyond measure, certainly beyond one selfish man's attempt to bring glory to himself.

And this was the subject Hau and Major Chau had discussed earlier: trying to find a remedy or a solution to this problem. It would be easy enough for Major Chau to request another senior advisor. His reputation alone would justify a request to kick White's ass out of Di An forever. The province senior advisor would have no choice if Major Chau chose such a course of action.

My instincts told me there was more to it than this, that I figured into the scheme of things somewhere, and now I saw exactly where it was. If I was in favor of getting rid of Major White, he would be gone the next day. I was certain of this. I was just as certain now that Hau had been sent to "feel me out," trying to determine what I thought. What I didn't understand was why Major Chau was giving me this power.

Time was running out for Major White. This had just been established. But if he made no more serious mistakes, it was just possible that he could be saved. He was still my boss, and I owed him a certain degree of loyalty, but I owed much more to the district. I realized Hau was waiting for an answer.

"I don't know, Troung Uy," I said. "Perhaps today we do not deserve such a man, but maybe tomorrow we will. Maybe we should wait and see. What do you think?" I asked.

"You are my advisor, and I think I will take your advice," he replied. There was no smile this time, only honesty.

I had bought Major White a little time; the rest was up to him. I knew one more serious mistake like the truck, and that was it—nothing could save him then. As we left the restaurant and headed for the alley, I was afraid for the first time of the power I now possessed.

November brought the rains as it had always done, answering the farmers' prayers. The blinding dust was now replaced with mud, making travel by jeep to some of the most remote hamlets impossible. But the ground operations continued all over the district as before. Nothing altered or interferred with them, for our safety was secure only as long as they continued, thus preventing the enemy from a major buildup.

Unlike his predecessors, Major White never participated in them. He left this task to the rest of the team while he concerned himself with other, less important problems. But we didn't mind; if this was his policy, then so be it. The Vietnamese, however, noticed that Major White never went on operations. They noticed everything, and this only added to the split that was steadily widening each day.

In early November, I attended a meeting at Bien Hoa with Major White. The purpose of the meeting was to bring the province senior advisor, Colonel Gardner, up to date on what the districts were doing. Major White used the meeting for a sounding board to berate the district, accusing the Vietnamese of not cooperating with him or accepting his advice. When it was noted that Major Allen had never complained of such problems, Major White indicated that Major Allen "was unaware of the conditions in his district," and hinted that the reputation of the district chief was "vastly overrated." When asked by Colonel Gardner if he had visited all the outposts in Di An, the Major replied that the district chief "showed no desire to have his outposts inspected." However, he was very careful not to tell the colonel why Major Chau took his present position.

It was a monumental effort for me to restrain myself, but I managed. I found it hard to believe that Major White could actually be saying these things, knowing full well they weren't true. When the meeting was over, we drove back to Di An in silence. The hopes I had once had of saving this man's position were quickly fading, along with my loyalty to him. It was a depressing subject to think about, yet there was no escaping it; if there weren't some changes made in a hurry, Major White's chances of finishing his tour would cease to exist. When we arrived at the compound, Tom had dinner waiting for us. It was a silent meal; most of them had been silent lately.

On the seventh of November, I was promoted to captain, one year to the day after my promotion to first lieutenant. I recalled the abuse that Captain Wentworth had heaped on two-year captains and it bothered me a little; he had been right in most of the things he had criticized.

Colonel Gardner drove down from Bien Hoa to pin on my bars. The ceremony was very brief, but that night Major Chau gave a party in my honor. Unfortunately, the party was not brief; however, it was a joyous occasion. For a few hours, the old spirit returned, and I was able to forget the friction that was growing larger everyday in this compound. I had to drink a toast with everybody, or at least I thought I did. It was a repeat of my promotion to first lieutenant, only more lavish. As usual, the food was excellent. Hau, Major Chau, Lieutenant Vo, Lieutenant Hoan, Dalton, Jackson and I were the die-hards, as we kept the party alive until two in the morning.

The hangover I had the next morning had been well earned, causing my first day as a captain to be miserable. I was supposed to feel different, but I didn't. I was told that I was now making more money, and if this was true, then it was the only tangible evidence that I had been promoted. But there was a possible complication created by my promotion that I really didn't care to think about.

I was now a captain, performing a function that was supposed to be handled by a lieutenant. Unofficially, I was the deputy senior advisor, but I was listed officially as the district Phoenix advisor, and this position called for a lieutenant. I was aware of this when I extended, and I discussed it with Colonel Gardner at the time. He had agreed to let me serve out my extension in Di An, much like Colonel Andersen had done as a lieutenant colonel in a major's position. The six months I had bought with my extension would end with November. The past six months had passed so fast that it took my promotion to make me realize that I was running out of time. I didn't want to leave because the thing was not finished, yet another extension could not be justified under the present conditions. I had no argument to offer to support my desire to stay—as a captain in military intelligence, I simply had no business being in Di An. It was the old story of being promoted out of a job; this was the complication.

If this wasn't bad enough, I had orders to join the staff and faculty of the Army Intelligence School at Fort Holabird. I had known this for over a month, yet I had really never accepted it as being fact. I had no desire to teach army doctrine to brand-new, empty-headed second lieutenants. The commanding general at Fort Holabird had sent me a personal letter telling me how much I would enjoy my new assignment, but I rejected that, also.

But now, with just a matter of days remaining, the reality of my situation was closing in. I had already been told, by Colonel Gardner, that my replacement had been requested, and that I would be going home.

"More than one extension is frowned on now, Cook," he had told me. "It's not so bad yet for the enlisted men, but officers should consider their careers. And, if by some miracle, DA approved a second extension for you, I couldn't hold you on the team, at least not in Di An."

"Where would I go?"

"Probably as a Phoenix advisor in another province. That's a captain's slot you know. But I don't recommend you even applying for another extension. Go on back to Holabird and take that job with the school. It'll look good for your career," he told me, thinking his fatherly advice was quite sound. Further discussion would have been pointless.

When he was finished I thanked him for his time and walked out. My war was in Di An, just as Wentworth's had been. This was where we had fought our dirty little war, and if I couldn't stay here, then I couldn't stay. Another job on another team would be unacceptable.

During the next few days, I knew the frustration Wentworth had felt during his final days in the district. The desire for one more big contact, one more big fight, became an obsession. Perhaps the bitterness I felt toward the circumstances that I had become a victim of could be drained out on the Viet Cong. It was because of this that I had agreed to go with Hau on an ambush with just over a week remaining in Vietnam.

The intelligence looked good, and if we were lucky we would do serious damage to a security squad that was causing trouble in Tan Hiep Village. It had been a long time since Hau and I had teamed up for an ambush, making us past due for a contact. Sergeant Davis wanted to go also, and so did Tinh, the faithful one. I decided to take an M-60 machine gun along, just in case we found something. There were twelve of us in all—Hau, Davis, Tinh, myself and an eight man squad of Popular Forces. Enough to be effective, yet small enough to escape if we encountered more than we were bargaining for.

Hau's agent told us the bad guys would be coming from the north, from Tan Uyen District, travelling south to Tan Hiep II, the smallest hamlet in Tan Hiep Village. Tan Hiep II was guilty of aligning itself with the government and accepting projects that were beneficial to the residents. In short, Tan Hiep II was allowing itself to become pacified and, to the Viet Cong, no hamlet could commit a more serious offense. The VC squad was coming to show the hamlet the error of their ways, to demonstrate what happens to hamlets that allow the government to influence them. Hopefully, we could demonstrate to the VC why it was in their best interest to leave the hamlet alone.

After dinner, Hau and I discussed the operation. Our plan was simple. We would be waiting near the most likely trail leading into Tan Hiep II from Tan Uyen. If our information was as good as it looked, we would blow them away; if it wasn't we would spend a long night feeding the mosquitoes. Chi had agreed to spend the night listening to the radio. I felt better knowing he was handling this end for us.

It was an easy load for Claymore—twelve people hardly constituted a decent load, yet this was mute testimony that things were slowing down. We were unloaded about a mile from the point where we planned the ambush, and waited for the night to settle. When it was dark, we headed for our destination by skirting the hamlet to the west and then proceeding east along a small stream. Then, as an insurance against being followed, we made two tight circles. It was completely dark when we finally settled into the position we wanted. We were using an L-shaped ambush with most of our fire power lying parallel to the trail. The base of the L, consisting of four men, was stretched across the trail and had the responsibility of halting the Viet Cong's forward progress, while producing an effective crossfire. Hau and Jackson were with the troops parallel to the trail, while Tinh and I joined the base.

Tinh was excited, as usual, and started his same old shit about "we kill VC." I had to tell him to shut up twice. Our position placed us almost directly in the trail, with a soldier on either side. This appeared to be the most logical deployment, since I had the machine gun. I appointed Tinh the assistant gunner, making him responsible for adjusting the bipods and linking the ammo belts together. He handed me one end of a belt, and I placed it under the feed tray. This would give me non-stop firing, if necessary, with Tinh adding more belts as they were needed. This was one of the beautiful things about the M-60; with an assistant gunner, even a half-ass like Tinh, I could fire until the barrel burned out. And the barrel could be replaced in three seconds.

Comfort was not a necessity on an ambush, but I made myself as comfortable as I could behind the gun, swinging the butt plate up and placing it on top of my shoulder. I pulled down on the stock with my left hand until it was firmly against my shoulder. This would reduce the recoil when firing and give me a place to rest my cheek while waiting. My right hand toyed with the safety switch, just behind the trigger.

Ahead of me to the left, I could barely see the dim, square outline of a Claymore mine. There were others farther ahead, but I couldn't see them. Nor could I see the rest of the ambushers hidden in the grass, waiting patiently to activate these awesome weapons. I shook Tinh periodically, making sure he wasn't asleep. He had picked up the bad habit of sacking out on ambushes, but I was determined it wasn't going to happen this time.

"If you go to sleep tonight, Tinh, I'll cut your balls off. Do you understand?" I told him before we left the compound. "I've already asked Major Chau, and he said I could."

"Tinh no do, Dai Uy, Tinh no sleep tonight," he promised, desperately trying to protect himself from a remote chance of being castrated.

We had been in our ambush position for well over two hours before anything happened. I was beginning to get the old familiar feeling of depression, a depression that always convinced me nothing was going to happen. This had been the case so many times before that it was almost routine now. But this time, things were different.

At first I thought my eyes were playing tricks on me. Then I heard them laughing and talking, as they walked down the trail towards the hamlet. As I watched the faceless forms advance on my position, I could only hope that Hau and the rest of the main ambush party were also aware of the strangers. A second later I discovered they were.

In the darkness, I could see one of the intruders stop by a Claymore mine—the one I had seen earlier. He picked it up, suddenly realizing in that split second what it was and what he had done and what the wire leading from it meant. And in that split second there was an awful silence, so deep that I could hear the ticking of my watch and hear my heart beating, as my brain replayed that first ambush with Colonel Andersen. On that ambush I had whiled away the night wondering about the enemy's thoughts, but I soon gave it up, concluding that he was thinking of nothing, certainly not dying. But now, seeing the man in front of me with the instrument of his own destruction in his hands I knew this night was different. There was no time to cover my ears, to protect them from the explosion that I knew was coming, yet there was time—too much time—for the doomed man holding the mine to die a thousand times. Perhaps he was thinking of his own death, realizing that his life had suddenly come to a screeching halt on a narrow, dark, trail leading to Tan Hiep II Hamlet, realizing also that he had been cheated—that he was dying for a revolution, and it wasn't worth dying for. And the ultimate horror may have flashed through his mind—that his death may go unreported and that his body, what remained of it, may never find its final resting place beside his father.

In the weeds to my left I heard the sickening click of the plunger that pumped life into the mine, at the same instant the man holding it disappeared in the blinding white flash. The other claymore exploded immediately as I instinctively pulled back the M-60's trigger. The sharp recoil reminded me the butt plate was not locked against my shoulder. The recoil stopped when I pulled down on the top with my left hand, and then I slowly raked the area immediately ahead of me, working first to the left side of the killing zone and then to the right. Every fifth round was a tracer, letting me see exactly where my fire was going. But the tracers weren't necessary, not this night.

It was ridiculously simple, almost unfair, yet this is what I had hoped for. I was still firing after the others had stopped, and I continued to fire until the belt was gone. The barrel was a light pink when I finished. Burnt up, I thought, and it was a brand-new barrel. The firing should have been in short bursts of six rounds each, the way it was taught on the machine gun range at Fort Benning. But I had laid into the trigger savagely, demanded that the gun perform my way, and it had. It had given all it was capable of giving without complaining, making me glad I had brought it along. The extra weight had been worth the extra effort.

When all was quiet, hand flares were fired above us. As they slowly descended, we viewed our handywork, lying on the trail. The ambush had been incredibly effective; the seven bodies before us were proof of that. This had been Davis' first kill, so I let him call the district and report it. We had to work quickly before the flares burned out. After pulling the bodies, including the bottom half of the man who had briefly held the mine, into the weeds beside the trail, we gathered up their weapons and settled into our position once again. For once, Tinh was on the ball and had already loaded a new belt of ammo into the M-60's feed tray. Tinh went crazy, trying to tell me over and over again, what I had just participated in. I finally had to pull him down in the weeds beside me before he would shut up. The machine gun was still good for a few more rounds, and there was a possibility that I would have another opportunity to fire it that night, but I didn't. Tinh and I took turns dozing, but I found it difficult to sleep.

The exploding mine had set off a ringing in my ears that refused to go away. It grew more intense as the night wore on, a searing reminder of the doctor's violated advice. He had told me to stay out of the field, avoid loud noises, keep it clean, etc. In one instant, I had disregarded everything he had warned me against. The thought of another ear operation was hard to push from my mind, but with the coming of dawn, the ringing had subsided, and as we examined the bodies, it was almost forgotten.

I was certain that none of the VC had escaped, yet we searched for blood trails leading into the jungle. Those that had received the full blast of the Claymores were badly mangled; three were beyond recognition. Five AK-47s were found, along with one K-54 pistol and a few hand grenades. Readable documents were scarce, but we found enough information to confirm our suspicions that this group was involved with tax collection. The task of identification would be handled by the Coordination Center in Tan Uyen, since this was where they had come from, but we would take credit for the kills.

After the search, I called the district to add the number of weapons to Davis' report. I also requested that Tan Uyen be informed so they could start the identification and evacuation of the bodies. We congratulated ourselves several times before we left; Hau was commended for his valuable intelligence, the PFs were complimented with their team work, and there were even a few praises for the way I had handled the machine gun. Already people were moving along the trail. Some stopped to peer intensely at the bodies while others hurried along, casting only a passing glance at the bloody forms, much too busy with their daily tasks to study what we had done. There were no weeping widows shedding tears on the dead this morning, no sad group to mourn their passing or stare at me with that hopeless, helpless look that I would always remember.

While we waited in Tan Hiep II for Claymore to arrive, we had coffee with the hamlet chief. Hau explained to him what the Viet Cong had planned for his hamlet and how we had been able to neutralize their plan. This seemed to please the old man, as if he was also responsible for our success. And maybe he was, for it was his hamlet that had been reluctant to pay taxes to the Viet Cong, thereby incurring the wrath of the tax collectors. This in turn, was the reason for the coming of that group we encountered on the trail. We had been fortunate because we had prevented this from happening. A cold chill settled around my spine as I imagined what would have happened had we not intervened; a hamlet's fate turned on such chance happenings. Of all possible situations my mind created, one thing stood out, beyond question—had we stayed in the District Headquarters the night before, we would not be drinking coffee and laughing with the hamlet chief of Tan Hiep II this morning.

With the coffee gone and the pending disaster averted, we returned to the district where Tom would have breakfast waiting for Davis and me, and where the Popular Force soldiers would be allowed to sleep until the afternoon. And maybe I would sleep, too.

Chapter Twenty-Six

THE CONFRONTATION

The ambush had taken place one week before I was scheduled to leave Vietnam. It had been partially successful about making me feel better about leaving, for it represented the parting shot, the last blow against the enemy, in my small, limited war. In the game of one-upmanship, I was one up. Yet the frustration was still there; the sense of failure and the agony it produced still gnawed away at me, and no symbolic victory resulting from our ambush could erase it. The slipshod attempt at rationalization failed, also. I could convince everyone but myself that I had accomplished all I was capable of achieving; my leaving would be justifiable to everyone but me.

And now my departure had to be planned; it could be postponed no longer. I would be leaving at the lowest point of our relationship with the Vietnamese, and this added to the feeling of frustration. Major White and Major Chau no longer talked to each other, but this was not a new development. Things had been in this condition for some time, and their chances for improvement were almost nonexistent. Yet it was beyond my ability to alter, so I tried not to think about it. I was determined to make the last few days I had left as pleasant as possible.

With three days left, I still had no replacement. There had been several parties for me during those last few days, but they weren't very enjoyable. I received four plaques, and they were all inscribed with nice statements about my accomplishments, statements I really didn't deserve but appreciated anyway. This was proof positive that I had been there, as permanent as the scars, yet far more attractive; here were things to show with unashamed pride for the rest of my life, beyond the influence of the shifting, changing values in the fickle world. As this partnership was about to be dissolved, I found that I was unable to stress the things I felt. My Vietnamese was far too limited for anything other than the most common expressions, and English does not lend itself to explaining the unexplainable. The

Vietnamese solved this problem by showing me with the plaques and the parties that I had been a part of their life, that I had been accepted, and that they had approved of me. Nothing, beyond that, really mattered.

Sitting in my room thinking of some way to return this expression that would convey my feelings, Sergeant Chi interrupted my mental search with the announcement that Major Chau wanted to see me in his office. Some last small gift, I thought, as I crossed the courtyard, something that I had indicated before that I wanted and now he would surprise me. He was famous for his memory and consideration; he would remember something such as this that I had long since forgotten. The messenger in the outer office showed me into Major Chau, then left, closing the door behind him. The district chief was writing when I entered, and after a few seconds he looked up, smiled for the delay, and asked me to sit down.

"Dai Uy (Captain), you have been with me a long time." It required no answer, only a nod.

"I would like very much for you to stay in Di An because you now understand about the district. I know what I ask is difficult and already you have done many things for us, but we still need you."

I was both flattered and shocked at what I had just heard. I had told him on several occasions before that the position for an intelligence advisor called for a lieutenant; an additional extension was out of the question. As tactfully as I could, I thanked him for his confidence and once again restated my situation. With a wave of his crippled hand, he dismissed my argument, as only the perfectly obvious can be dismissed, with the same ease as if I were telling him the sun was shining.

"This I know, Dai Uy. You tell me already. I do not want you to stay here as intelligence advisor. I want you to stay as the senior advisor in Di An. This is what I am asking you to do for me."

The shock was now replaced with a paralyzing numbness. It was impossible for me to fully comprehend all that this meant, yet some of the ramifications were immediately apparent. I stared stupidly at him for several seconds as I tried to put this together, desperately searching for a reply to his request, anything that would make sense, but the words wouldn't come. The only thing I could think of was that I had misunderstood him, that he really hadn't asked me what I thought he had. My mind was playing tricks on me, now that I was getting short. This seemed like a logical explanation, much more logical, in fact, than what I thought I had heard.

But there had been no mistake—I had heard him correctly. He pushed the paper he had been working on across the desk to me. It was a letter to Colonel Gardner, requesting that I be given the district and that Major White be removed immediately. The letter went on to explain why this action should be taken, in a strong, demanding tone. Major Chau had not listed the most serious incidents. Such action would have been counter to his well-defined sense of diplomacy. And it wasn't necessary, for there could be no mistaking the letter's uncompromising ring. I read it through twice before I handed it back, making sure I understood exactly what he wanted to happen, allowing myself to indulge for a few stolen seconds in the fantasy of being the senior advisor.

"This is very kind of you, sir. It makes me feel proud that this is what you want, but I do not believe that it can happen. A senior advisor must be a major. There are no captains in Vietnam who are senior advisors. And besides this, I'm an intelligence officer, and the job you're asking me to take calls for an officer from the combat arms, such as infantry, armor or artillery. So I do not believe my army would approve what you ask, sir."

I had been as candid as I could under the circumstances, with my brain toying at the idea outlined by this man. I had given all the reasons I could think of as to why it wasn't possible and, again, everything I had said was obvious to him. The structure of a district Advisory Team was common knowledge to any district chief, certainly to a man such as Major Chau. The question he had asked had not been answered; all I had given him were excuses.

"Dai Uy, will you stay with me? Please, let me worry about the things you speak of," he said, much like a man who was bored with dealing in trivial matters.

"Many things can be changed if you agree with my plan. If you do not agree, I will understand. Already you have given us much, and I know you would like to see your family. Life here is difficult and uncertain, which you know. If you tell me now that you cannot do what I ask, then it will be forgotten—only you and I will know what we have talked of."

The prospect, remote as it was, scared me. I honestly did not feel I was worthy of consideration for this job, much less receiving it. Yet here was a man who I respected beyond measure—a man I would follow anywhere without question, a man I had observed for a year and a half and had grown to trust completely—and he thought I was worthy. He had observed me also during this period, had watched me stumble about during my first few months as I desperately tried to get my feet on the ground, knowing full well that during this period I was critical of many things his people did. And I had stayed longer than my obligation because, ironically, I had no choice. Perhaps he knew more about this than I did—that possibility did not seem inconceiveable to me in the least.

At any rate, and for whatever purpose, he was asking me to stay and serve as his counterpart, as his equal, in Di An District. That I could be his equal in this district or any district did strike me as being inconceiveable; I had grown too realistic to entertain such a notion. It was a fantastic, overwhelming possibility I had been offered, and I knew in the end I could do no less than accept it, not because I was seeking it, but because this man had offered it.

"Yes, sir, I will stay if it is possible. If you can somehow arrange the things we have discussed, I will be honored to serve as senior advisor.

That was it; there was nothing else of importance that needed to be said. We said goodbye, shook hands and I left, knowing full well that I had just engaged in a conspiracy, and whether I wanted it or not, I was now deeply and morally involved in a power struggle in the district.

That same day Major Chau went to Bien Hoa to see Colonel Gardner, making sure that the letter he had written was explained in detail. I estimated the time at about two hours before I would hear from Colonel Gardner; I was off by five minutes. The request that I be in Bien Hoa as soon as possible was desperate and urgent. When I arrived at the Province Headquarters, I was immediately called into Colonel Gardner's office. There, on the middle of his desk, was the same letter I had seen in Major Chau's office a few hours earlier. It looked strangely out of place among the neatly typed pieces of paper on the colonel's desk. Everything else seemed to belong where it was—everything but the sad looking little note from Major Chau. Yet that little scrap of paper was responsible for me being in the colonel's office. The colonel had a wild, frightened look about him.

"Have you seen this before?" the colonel demanded, pointing a finger at the letter in question.

"Yes, sir, I have. It was earlier this morning in Major Chau's office."

"Are they true, the things he said?"

"Yes sir, everything he said is true."

For just a second I felt a sudden surge of anger at the implication that Major Chau was possibly lying, yet my answer seemed to be a relief to the colonel. He had been standing before, but now he collapsed in the swivel chair behind his desk as he waved me to a large easy chair. The questions he asked were straightforward, and I answered them as best I could. It took over an hour to tell him about the deteriorating relationship in Di An and why the problems were as serious as I made them sound. It wasn't until I was ready to return to Di An that the conversation turned to me.

"You leave in three days don't you, Cook? he asked.

"That's right, sir."

"Do you really know what this means?" Again he pointed to the letter.

"Yes, sir, I do, but I realize that what he's asking for is almost impossible."

The colonel smiled at this.

"For anyone but him, perhaps what you just said would be right, Cook. But nothing Major Chau wants is impossible. Hell, if he didn't get it here, he'd go to Saigon, but he'd get it," he told me. "He wants you as his senior advisor and that's what he's going to get. Unless you change your mind. That's why I called you up here today. We don't have a hell of a lot of time to play with, and I want you to understand exactly what this means to you. It means another six months in Di An with you being responsible for everything that the team does or fails to do. I'll expect as much from you as I do my other senior advisors, if not more because you've been around longer. I'm overlooking the fact that I have other senior advisors old enough to be your father. If you're good enough for Chau, you have to be good enough for me," adding as an after-thought, "I just wish to God I had never sent that son of a bitch down there to screw things up the way he has."

It was happening, and it wasn't a dream. The considerations were now serious, deadly serious. The matter of gaining official approval for my extension had to be worked out, but Colonel Gardner had the necessary papers prepared before I arrived. He told me that Washington would be notified that night. The final word still had to come from Department of the Army, but he seemed confident that they would go along with his request.

"I'll let you know tomorrow what the word is, but under the circumstances, I don't think DA has any choice. That's all I have for you now."

"What about Major White, sir? He'll want to know why I was called up here and I have to tell him something."

"I'll take care of him tomorrow, Cook. But for today, tell him," he paused, as if searching for the exact words, then continued, "tell him I would like to see him here at nine tomorrow morning—with his bags packed. And tell him the rest of it if he asks. Tell him you are his replacement, the new senior advisor in Di An."

I thanked the colonel and left. As I drove back to the district I thought of the possible ways I could break the news to Major White. I knew he was going to raise hell when I told him his job was gone. Yet there was no other way, there were no other choices. It would be easier on him if he didn't ask why I'd been called to Bien Hoa, but I knew better than to believe he wouldn't ask. The major always asked, even demanded, what was going on in Bien Hoa. This day would be no different as far as the questioning was concerned; the answers, however, would supply the big difference.

It was late when I returned. Tom was clearing away the dishes, but he had save some chicken and potatoes for me. Major White walked in while I was eating. I could read the eager anticipation on his face, knowing his questions before they materialized. It had been a long hard day, a day that should have ended then and there. As the major asked his questions, I tried to feed him short, simple answers, hoping that the more serious details I had to relate could wait until we were alone, or at least until I had finished eating. Then he asked if the colonel had given me any messages for him.

"Yes sir, he did. He wants to see you in Bien Hoa tomorrow morning—with bag and baggage."

He stared at me for several seconds, as if he was looking at me for the first time.

"Don't joke with me, Cook. I'm in no mood for it."

"It's no joke, Major; that's what he said. Tomorrow at nine

o'clock with bag and baggage."

"But why, did he tell you why?" A touch of hysteria had slipped into his speech now.

"Yes sir, he did. Di An is getting a new senior advisor."

"Who? What's his name? When does he arrive?" The questions were desperate, running together.

"Me, Major White, I'm the new senior advisor for the district."

He looked at me as though he had been struck between the eyes with a pole axe. When he finally recovered his ability to speak, all he could manage was, "I see, I see," over and over again, as if in a daze. But that daze didn't last long. A minute later I was accused of plotting against him, accused of making him look incompetent as an advisor.

"What about the Sunday afternoon, Major, when I tried to tell you what was going on, and you told me to mind my own business? What about that? Do you remember that?" I demanded. There was no response.

"And why was everything that was done before you arrived 'all wrong?' Why were your ideas the only ideas?" I continued.

"Is that why you are getting ride of me, Cook, because of my ideas?" he asked.

"No, I'm not getting rid of you; you're doing that yourself. You've been doing it since the day you arrived."

I wanted to say more, much more but it would have made no difference. If it made him feel better, then I didn't really mind the accusations, in fact, I was sort of proud of them, to think that I had this power. I walked out of the kitchen and left him standing there—it was pointless to continue the conversation. Nothing worthwhile could come of it.

The scene I had hoped to avoid had happened; the damage was done. I had hoped that I could have possibly found some easy way to say the things I had said, but that was impossible. There is no easy way to tell a man he's lost his job because he doesn't understand it, and then be replaced by a subordinate. What would happen to him now? Would Colonel Gardner keep him in the Province, or would he be shipped out? And how would this look on his efficiency report? For the first time, I thought of these things and realized that a man's future was at stake. Though not nearly as important as the mission of the Advisory Team, it was, nonetheless, worthy of serious reflection. But this was his problem now. Maybe I was trying to read too much into the situation, at least more than the facts would allow. Perhaps, in the end, the war had simply produced another casualty and no other explanation was justifiable. Before I went to sleep that night, I heard Major White packing his things. The power struggle was over.

The next morning, before Major White left, I received a call from Colonel Gardner confirming my extension. The atmosphere was strained as Major White said his goodbyes, but there were no more scenes. Even the farewell to Major Chau was handled with as much dignity as the occasion required. Davis drove him to Bien Hoa for his fateful meeting with Colonel Gardner. In an incredibly short period of time, it had happened, and now it was all over. I had no idea where to start putting the pieces together again, but for the first day in a long time, I felt relaxed, a feeling that comes only when a major crisis is behind you.

It was near the end of the month, and all the reports would be due from the districts in less than a week. I decided to spend the day with Mr. Quy preparing these reports in order to avoid a last minute rush, when one of Major Chau's bodyguards interrupted us. Major Chau had invited me to a restaurant in Dong Hoa for Chinese soup, and the guard wanted to know if I could make it.

"I must go with him, Mr. Quy. We will continue when I return. It is the first invitation. . . ."

"Yes, Captain Cook, I understand. Please go. I will stay with the reports."

I took my jeep, or the jeep that was now mine since Major White was gone. It was the newest jeep the team had, yet it was beginning to show the wear and tear of the trails and back roads, growing old before its time. It was only three miles to Dong Hoa but we took our time, stopping by Ap Tay Hamlet to say hello to the hamlet chief. Major Chau visited each hamlet at least once a month, personally gathering the information necessary to complete his monthly reports. Now, I would be making these visits with him, because it was my responsibility, also. Suddenly I didn't feel as relaxed as I had earlier, as I had visions of the requirements and responsibilities stacking up, trying to smother me. These things—the administrative duties, the visits, the meetings in Bien Hoa, the Pacification Program, and a thousand other things—would demand most of my time, forcing me to relinquish or severely limit the time I had spent before on operations. It would be different, much different than it was before.

As we were eating our soup, I was unable to keep these thoughts from seeping into my brain. Hau would no longer be my counterpart, and this disturbed me. I had been pulled away, by the very nature of the position I now held, from the man that had first accepted me, then befriended me, and served as my constant, faithful companion through countless crises and untold agonies. I would still work with him, see him, drink his coffee, but it was different now. And Major Chau knew what I was thinking.

"Do not worry too much now, Dai Uy. There is always time for that later. You have many friends—they will help."

"How do you know I am worrying? Does it show that much?" I asked.

He smiled his quick smile, "No, it does not show. But I know the feeling you have. When I come here as the new district chief, I asked myself the same question you now ask. After awhile, the answers come—all but one, and I still have not found that answer. Yet each day I still ask the same question."

"What question is that, sir?"

"I ask myself if I should have this job—if I am worthy to be the district chief. If I stop asking this question, then I know I should not be here. So you see, Dai Uy, you are not alone in your questions and doubts, but most of them will pass in time."

We had finished our soup, and the flies had started buzzing around the empty bowls, trying to determine if we had left anything worthwhile. I tried to persuade Major Chau to let me pay for the soup, but he refused. He motioned to the two bodyguards seated at a table next to us, and one of them took a crumpled piaster note from his shirt pocket and paid the young girl behind the counter. The other one went outside to start the jeep. As we stood up to leave, I noticed the flies had stopped their buzzing and had settled in the bottom of the bowls, realizing that we were leaving and there was nothing to fear.

Chapter Twenty-Seven

NEW MANAGEMENT

The first few days as senior advisor passed quickly. True to his word, Major Chau offered much assistance. He was never too busy to discuss a problem or listen to a complaint. I found myself spending a large part of each day with him as we visited hamlets and inspected the pacification projects. The pig and chicken projects needed constant supervision, and plans were being discussed in Bien Hoa to build a dam in Tan Hiep Village. When completed, it would provide irrigation for four other villages during the dry season. In addition, operations had to be planned each day, and this required close coordination with the base camp. There were a thousand things that had to be done each day, which kept all of us running.

But we were a team once again, a team that depended on each other for support, a team that felt needed once again, and because of this, the long hours didn't matter. The only advisors left from the original team I had joined, were Dalton and Jackson. The others had gone home to their wives and families, trying to forget the things they had seen and done here. Only Dalton and Jackson had refused to leave; Dalton stayed because he had nothing to return to, Jackson stayed because he didn't want to return to what he had. Their reasons for staying were their own, and I was glad they were with me. I couldn't afford to part with their experience.

And, true to his word, Colonel Gardner had a replacement for me and I was pleased. However, since I was now staying, I decided to make him my deputy, and if he worked out well in this position, then I would gradually ease him into the Coordination Center. Under these conditions, Lieutenant James Garland became the newest member of the team. Fresh out of the two-week Phoenix School that had moved to Vung Tau since I had attended it, Lieutenant Garland was eager and determined to put the principles he had learned to use. He was shocked when I explained to him that, for the most part, the Viet Cong infrastructure ceased to exist in Di An. I told him the story of To Van Phoung and how he met his end. I explained that this action had lead to heavy defection among the party in Di An, a direct tribute to the faith the party had placed in the late Mr. Phoung. With him gone, there was a general loss of morale among his supporters. I made certain Garland was aware of the effort Lieutenant Hau and the rest of us had put into the Center; otherwise I was afraid he may have gotten the impression success comes naturally with time. But Garland seemed to be sharp enough to understand what I was telling him. And this gave me cause to feel encouraged. There was much he would have to learn and little that he knew. It made me think of him as being a great deal younger than me, but, at twenty-six, he was two years my senior.

The arriving and departing was constant, yet somehow, the continuity survived, and the team retained its identity. And with each's man's passing, his mark was stamped on those remaining. He was remembered, his influence was noted and recorded, and he moved on. By the time my extension would be up, both Dalton and Jackson would be gone, leaving me as the sole survivor of three generations of advisors. I thought about what I would do then, but it was so far in the future and so much had to be done before that time arrived, that it occupied little of my time. There was not time at this point to waste, looking backwards. But there were occasions when I became reflective and looked back. During those first few weeks as senior advisor, I found myself wondering what Colonel Andersen or Major Allen would do in a similar situation I was facing, and I relied heavily on the experience and past performances of those men.

Christmas that year was a joyous occasion. Dalton managed to liberate a twenty-five pound turkey, complete with dressing and all the trimmings, from some unsuspecting mess sergeant. We invited Major Chau and his family to have Christmas dinner with us, and he was delighted to accept. A week later, we had a combined New Year's Party in the courtyard and bid goodbye to the sixties. We welcomed the new year with a renewed sense of hope—hoping that it held the promise of peace, hoping the peace would come from our victory, but balancing the hope with a liberal amount of realism, knowing full well that what we achieved and hoped to achieve would not be easy.

As the enemy contact continued to dwindle, Major Chau and I concentrated on the Pacification Program. With the serious enemy threat eliminated, it was vital that we fill the vacuum with governmental influence, strengthen the confidence the people had in us to protect them, and make life a bit easier to bear in the process. There was no guarantee that the Viet Cong would not make a strong attempt to regain the hamlets we had won, and if they did make this attempt, we wanted it to be as difficult as possible.

During January, we were having trouble finishing the pig project that had originated the year before. The difficulty was caused by the lack of feed for the pigs. As a result of poor planning on the part of Bien Hoa, there was no money allocated for feeding the pigs. The administrators had declared the project completed as soon as the pigs were purchased and the pens constructed. Now, however, we were faced with the task of providing feed for the pigs until they reached maturity. If this did not happen, two hundred and thirty pigs located in thirty different hamlets would be prematurely roasted.

At the outset this seemed like a fairly simple complication, one that I could handle without any difficulties. After discussing it with Major Chau, I told him I would request assistance from Province Headquarters. This was the established course of action for me to take. However, it was not that simple.

When I presented my case to the Province, I was told that the request could not be met since the project in question was complete.

"Your pig projects were approved and completed in 1969, Captain Cook. Our resources are now being used for 1970 projects," I was told by Mr. Rosenthal, the balding, overweight authority on civic action.

Patiently, I explained the flaws in the previous year's program, but it did no good. I was told that each request for assistance such as mine had to be approved by the province chief. This seemed incredulous to me, that a Vietnamese at province level would have the final say as to where American assistance would be utilized, to the point of actually denying this assistance to a particular district. Yet, there were more incredible things to discover as time went by. I was inexperienced in the political interworkings of the province administration. My former position in the district had not prepared me

239

for this; in dealing with the Viet Cong, the options had been decisive and clear cut, now they were not.

The problem was not a shortage of corn, for there was a warehouse full of it. It was more complex than this. It involved reports and invoices and justifications and explanations. How, for example, could an administrator, justify allocations of corn to a project declared complete? Not only would this be an admission of poor prior planning and administering, it would also be considered a failure, and failure has a tendency to cloud a rosy picture. Based on this logic, or lack of it, it would be much more desirable to allow the corn to rot in a warehouse than grant my request.

But all this was unknown to me at the time, so I asked Mr. Rosenthal to explain the official procedure I should follow in submitting my request. He gave me a handful of forms, carefully placing an "X" by each item that had to be answered. He also indicated where I was to sign and where Major Chau had to countersign. The fact that I had been given the forms and explanation of their usage was encouraging.

I took them back to the district, studied them religiously, provided all the required information, and had Major Chau sign them. I checked and rechecked my computations used to determine the exact amount of corn required to feed two hundred and thirty pigs for six months. I arrived at the figure of forty tons. This seemed like a lot of corn, but it was no more than the project demanded. In six months, the pigs, would be at their prime market value, and I was shooting for this.

Mr. Rosenthal had told me to submit the requests through official channels, which was routine. This I faithfully did. A week later, I was notified that my request had been disapproved officially, which was also routine. At the bottom of the disapproval slip, Mr. Rosenthal had penciled his equivalent of "I told you so," obviously to discourage any such future requests.

The next day I appealed directly to Colonel Gardner to intervene on behalf of the district, but he said there was nothing he could do. This was strictly a pacification matter and, although he was directly responsible for the success of the pacification program as well as the military operations, he was committed to "supporting his staff on matters such as this."

Normally, this should have been the end of the matter, for the channels open to me for support had been officially closed. As the district senior advisor, I was required to do no more than this. Yet I knew I had to keep trying even if the attempts for aid took me outside my official channels, a risky course of action at best. I explained this to Major Chau and he understood; he had been dealing with the "system" much longer than I. I promised to keep trying, that somehow I could try to find a way to get the corn, but it wasn't very encouraging. Other pressing considerations were taking our time.

Elections were scheduled to be held in March, school houses were under construction as current projects for 1970, and marketplaces had to be built in hamlets that did not have them. Also, several of the roads and bridges had to be repaired, and it was my responsibility to solicit engineering aid from the American units in the area to accomplish this. From the military side, there was an urgent need for RF and PF housing, not only for the soldiers, but for their dependents as well. The newly organized People's Self Defense Forces, a home guard for each of the hamlets composed of the hamlet residents, had to be trained in the use of the weapons they would soon be issued. These people ranged in age from sixteen to seventy, and there were over eight thousand of them in the district. And several of the outposts manned by the district soldiers were scheduled to be abandoned, a move that would allow the soldiers to move in close to the population for more effective protection. We hoped this action would prevent one of the enemy's most successful tactics—that of simply slipping by the outposts at night and getting into the hamlets for terrorists raids and tax collection. By eliminating the outposts, we were denying the exact location of our forces.

So that was enough to keep us all busy, much too busy in fact to allow me to spend much time on the corn problem. But it was far from forgotten. As the problems stacked up, one on top of the other, I was plagued once again with the same self-doubt that had tormented me as an inexperienced intelligence advisor. Too much was happening too quickly, and I was running to keep up. But I was learning, the hard way perhaps, but learning nonetheless. I leaned heavily on Mr. Quy, Chi, Dalton, Jackson, and most of all Major Chau. These were the people who had passed the test of time—the ones I knew I could count on when I needed them.

Decisions determining which hamlets received what had to be

241

made quickly and often. Was it more important for Tan Hiep to have roads that were passable year round, than it was for Binh Tri II to have a new schoolhouse? Should Dong Hoa get a new marketplace, or should the money be spent in Binh An for a health station capable of delivering babies? There were not enough resources for everything. Some pressing needs would have to wait for the next year, or the year after, or the year after that. And always, I was faced with a question of priorities. What could wait no longer? What had to be taken care of today? At Bien Hoa I was expected to be able to answer these questions and a thousand more like them, for I was supposed to know more about Di An district and its needs than any other American in the world.

But we did what we could. It wasn't unusual for us to put in sixteen hours a day trying to solve our problems; some days were longer than others. Each success, no matter how small, was cause for renewed hope and inspiration. Yet the things we did failed to offset the agony caused by the things we could not do.

As the administrative responsibilities mounted, I was pushed further away from the day-to-day activities of the Coordination Center, yet it was here that I still felt the strongest sense of belonging. Hau and I still had our coffee and discussed operations with the same ease we always had, and when I felt a strong urge to escape from the pressure of my new job, I could always find a sanctuary in the Center. When I could spare an hour or two, I would try to spend it there. I would usually find Hau or one of his understudies interrogating a peasant who had information concerning a tax collector or an assassin. This was not unusual—it happened quite often in fact. The peasant wanted to be free from the influence of the Viet Cong for all the good reasons peasants everywhere want to escape from repression, yet the possibility of the Viet Cong discovering who had talked—and the action this could bring—made the peasant reluctant, afraid, uncertain. It was the same story, and I had heard it countless times, yet I was still fascinated. And when I became engrossed in my latest mission, this served to remind me exactly where the war was really being fought. The peasant would usually ask for promises that would guarantee his safety, yet realistically they could not be given. Those who gave information knew the grave risk involved, knew full well we couldn't protect them completely, yet they still came. And this phenomenon fascinated me, for what they were doing defied logic. There was more than enough evidence supporting past acts of the Viet Cong to make any level-headed, reasonable man think twice about aiding the government.

But there must be a point a man reaches when his own survival is not the most important thing in life, a point where he must strike out against his tormentor, regardless of the consequences. We had counted on, even banked on, this point being reached in areas where the Viet Cong were strong, and when it happened, we took full advantage of it. Yet we never really had the right to expect this to happen—it was beyond the thing one can reasonably expect a man to do. Scenes such as these in the Coordination Center were enough to restore my faith, if it had been shaken, and allowed me to return to the hectic world of the senior advisor. After bearing witness to such happenings, I was much better prepared to deal with the problems of corn, schoolhouses, bridges and health stations.

Chapter Twenty-Eight

CORN FOR THE PIGS

During the first week of February, an opportunity presented itself—from an unexpected source—that had the potential for solving my corn problem. I looked up from my desk that morning and discovered I was staring, eyeball to eyeball, at a beautiful American girl. Staring in this case was justified, for this didn't happen very often. In fact, it had never happened before. She introduced herself as Laurie Petrich, a secretary with the USAID complex in Saigon.

Her reason for being in the district was pure chance, since all she had in mind was seeing a typical district, one far enough from Saigon so as not to be influenced by the stiff commercial competition the city produced, yet close enough to get to by jeep. If there was such a thing as a "typical" district, it was her desire to explore it—firsthand. I quickly assured her that Di An was as typical, in many ways, as any district in Vietnam, and this seemed to relax her.

The favor she was asking of me was really a joy. Would it be possible, she asked, for me to take a little time from my busy schedule, and perhaps give her a guided tour around the district? She would be most grateful for this, she assured me. Obviously planning on her requests being granted, Miss Petrich had brought along two cameras and several rolls of film. At the time, I failed to see the connection between Miss Petrich and my corn problem, for I was accepting her at face value—a young lady who was asking for my assistance. The day happened to be a Saturday, and there wasn't much going on. I needed to visit a few hamlets anyway, and I couldn't think of a more pleasant way to go about this. I quickly agreed to her request, and leaving Lieutenant Garland in charge, we left.

It was a perfect day for driving in the district. The sun was just right, with the cool breeze blowing down from Tan Hiep. I was rambling on about the purpose and mission of the Advisory Team when we left the compound, glancing occasionally at Laurie in the seat next to me. The breeeze was blowing her long, brown hair back over the seat, triggering her futile, subconscious effort to keep it in place with her left hand. Her quick, spontaneous smile was completely disarming, and in a few minutes I found myself confiding in her the problems I was confronting. There was a certain interesting beauty about her that made her seem strangely out of place in the district, and this only strengthened the appeal she generated.

As we drove from hamlet to hamlet, it became increasingly difficult to concentrate on the stated purpose of our trip. I was thinking of a world I had left behind almost two years earlier, a world that had been filled with beautiful girls with long brown hair and disarming smiles, girls who could project a certain innocence over their environment and create joy and laughter, a world far removed from the uncertain, uneasy peace in Di An, South Vietnam.

In Binh Dong hamlet we looked at the lucky pigs, the ones that had survived. In a brick pigpen constructed to accommodate eight pigs, there were only four left. I explained to her that at one time there had been more pigs and apologized for the present small number. I hadn't planned on telling the story of the corn and my unsuccessful confrontation with the "system," but she was sincerely showing interest in the project that was now in serious danger of being a failure. It was a long story, and I told it as simply and truthfully as I could, leaning over the pigpen and staring at the four survivors rooting around in the pen, completely oblivious to their uncertain future. When I had finished, she told me of a program I was unfamiliar with—Food for Freedom.

Under this program, the American people donate money to purchase much needed commodities such as corn for needy nations such as Vietnam. The only cost to the government was transportation. She told me that in Saigon the two programs, USAID and Food for Freedom, were administered separately, yet the objectives of both were basically the same. If USAID was unable to assist me, she felt certain that Food for Freedom would be willing to solve my problem. I mentioned the bewildering maze of documents that I had waded through, just to apply for assistance. She laughed at this.

"Don't worry about the bureaucracy. If you apply through normal channels,you would never see the corn, and besides, you don't have to. I'll take care of all of this if you like, but it's going to cost you."

"How about some dinner when we get back?" she propositioned.

"You have a deal, and you're getting the short end."

We looked at some more hamlets, and Laurie took more pictures. She was particularly fascinated by the children, the little barefoot boys and girls who stared silently at her from behind their bigger brothers. With her cameras around her neck, her long brown hair, fair skin and blue eyes, she was as alien as a visitor from Mars. But in a few moments she was able to win them over as easily as she had won me. And she took advantage of this, snapping closeups and group shots as the children laughed and smiled, coming ever closer to this strange visitor who appeared less strange as time went by.

As we were preparing to leave Binh Tri, one little boy rushed over to the jeep, quickly touched her arm and then ran back to the collective safety of his peers. The startled expression on her face demanded an explanation.

"They've never seen anything like you before. He was just checking to make sure you're real."

The last picture in Binh Tri was a group shot, taken by me of_ Laurie and her newfound friends. As we drove away, we were escorted to the edge of the hamlet by this group of laughing, waving kids who seemed to be unaware of the dust generated by the jeep. Only when we passed the last house did they drop behind, allowing us to continue on our way.

Back at the compound, Tom had prepared one of his favorites—roast beef. Laurie was surprised that we had most of the luxuries of Saigon without the smog and traffic congestion. The fact that Tom could handle most American dishes without difficulty impressed her and helped destroy the preconceived idea that rice was the only thing a Vietnamese was capable of preparing.

"Too bad you won't have a chance to try Tom's broiled lobster," I mentioned casually.

After dinner, I asked her more about the Food for Freedom program, trying to get the facts and details down pat. After it was explained fully, we hashed out the mechanics of transporting forty tons of corn from Saigon to Di An. The transportation had to be handled by me, but it would be no problem. Trucks would be requested from Province for this task, just as they were requested for support of our operations. Laurie, being the personal secretary of an

246

executive in the USAID empire, was our ace in the hole. She was in a position to minimize the paperwork, and since both of these agencies worked hand in hand, she was as familiar with the interworkings of one as the other. Of course I would not be able to report this to Bien Hoa, since I had been told officially to forget about the pigs, the corn, and everything else from the 1969 plan.

As we conspired to beat the system that was bogged down by the never-ending bureaucracy, I realized how ironic my situation was. By exhausting every channel open to me, I had accomplished nothing except waste valuable time and become disillusioned. Now quite by accident, I had stumbled on the promising avenue of success with virtually no effort on my part.

It was late in the evening before we had it all worked out. Laurie promised to call me Monday morning and let me know if she had succeeded. If she had, I would request the trucks at that time and tell Major Chau. I decided not to tell him about our plot unless it worked. There was no point in having him believe something good was going to happen and then have it fall apart. Unless I could make him a commitment I could keep, I was going to make no commitment at all.

It was getting late, and I knew she had to get back to Saigon, yet I wanted her to stay. The months in Vietnam, with other things to consider besides women, had produced a numbness that replaced desire, almost. I had felt something strange about this girl most of the day, but by concentrating on showing her what she wanted to see and then discussing the corn, I had been able to force this feeling into subconsciousness. Now that she was leaving, there was nothing to suppress whatever it was I was feeling. For the first time that day, we were alone as I walked out to the jeep with her. Once again she promised to call me, and I thanked her for coming, even if our plan failed. And I asked her to come back when she had a chance; as soon as possible, I quickly added. And that's when she invited me to Saigon.

"I would like to return the favor. If you come to Saigon, maybe we can even the score," she told me.

"Do you mean it?"

"Just as much as I mean I'll help you with the corn. I owe it to you, and I like to pay my debts." Again the disarming smile. "Will you come?"

"Yes, I'll come. Where do you live?"

"I'll tell you Monday when I call. Okay?"

As she climbed in her jeep, I nodded and thanked her again for coming. Another round of goodbyes, and she drove away.

"What do you think of the American girl, Chi?" I asked after she had disappeared.

"I think she is very nice. She wants to help us, so that makes her nice, Dai Uy. Do you think she can do the things she speaks of?" he asked.

"Yes, Chi, she can do those things. And I agree with you. She is nice."

That night, I had trouble sleeping—trouble clearing my mind of the images it produced. Like so many short film clips, I saw Laurie in a hundred different situations and each situation involved me. As the night dragged on, I was unable to draw the line between conscious thought and sleep, for the dream I had was a rerun of the dream my conscious mind had created, and it was a fitful, wonderful, agonizing night, spent in a web of warm flowing sensations that engulfed me, smothered me, then threw me on the cold beach of awareness for a few moments, only to sweep over me again.

Monday morning Laurie called. She had had no trouble selling my request to the system. By going directly to the top and bypassing all the levels in between, she had overcome the most awesome of the system's defenses—the "proper channels," striking where the organization was most vulnerable. Even though she had promised to do this—and I had believed her—it was still a shock to me that she was able to accomplish with so little effort what I considered a formidable task. All I was required to do was come to Saigon, pick up the order at her office, take it to the warehouse at the Newport Dock on the Saigon River, and get my corn. I assured her that I would be after it as soon as possible, which would be the next day, and she gave me the necessary instructions to find her office. It was near the center of the city, just off Tran Hung Dau Street. Just in case I couldn't find it, I took her phone number, but she cautioned me against talking to anyone else in her office.

"Whatever you say, wonderful lady," I told her. If she had asked me to stand on my head and salute her typewriter, I would have done it, because I had come too far with this thing to have it blow up now. And the less I knew about what it had required to get that order moving, the better I liked it. Perhaps at a later date she could help me with some other problem.

I was considering the possibilities of this as I walked over to Major Chau's office to tell him the latest development. I found him working on an operation plan for the next day.

"I have good news, sir. Tomorrow we get the corn for the pigs."

He looked at me as if he had misunderstood what I was saying. "The corn for the pigs tomorrow? All of it, Dai Uy? How?"

I told him the story of Laurie Petrich and how she was able to swing it in Saigon. He was obviously delighted at this news, yet he showed none of the excitement I expected.

"We are very lucky, the way this has worked out. Now all I need from you are the trucks to haul it in."

"That is no problem, Dai Uy. When?"

"Tomorrow morning, sir, I would like to get it all hauled tomorrow, and if we get only two or three trucks, we will have to make more than one trip."

I figured roughly on putting four and a half tons of corn on each truck, which would come to about ten truck loads. We would work this problem out in detail the next day, after the trucks arrived.

He sent his aide for tea, and when it arrived, I told him the story once again, as much for my own benefit as his. I didn't mind telling him that I had almost given up hope for getting the corn after the dismal resolution we had received from Bien Hoa. He smiled when I told him this, and I immediately interpreted his smile to mean he shared my outlook, but I was wrong.

"I never gave up hope, Dai Uy. I know that we would get the corn, so I never worried about that."

If he had pulled a pistol from his desk drawer and demanded my wallet, it would not have had greater impact.

"How? How did you know we would get the corn, sir?" I asked quickly.

"Because you told me, Dai Uy. You told me that somehow you would find a way to get the corn and you have. Do you remember?"

I remembered, and it scared me. The leaning was going the other way now; my apprenticeship as senior advisor was behind me. I was being listened to and believed by this man, who listened to few people making promises and believed even less. This made me feel better than the news from Laurie, but I made a mental note as I left

Major Chau's office to be more careful in the future of the things I promised. I just hoped I would be able to stick to it.

The next morning, all was ready. Major Chau had managed to squeeze four trucks from the Province support company. If I was lucky, I would be able to get away with making only two trips to the Newport Dock. By eight o'clock, my convoy was ready to roll. I took Mr. Quy along in case I was unable to find Laurie's office.

There was no need for the trucks to follow me to Saigon for the order, so I left them at Newport, and Quy and I went into the city alone. I carefully threaded my way through the traffic with Quy as navigator. Following his advice concerning a shortcut, I maneuvered the jeep through an endless maze of back streets and alleys that eventually led us to a parking place across the street from the address Laurie had given me.

Her office was on the third floor of a respectable looking, fairly new office building, complete with elevator operators. Except for the guard in the lobby who checked my pistol, there was nothing to distinguish this building from one in downtown Baltimore. Girls and office boys hustled by us as we waited for the elevator, oblivious to everything except delivering the papers they were carrying. Maybe they're delivering requests for corn, I thought idly, as the elevator doors opened, and Quy told the girl operator where we were going. In the elevator I tried to brush most of the dust and dirt from my uniform, but I made little progress. My actions drew a smile from Quy, who had never seen me concerned over dust before.

Laurie was sitting behind the typewriter when we entered. The short, light blue dress she was wearing did more for her than the blouse and jeans she wore on Saturday, leaving no doubt of the quality of her beautiful, suntanned legs. She gave me a warm greeting, and I quickly introduced Mr. Quy, who now understood the dusting bit in the elevator. There was no one else in the office, which suited our plans fine. Her boss, a Mr. Brooks, was in a meeting across town, and the only other secretary in the office was taking the day off.

Laurie offered us coffee, but I explained we were in a hurry. The necessary forms were ready on her desk. She assured me they were in order and that she had personally called the warehouse to make sure there would be no confusion. She handed the forms to me, and I passed them to Quy.

"You haven't forgotten about our little agreement, now that you have what you've come after, have you?" she asked, with that same disarming smile.

"What makes you think I have what I've come after?" I replied, trying not to look at her legs. This time there was no simple smile to mark our parting. There was something deeper, more meaningful expressed on her face as I was leaving, that told me, plainer than any words, that what I had not received this time would be waiting for me on my next trip. I knew then that I would be back. She jotted her home address on a slip of paper and gave it to me.

"Just across the street from the USO. No trouble finding it," she said as I moved to the door.

"And call me, to let me know when you're coming," she added as an afterthought. I told her I would and thanked her again as she slid back behind the typewriter.

Mr. Quy had been waiting in the elevator, examining the forms. He was obviously pleased by the way they were filled out finding no mistakes. One of the pleasures life held for Mr. Quy was a properly completed form. As an administrative specialist, he was fascinated by procedures, as all administrative specialists are. The fact that this was only a means to an end, and not an end in itself, made little impression on Quy. It was the mechanics that were important to him, and in his dealing with me, he had little opportunity to examine a form perfect in all the required administrative details. I think this was a holdover from his experiences with the French system. At any rate, it pleased him, and this pleased me.

We worked our way back through the same alleys and sidestreets to the docks where we'd left the trucks. We found the drivers squatting in a circle, playing cards. Once again the convoy was formed and I led them to Warehouse 3, the one for corn. I showed the guard at the gate the proper form, and he allowed us to proceed. At the warehouse, we were met by a Korean national who looked at my papers, stamping some and signing others. When this was completed, he directed the first truck into the warehouse. As far as I could see in the cavernous building there was corn stacked to the ceiling, leaving only enough room for movement about the mountainous stacks. I had expected to see a lot of corn, but this boggled the mind, defying description.

It was nearing lunch time and a number of laborers, employed as loaders, were stretched out on the stacks. A sharp command from

251

the Korean had a crew on their feet in seconds, wrestling with the one hundred kilogram sacks. Two of the laborers would grab a sack and heave it in the truck, where it was juxtaposed by two more laborers. When one truck was loaded, another took its place, and the procedure was repeated.

And so it went, until all four were full. The trucks had been filled from a single stack yet, when it was over, the stack looked the same as when we had started. Our four trucks had failed to make a dent in the mountain of corn, and with the exception of the laborers' sweat, there was no visible evidence we'd been there.

On the way back to Di An, I couldn't help thinking how easy it had been, almost too easy, in fact. One lesson I had learned over the months was that few things come easy to the advisors, even those who had the full support of their counterparts. Had I been a believer in the system, I would have placed my faith in the chain of command—the chain that had been established to support advisors like me, on the bottom rung of the ladder. Theoretically, all the resources and assets of the United States government were behind me, and all I had to do was request assistance through the system—again, theoretically. But it had failed to work that way—in fact, it had failed to work at all—and a blue-eyed, brown-haired girl in Saigon had accomplished all that the system had failed to accomplish. This had jolted my faith in the system, yet I could dismiss it as an isolated case, rationalizing that other people in my business had faired better with their requests than I. But after seeing the amount of corn that had not been delivered, lying there in the warehouse, I began to consider the possibility that perhaps I wasn't an isolated case. And this disturbed me, for it was only through sheer luck that I had been exposed to the inner sanctums of the system. How many other advisors' requests for food were never filled I would never know, yet one thing I did know for a fact—there was something seriously wrong with the distribution system that allowed goods to pile up as they did at Newport Docks. I could have spent my remaining time in Vietnam trying to get assistance and never been aware of the support available outside my "chain." And if this inefficiency in distribution was occurring with corn, what other goods and materials were being affected? Being on the bottom I had no way of knowing; the big picture, if there really was one, was reserved for those above me—the same ones who would decide the priority and completion of each pacification program.

I should have been happy with my success, but I wasn't, for I had suddenly realized that, although my district was the most important thing I had, success in Di An would be meaningless unless it was coupled with success elsewhere. The same things we were doing in Di An had to be done in other districts. The only place it could exist alone on a separate plan was in my mind. The belief that this district was vastly different from its neighbors was only a belief, yet it was this belief that was at the core of every success we achieved. It was behind the faith Major Chau had in me to get the corn, and this belief, that we were something special, pulled us together. But I couldn't think of these things at the time. Maybe tomorrow, I thought. The corn was my mission that day.

Major Chau was in the compound when we arrived.

"Did you have any trouble, Dai Uy?" he asked.

"No, sir, everything went fine, but we must make another trip for this is only one half of what we need," I told him.

We had agreed the corn would have to be stored in the district warehouse until the hamlet officials came after it. The unloading was performed by a Regional Force company that had just returned from an operation. As soon as the trucks were empty, the convoy was ready to roll again. I sent Sergeant Dalton on the return trip with Mr. Quy, while Major Chau and I planned the distribution to the hamlets. It was better to get the corn out of the district as soon as possible, for if it was discovered by someone from Bien Hoa there would be a lot of questions that I didn't want to answer.

We went over the computations I had made earlier based on the needs of the pigs for a six month period, trying to determine how much each hamlet would get, per pig. It was at this point I discovered the mistake. It wasn't a very serious one for it had been made in our favor. I had overestimated our needs by about ten percent, which gave us a surplus of some four tons. After the second load arrived I counted the corn, just to make sure we really did have a surplus, and then recomputed my figures. Sure enough, there were forty 100 kilo sacks over and above the liberal estimates I had made initially. Problems such as this were rare occurrences, and I knew I would have no trouble solving it.

The next day, Major Chau passed the word to his hamlet chiefs

253

that the corn was available for pickup. Before the day was over, each hamlet had picked up their allotment. A wide assortment of vehicles, from three-wheeled lambrettas to oxcarts, were used to transport the corn from our warehouse to the hamlets. Each sack of corn was counted, and the man responsible for its transportation signed a receipt stating exactly how much he received. The whole operation was handled smoothly and efficiently, with hardly a hitch. And when it was done, I felt relieved, knowing that we had accomplished something worthwhile.

Chapter Twenty-Nine

PIGS FOR THE SOLDIERS

A few days after the corn operation, Sergeant Chi and I were out inspecting the pigs in Binh Tri. The thought suddenly occurred to me that what was being done by the civilians in the district should also be done by the soldiers and their dependents. It was no secret that the soldiers, the Regional and popular Forces, were on the bottom of the economic and social ladder. Perhaps something could be done to start them in the pig business, also. I decided right then to use the four tons of surplus corn to start them in the business. Chi seemed to think it was a good plan; at least it was worth a try.

That night I discussed it with Major Chau, and he liked the idea immediately. We had no money to put into the venture, but I proposed trading some corn to a commercial pig grower in Dong Hoa for a few young pigs. The pig owner I had in mind controlled the largest private pig farm in Southeast Asia, and all the feed for his pigs was imported from the states at considerable expense. It was my opinion he would welcome a chance to trade a few pigs for a couple of tons of corn. My proposal was somewhat illegal, for commercial organizations were not supposed to receive support of this nature. In addition, I had agreed to use the corn for projects in the hamlets. I was violating the letter of my agreement, but I considered myself abiding by its spirit. .

Mr. Quy was chosen to make the deal, since he was a friend of the pig farm owner. If we could get ten medium size, ten-week-old pigs for two tons of corn, we would be in business. This would leave two tons for the soldiers to feed them, along with scraps from the kitchen. I figured this should get the pigs through to market age or at least to a point where it would be profitable to slaughter them.

The next morning, Chi drove Mr. Quy to a pig farm to present our proposition. The owner accepted and sent his truck to pick up the corn that afternoon. The transaction was so quick, I didn't have time to select the units that would participate in the experiment. I left this to Major Chau, and he chose the 874 RF Company, located just outside the compound, and a Popular Forces platoon, stationed at Dong Hoa. The company received seven of the pigs, and the platoon took the remaining three. As soon as these units were notified, they began the construction of pens.

Two days later, they were prepared for delivery. Major Chau and I inspected the pens, constructed of poles, barb wire, and engineering stakes. I was not nearly as impressed with them as the unit commanders were, for it appeared that an ambitious enterprising pig with just a bit of initiative would root his way clear of these confinements, but I said nothing. I hoped they would prove to be more restrictive than they appeared, and I granted my approval based completely on faith. Perhaps this pathetic attempt was symbolic of how far the Vietnamese still had to go before advisors would no longer be needed. But I could not fault their enthusiasm or motivation, and if their efforts caused me frustration, it was frustration with myself more than with them. Perhaps I could have done more, produced more, advised more, been more involved. And frustration had never been a stranger anyway; I could live with it.

I had long believed that much more had to be done for the soldiers if the pacification plan was to succeed. Yet in a political war, such as Vietnam, the emphasis and attention was placed on the people, and the soldiers—to whom the task of defending these people fell—remained in the background. The only attention they ever received was in the form of criticism; being accused by the press and news media of lacking aggressiveness and spirit, being "unwilling" to fight, and unable to pass the big test of the American withdrawal.

Often they were compared with the Americans, and in this surface comparison, they were found wanting. But it wasn't a fair comparison. To begin with, the average Vietnamese soldier earns thirty dollars a month, and he is forced to compete in an inflated economy where the price of pork is roughly two dollars a pound. There is no incentive for him to count the days as they pass, for the passing days do not bring the war to an end for him. It ends when his life ends or when he is no longer able to fight, which ever comes first. And today is no different from yesterday, except that he is one day older and one day closer to "running out of time." If he's lucky, he receives a wound that will only disable him, ending his involvement in the war. And if he's extremely lucky, he will be evacuated to an American hospital.

But the average wounded Vietnamese soldier is not this fortunate. His wounds are treated at government hospitals, such as Cong Hoa in Saigon, which are little more than glorified butcher shops, where the doctors practice the theory that amputation is the most expedient form of surgery. Soldiers die routinely, everyday, in the corridors, without even seeing a doctor, without even receiving a bandage or morphine for the pain.

But he continues to fight, knowing full well that a moderate wound could cripple him for life; knowing too, that support for him at best is pathetically inadequate, and that each day his burden of defending his country grows as the Americans leave. The simple fact that it is his country and his responsibility to defend it is not justification to expect miracles of him.

As long as the average soldier can remember, there has been a war, and he has been involved. This condition has produced a certain philosophy often mistaken for indifference, and more often than not, reported as a lack of motivation. His philosophy is quite pragmatic and goes something like this: the war will not end today or next week or even next year. His energy must not be expended on such luxuries as enthusiasm and inspiration, for they eat away so much and produce so little. Surviving and operating and ambushing from day to day is the best course of action, for they must outlast an enemy that is prepared to last forever, an enemy that considers time its greatest asset. And this is a facet of the Asian mind that causes Americans much confusion and frustration because it does not allow the quick and easy victory—something Americans always expect from war.

And on it goes, the soldiers with nothing except the impossible mission, shunned by everyone yet vital to everyone, risking the ultimate sacrifice everyday for thirty dollars a month. Through it all, he still sees much good in his world, still sees humor in his miserable existence, still accepts his lot with a minimum of complaint. His children are raised in sandbagged bunkers and dirt floor huts, lacking the advantages other children enjoy, yet they survive. And they will grow up to be soldiers like their fathers; there is little else they can look forward to.

I realize I could do little to alter this trend, but what I was capable of doing had to be done. The ten pigs were a start. With a little luck and a lot of initiative, this enterprise had a chance of being successful. At the very least it would provide those involved with a few decent meals; even this would give me satisfaction. And it was with this attitude, neither pessimistic nor idealistic, but pragmatic like the soldiers, that Major Chau and I officially "dedicated" the pigs to their pig pens. Our celebration drink with both the 874 RF Company and the Popular Forces platoon was warm beer provided by the soldiers, who gazed hungrily at the pigs.

Chapter Thirty
THE RAID

As the pressure and initial shock of being the senior advisor began to wear off, it became easier to relax and have a little fun. Many of my previous relationships returned to normal or near normal. My relationship with Hau was still basically the same. I still sought out his opinions and advice, and I saw no reason for this to change. I still listened to his opinions as intensely as ever. The mutual trust that had developed over the months was in no danger of disintegrating; it was just that my new job kept me away from the Center more than I preferred.

So it was under these conditions that Hau presented his latest proposal to me. For some time we had been aware of the activities in the shacks of Binh An, along Highway 25. It was well known that the girls in these houses were prostitutes or "short-time girls." It was also known that the Americans on the truck convoys to Cu Chi and Lai Khe were patronizing these establishments rather frequently. They had worked out an elaborate plan to achieve this: on the way to their destination, the assistant driver would hop out at the house of his choosing and have a ball until his truck returned. Then he would ride back to Long Binh with the convoy under the pretense he had been serving the army all day. The next trip would be his turn to drive, and his buddy would have some fun.

This was all known to us, but it was of such a low priority that we didn't concern ourselves with it directly, being content to pass this information along to the MPs at the base camp and let them take the necessary action. But they took no action, and the situation continued, unchecked.

Now we had discovered that those who visited these houses were remaining overnight in ever-increasing numbers, and still the MPs did nothing. This placed a different wrinkle in the horn, for it left the district extremely vulnerable to a terrorist attack. It would only be a matter of time before the Viet Cong caught the Americans in

259

Binh An with their pants down, and there would go the "B" rating that had taken so long for us to achieve. The chance of this happening in the daytime was remote but at night, as experience had shown, it wasn't a chance—it was a certainty, and I couldn't afford to let it happen.

Hau's plan was simple. He suggested we take a platoon of Popular Force soldiers and raid all the short-time houses in Binh An. We would take two trucks along, one for the Americans and the other for the girls. Hau would take charge of the girls and deliver them to the Police Chief, while I would deliver the GIs to the Provost Marshal at the base camp.

I was impressed with this plan, and the more I thought about it, the more it appealed to me. The things Hau told me were true—it could be done, perhaps not as easily as Hau made it sound, but it was possible, nonetheless. From a purely tactical point of view, the raid was a necessity. Some action of this sort would have to be taken, and the sooner the better. But aside from its tactical necessity it sounded like fun.

I decided to take Dalton with me, knowing how much he would appreciate something like this. Since the raid had now been elevated to the status of an operation, it was reported to Bien Hoa on its tactical merits, just as an ambush or any other night operation would be reported. We decided to wait awhile after dark before we moved out of the compound. The Americans we wanted were the ones planning on spending the night, so there was no need to hurry. In fact, it would be much easier if we gave them a chance to "settle down." By waiting, we hoped to have the element of surprise with us.

Hau called the police chief over and briefed him on our plan. This was a necessity, for there would have to be some place to put the prostitutes we were picking up. In order to clear the jail, the chief released three men jailed the night before on the charge of drunk and disorderly. After this was done, the chief insisted on coming along for the raid. He thought it was funny, too.

It started to rain just before dark—not much, just a drizzle. But when the time arrived for us to leave, it had become a steady downfall. Chi, Lieutenant Hau, Dalton and I rode in Claymore, the vehicle we planned to load with Americans on the return trip. Following close behind was the two-and-a-half-ton truck carrying the platoon of Regional Forces. This was the truck for the prostitutes, if all worked according to plan. The police chief drove his own jeep.

The houses we were interested in were in a straight line along the highway running through Binh An, directly across the road from the public works. The rain was still falling when we arrived. It was an advantage since it forced everyone inside and covered the sounds of our movement. The trucks were parked about two hundred yards below the houses, out of sight. We stayed in the tall grass that was growing beside the road as we sneaked up on our objective, carefully keeping in the shadows.

About ten yards from the first house, Hau signaled a squad leader, and the leader took his squad behind the row of houses. This squad would serve as a blocking force, preventing escape into the open area to our left. Another squad sealed off the houses from the north, the only other likely escape route. We left five men in position to block any attempted escape to the south, and the rest of us moved out to start the systematic search. I expected at any moment to hear a dog bark, announcing our approach, but it didn't happen.

At the first house, Hau knocked politely on the door. A few seconds later, it was opened by an old lady trying to look annoyed at being disturbed. The back door was quickly covered as Hau and the old lady conversed. She seemed reluctant to have her house searched, but offered no further resistance when the police chief emerged from the shadows. In the two back rooms we found what we were looking for—a GI in each room, in bed with a short-time girl. The first GI offered no resistance as I explained that he was in an off-limits area and would be taken to the Provost Marshal's Office. He put on his clothes and was led down the road to the waiting truck. The second one, however, questioned the authority of Sergeant Dalton, angrily stating that he was well within his rights to be in the house. Without arguing, Dalton leveled his shotgun at that portion of the GIs stomach hanging over his belt, and told him to move. The soldier meekly complied with Dalton's demands, his rights no longer in doubt, and buttoned his shirt as he left the house. The two girls were handled in much the same way. They seemed to be more upset by the rain frizzling their hair than anything else. I was surprised to discover that neither soldier had a weapon, but I had no right to be. Anyone stupid enough to spend the night in Binh An Village at a short-time house, could not be expected to prepare himself against a possible enemy attack.

At the next house the procedure was the same—the surrounding, the knock, then the search. We wanted to be as polite and orderly as possible, using force as a last resort. The rain muffled the noise from the first house, allowing us to surprise the second one. We found only one American and one girl here, neither of which opposed our actions. The smoothness of the operation impressed me, and I enjoyed it despite the rain.

It was a rude awakening to those pulled from a warm bed and shoved in the back of a cold, wet truck, and perhaps a valuable lesson that would someday save their lives. The raid proceeded without incident until we reached a house near the end. The house was constructed much like the others—walls of tin and plywood, covered with tarpaper. There was a poker game going on in one of the back rooms involving four Americans and a number of girls. The girls weren't playing, only watching. Dalton, Hau, two soldiers and I walked into the room, attracting hardly any attention. One of the soldiers saw an M-16, minus the magazine in the corner, and picked it up. A quart bottle of Seagrams was in the middle of the table, more than half gone. And beside the bottle was a small pile of military payment certificates.

I explained our presence as simply as I could and told the GIs they would have to come with us. There was some grumbling and complaining, but they complied with our demands and started putting on their boots. We gave them a few minutes to gather up their belongings. Since we had not found the girls in bed with the GIs, Hau let them stay. As we were leaving, one of the Americans had a sudden change of heart and made a dash for the back door. Before he could cover the distance, Dalton blasted a twelve inch hole in the floor between the wound-be escapee and the door. Dalton quickly pumped another round into the chamber, but it wasn't necessary. The former gambler wisely decided the odds were not in his favor, not with Dalton looking for an excuse to blow him away. He went quickly to the waiting truck, and we continued our raid in the rain.

When it was all over, we had twelve GIs and nine very wet, very mad, short-time girls. The girls were hurling abuses at the Regional

Forces, which the soldiers thought was very funny. A couple of the girls tried pleading with Lieutenant Hau, insisting that he made a terrible mistake, trying to convince him he should let them return to their houses. Hau listened intensely, as though he was seriously considering their argument, and then he laughed. This really pissed the girls off. The GIs, for the most part, accepted their situation, moaning and complaining that a man "can't even get a little bit in this damn place without taking a lot of static." They did agree that what had happened was "a bad scene," one more example of the "system" descending on their heads, and so on.

But there was nothing serious. Any plan or idea they may have had involving an escape was gone now, after Dalton's demonstration in the house. There was something about his calmness that conveyed a certain sense of purpose, a seriousness that should not be tampered with. And there was a lot of respect for his twelve gauge shotgun; perhaps it was the weapon that gave him his special qualities. At any rate, we delivered them to the Military Police at the base camp, where I brought against them the formal charge of being in an off-limits area. After that, their fate would be decided by the Provost Marshal and their commanders.

The girls, still shouting abuses and obscenities, were hauled down to the jailhouse to occupy the place prepared for them by the police chief. I couldn't understand all they were saying, but I did understand "number ten," meaning that we were very bad people, and "dinky dau," a common expression of insanity, again directed at us.

But it was all enjoyable. It had provided a diversion that we needed, and hopefully, it would discourage the GIs from sleeping in Binh An Village. By doing this, it may have prevented a Viet Cong terrorist attack, thereby preserving the high rating that we had earned in that area. These were imponderables of course; only time would tell us how successful we had been. But one thing was certain—we had shut down the short-time houses along Highway 25 for the time being, and that was about all we could hope for.

Chapter Thirty-One
IN SAIGON

During April the Hamlet Evaluation System showed a drastic improvement. With the new projects for 1970 being implemented, I was able to report thirty category *A* hamlets out of a total of thirty six. The remaining six were rated *B*. This reflected a tremendous change from the situation two years earlier. It also reflected the virtual destruction of the Viet Cong's political apparatus that at one point had threatened to strangle the life out of the district. And because of this success, those of us remaining felt justly proud of our accomplishments. The people at the base camp who had given us support had to receive some of the credit for what had happened; the advisory team had made many requests of them, and we were never refused assistance. But in April, the First Division, "The Big Red One," was on its way home, and the base camp would be turned over to the Eleventh Armored Cavalry Regiment, who would be unable to support us as the First Division had done. Each day we had to rely more and more on our own resources. As a part of the "Vietnamization Plan," efforts were being made to make the Vietnamese self-sufficient in order to coincide with the President's withdrawal scheme. Due to this shift in emphasis, it was doubly significant that our district showed progress.

But April was also a month of loss. On the 18th Sergeant Dalton left us. He had been on a team when I had arrived two years earlier, and he would have stayed longer, but his third request for an extension was disapproved. Dalton was one of those rare men who is beyond replacement, who did his job so well that it was taken for granted; an exceptional man who worked miracles and saved lives as routinely as he drank his quart of Seagrams each day. He had taught me about motivation and professionalism and dedication. Yet he carried these qualities easily, as if they were an invisible part of his faded jungle fatigues, as if they were common issue for the combat medic. The usual ritual of parties and dinners and drinking bouts preceded Dalton's departure and terminated with a gathering given in his honor by Major Chau. This one, the last one, was conducted with much dignity. Major Chau showed his appreciation the only way he could; he presented Dalton with the Vietnamese Gallantry Cross for his service in Di An District.

Reluctantly Dalton turned his medical operations over to his replacement, SFC Adams, who came to us highly recommended from the Province Team. Adams was aware of Dalton's performance and accomplishments, and he told me quite honestly something I already knew: Dalton's act would be hard to follow. Miss Lai knew that Dalton was going home. She had known for some time, but there was nothing she could do to alter the impending events. And Dalton had known all along that it would end like this someday, even when we had talked of his plans to marry Miss Lai during those long nights on radio watch. Now, unable to stay any longer and no where else to go, he was going home. I asked him if he wanted to spend the last night in Saigon, but he declined the offer for reasons known only to him.

So he spent the last night with us, much like he had spent the others, drinking and talking until late at night. His twelve-gauge shotgun was left to Sergeant Chi. It was unusual to see any Vietnamese show a preference for such a terrifying weapon, especially a Vietnamese as small as Chi. But Dalton's handling of the weapon had impressed Chi, who had before been content to carry only a .38 caliber.

On the morning of the eighteenth, Chi and I drove Dalton to Saigon. His plane was not scheduled to leave until late that night, but there were several administrative details that had to be taken care of. These details were known collectively as "outprocessing," the reverse of the administrative details required on arriving in Vietnam, "inprocessing."

We dropped him off behind the huge MACV complex at a group of buildings known as the MACV annex. All the outprocessing required would be handled here, and from this point Dalton would go directly to the airport and be on his way. There was a constant stream of advisors through these buildings—some just arriving and trying to get their records in order, and others, like Dalton, going home. Chi and I helped him carry his bags inside the building that served as the Customs Inspection Station. Then we told him goodbye and left him there by the annex, looking pretty much the same way he had looked the day I arrived in Di An, his flop hat hiding most of his face, and a Marlboro dangling from his lips.

That's the way I wanted to remember him, for I had known him no other way. He would appear different in his starched khaki uniform with his chest full of medals and, as soldiers go, he would look "sharp." But he would lose something when he discarded that faded green, thread bare, jungle uniform, and I didn't want to be there when it happened.

On the way back, Chi and I stopped at the USO in Saigon. A milk shake and a hamburger was just what we needed before the drive back to Di An. But I had another reason for stopping at the USO, a reason far more important than the hamburgers—Laurie lived across the street, and I wanted to see her again; so while we waited for our order, I called her. She seemed surprised and genuinely happy that I was in town just across the street. She said she would be right over, and we had our hamburgers while we waited. It was sheer luck that she had been home. There was no way I could have known that this was her day off. She was wearing a pair of blue shorts and a white blouse, making her appear very relaxed and casual. The dark glasses she was hiding behind did little to conceal her natural, vibrant beauty. And when she joined us, she greeted Chi and me as if we were long lost friends.

"What a pleasant surprise!" she exclaimed.

"Didn't I tell you I'd be back?" I replied.

"How's the pigs?"

"Getting fat on your bootlegged corn," I replied. This pleased her.

"How long can you stay?" she wanted to know.

I told her we should be home before dark, but darkness was hours away. Laurie invited us over to her apartment for a couple of drinks and I accepted immediately. Chi wanted to see his family while in Saigon, and he was sorry to decline her offer. Laurie said she understood, and Chi left in my jeep, promising to be back at five o'clock. I was grateful to Chi for being so loyal to his family.

It was only a little after two when we left the USO, making it three hours before Chi returned. I had wonderful plans for those hours and the plans began to turn over in my mind as we walked up the steps to Laurie's apartment.

"It isn't much but it's home," she explained as we entered. Her remarks were hardly appropriate. As far as I was concerned, it was a luxury suite in the Waldorf. The faint, sweet smell of some unrecognizable flower perfume added a sense of intimacy to the room and the light green, wall-to-wall carpet gave a quietness I had long since forgotten was possible. The heavy drapes were pulled, blocking out the harsh, white sun, causing the air conditioner to gently swirl the cool air throughout the room. I was enjoying the sights and sensations about me that spoke unmistakenly of a woman's presence, while Laurie rattled on about the adjustments a girl had to make in Saigon. I was unaware that she was preparing our drinks and trying to determine what I wanted. I heard her question the second time.

"Will scotch be all right? I think it's too hot for anything else."

"Fine, Laurie, scotch is just fine." Cactus juice would have been fine, also, if it had been offered. I took the glass she offered and continued to look around the room, keenly aware of her presence behind me, aware of the long, tanned legs in the blue shorts and the white blouse stretched tight across her breasts. I was aware of the cold glass in my hand with the floating ice cubes, and the stillness of the room was a constant reminder we were alone.

I knew what was going to happen and it made me weak with anticipation. It was her move, I kept telling myself. Let her have it her way—slow and easy, with the lights out and the air conditioner drowning out everything from the world outside. But it didn't work this way. I turned to ask her about a painting that I really had no interest in, and she touched my arm. My scotch was taken from my hand, and she put her arms around me, silently, as if she had been doing this for a long time. Instinctively, I pulled her close, without speaking, crushing her firm breasts against the buttons of my shirt, searching for and finding her eager lips, held up to me with her eyes shut. And I kissed them feeling the terrible need they betrayed, feeling her heart pounding under her blouse, feeling her arms tighten around my chest, feeling her legs stiffen as she reached up on her toes to push her warm, wet tongue between my lips, darting it in and out. I pushed her back on the couch, still holding her.

"Do you want me?" she asked. It was a hell of a question and a hell of a time to ask it.

"What do you think?" I replied.

"I think you do. And I'm afraid. I don't want to get involved with somebody like you, somebody that would just think of me as a roll in the hay."

"Why do you say that? Is that what you think, Laurie?"

"Is there more to it than that, John? Please tell me what you think . . . about me. Tell me what we mean to each other."

She wanted to talk of the day in Di An when I showed her around and the day in her office with Mr. Quy. She wanted to talk of these things, give them a meaning they did not possess, talk about their potential and our future, as though we had one. And she was right—I did want a roll in the hay, but I didn't need the questions.

"I don't want you to think I'm in the habit of doing this, bringing men to my apartment, I mean," she explained.

I told her there was no danger of that; I knew she wasn't. She accepted without question this mysterious knowledge and plunged on. What do you think of me? Do you respect me? Will you be coming to Saigon more often to see me? And so on. I answered each question as tactfully as I could, trying to anticipate the reply she was looking for and giving it to her, if I could. I wanted to get on with it, to do what I thought we had come to do, but the questions kept coming.

She asked me what the war meant to me, and I tried to tell her. I told her about the rice farmer who gives half his crops to the tax collectors. I told her about the murders in the hamlets and the bombing in the marketplace, and I tried to explain to her the outrage of these acts. And I told her about the things Mr. Quy had told Wentworth and me—how the greatest freedom, the one that costs the most, is the freedom to quit. I talked about this for a long time but it had little impact on her. Somewhere, in the explanation, I had lost her, and it was just as well.

I told her it was my war now, and she wanted to know why I felt this way. No one had ever asked me this, to justify this feeling of attachment to what was going on in Di An. I told her about the people who lived there who had influenced my life—Hau, Major Chau, Chi and Dalton—and that there were more reasons why I couldn't quit. The hatred I felt for the Viet Cong and North Vietnamese was a bigger reason, and I told her so. She wanted to know if the salvation of South Vietnam was worth my dying for, and I told her it was. She wanted to know if I knew I could get killed there, and no one would remember or care and that, perhaps

268

in the end, the South Vietnamese would lose anyway, and would this make a difference to me? I told her these things would be determined by time and determination and commitment and will, and that they were beyond my field of vision. Yes, she asked, but suppose you knew right now it was a losing proposition, would you still insist on fighting. And I told her yes, I would because there was no other course for me. And is this war the most important thing in your life now, she asked, and I told her it was, and when I told her this, she was silent for a long time. She walked to the window and appeared to be looking through the blinds onto the street below, but I knew, by the gentle shaking of her shoulders, she was crying.

I could've lied to her, told her it was much more important to make love in a hotel in Saigon than getting shot in a rice paddie, but she had asked honestly, and the truth was the least she deserved. The questions and the answers to the questions had eaten up all the time I had. There was no desire left now, and the illusion of the room being beyond reality began to fade. We had said nothing of the hope of a permanent relationship and possibly more than that. And there had been no talk of love or what we meant to each other.

I told her it was time to go, and I left. The noise and heat of the afternoon sun hit me immediately as I stepped into the street below and worked my way through the traffic to the USO. I was reading a week-old copy of the *Overseas Weekly*, discarded by its owner, when Chi arrived. We had a coke and he told me about his family. Before he could ask about Laurie, I told him she wasn't feeling well and that she apologized for not being down to see us off.

"Maybe she will visit us again in Di An," he speculated.

"Perhaps Chi," I offered, knowing she would not. There would be no point in it, just as there would be no point in my coming back to Saigon. And there was no point in explaining to Chi why this was so. I realized then that there was really very little difference between what one actually gives up for a cause and what one is prepared to give up. In the end, the sacrifice has to be the same. I felt no anger as we drove back to Di An, only sadness—the kind of sadness that comes from a conviction that costs a great deal to maintain, and the stark realization that the conviction could be supporting a goal no longer possible. But neither that nor the possibility touched on by Laurie mattered now. Maybe the time had come for sacrificing on a grander scale—the sacrificing or offering up of a nation by those grown tired of fighting and resisting. Perhaps a roll in the hay with an American girl in Saigon was all there was to it, perhaps there really wasn't anything else, but I knew I could never embrace such a simplistic philosophy.

Chapter Thirty-Two

SPRING—1970

The day after Dalton left, Major Chau and I inspected the site of a new dam at Binh Tri. Work had started earlier in the month, but very little had been done. Our plan was to complete it before the rainy season—which had just started—was over. It would rain almost every day until November, and if we could complete the dam by August or September, there would be enough time for it to fill and provide water for the rice farmers during the dry season. But the rain, which we hoped to save, was coming everyday, and this delayed progress. There was little we could do except wait for breaks in the rain and then make sure we took advantage of them.

The Americans at Bien Hoa were screaming for results that would justify their diverting funds for my dam from other projects. And the pressure was being applied to Major Chau through his channels. The concern at Bien Hoa, unfortunately, was not so much for the rice farmers who would benefit eventually, as it was for tangible evidence that would benefit the Bien Hoa hierarchy directly. It was a game, as blatantly political as any played by American politicians in an election year, and I played it with them because it was their money I was spending, and I had to keep them happy.

So when there was no progress and they grumbled, I travelled to Bien Hoa and told them why. Major Chau played the same game, only more skillfully, displaying more tact, and always saying the right thing. Before either of us went to Bien Hoa, we always conferred, regardless of the project in question, insuring we were both on the same frequency, thus avoiding mutual embarrassment. By neglecting to take this simple and logical precaution, many senior advisors lost their job and rightly so, for regardless of what else it indicated, it showed a definite lack of common sense.

The "united front" constantly displayed by Major Chau and me became one of our most distinguishing characteristics, and we took a lot of pride in it. The fact that I had been in the district so long stood me in good stead when I had to attend these grill sessions.

There were few questions concerning the terrain, religion, health conditions, schools, economy, attitudes, and sympathies of the people I could not answer. And if I didn't know the answer, I was secure in the knowledge that Bien Hoa didn't know either, and in these cases I told them whatever would be the most beneficial to the district.

It worked every time, resulting in the approval of projects that repaired schools, built roads, created marketplaces and a dozen other things. Under Major Chau's guidance, I was soon able to play the political game very well, not as well as he, but I didn't have to. The Americans weren't supposed to be as skilled as the Vietnamese in this endeavor, and they never were—at any level.

By the end of April, thanks to a couple of god sent rainless days, the dam took form. The canal to divert the stream was dug, and the foundation of the retaining wall was poured.

We had deliberately overestimated the amount of cement needed for the dam. This surplus was used to build new, decent housing for the Regional Force Company at Bien Tri outpost. In return for this, the soldiers provided much of the labor needed to build the dam. The money we saved in labor was used to buy pigs for the soldier's dependents at Binh Tri. By using the money that was supposed to go to this project, we built a bridge in Tan Hiep. Legally, we could get no assistance to build the housing, for it was not one of the "approved projects." So we did the best we could with what we had, which had always been the mark of an advisor.

Sergeant Jackson left on the last day of April. Like Dalton, he had requested an additional extension, and like Dalton, his request had been denied. It was part of General Westmoreland's policy to give as many people as possible experience in Vietnam. The fact that Jackson was far more valuable to me than the man about to replace him had no impact on such decisions in Washington. And the fact that Jackson wanted to stay with me, and the man replacing him wanted to stay at Fort Bragg, made no difference either.

His departure had a special meaning to me, for it had been Jackson who picked me up in Bien Hoa on that June morning almost two years earlier, and the first member of that old team to welcome me to Di An. We had been on more operations and ambushes than either of us cared to remember, but unable to forget, some productive, some not. He had taught me how to plan operations and coordinate support the way it should be done, not the way it's taught at Fort Benning. And he watched me progress from a green, dangerous, second lieutenant who knew nothing, to the top spot on the team. And we both knew this could never have happened had it not been for people such as Jackson, Dalton, Chi and Quy—people who had more faith in me than I had in myself, and stood behind me when I needed them the most.

There would be no Americans left after Jackson, who could feel the same as I felt about Di An. He was the last who held the same frame of reference as I, who had experienced our greatest successes and witnessed our most tragic losses. To the newer men on the team, the dark days of 1968 and early 1969 were only stories and, because of our present success, it was hard for them to relate to that time period. It was much easier to take the smoothness of our current operations for granted. But Jackson knew better, and he constantly cautioned the new advisors of the danger created by a false sense of security. With him would go the irreplaceable combat experience that adds vital continuity to an advisory team, leaving me with a team untested under fire.

During those past few months, the Viet Cong had given us few opportunities to train the newer members under the guidance of the combat veterans like Jackson. And this scared me, for it created a weakness—a weakness caused, ironically, by our success at virtually destroying the enemy's threat. But there was no guaranteeing conditions would continue as they were. If we were unable to fill the vacuum in the areas cleared of the enemy, if the pacification program (now becoming widely known as the Vietnamization Program) bogged down through inefficiency of bungled administrations, there would be little to prevent the enemy from regaining lost ground. This would force us to become engaged once again in violent contact with the enemy, requiring experience and cool-headed advisors. With the reduction of American forces, the pacification program would undergo many tests; some I had no doubt the program would pass, others I was afraid of. The loss of advisors of Jackson's caliber scared me more than the loss of American combat units, but I would have to live with this fear.

His replacement, Sergeant First Class David Singer, had served a previous tour in Vietnam with the Ninth Division. He had been a platoon sergeant for awhile, but most of his experience in the war

273

zone had been in the motor pool. If I was disappointed in his combat record, there was some consolation in the fact that with his experience in the motor pool, he could keep our jeeps running, and this was nothing to be sneezed at.

As part of the unshakable tradition strictly complied with in the district, Major Chau had given Sergeant Jackson his final farewell dinner. These occasions were never allowed to become routine or trite. There was a certain, simple dignity about the way Major Chau conducted them—and himself—that did justice to the affair. He could say things about an advisor that would sound overblown or flowery anywhere else, things that would embarrass both the speaker and the guests.

But the honesty of Major Chau's praise was unmistakable as he spoke of the only thing that could justify the sacrifices made by Jackson and other advisors—that his work in Di An had not gone unnoticed. Major Chau was grateful for the things he had done, and he was sorry Jackson had to leave. There were gifts and plaques bearing the date of his arrival and departure; souvenirs for him to take home as tangible proof of his service. But it was the words of the crippled district chief that carried the greatest impact. On the thirtieth of April, Sergeant Chi drove Jackson to Saigon.

We had performed well during the last two years; there was no question of this. The fact that I could now drive, alone, anywhere in the district was proof of what we'd done to the Viet Cong's organization. By making Di An a "better place to live," we had accomplished most of our purpose for being there. It had always been the advisor's objective to work himself out of a job, to reach a point when his services are no longer needed and his advisees can stand alone. This simple truth was often overlooked in the day-to-day life of the district. The closeness of our association with the Vietnamese erased the long-range objectives that had created the association in the first place. Like other advisors, I was guilty of forgetting exactly why I was in Di An District, at least the part about working myself out of a job. There was something cold and impersonal about this objective, so I rejected it. Therefore, it was a shock when the colonel told me, early in May, that I would have to give up four of my seven advisors.

Di An had been selected as the first district in Three Corps for reduction of the advisory effort. The reason behind choosing Di An was the success we had achieved. I should have been proud to be involved in this experiment, but it had been so sudden I automatically rejected it, complying only because I was ordered to. The plan was scheduled to be implemented in two weeks, leaving me very little time to reorganize my shrinking organization.

I was directed to decide, rather quickly, which advisors I would give up. It wasn't the kind of decision I liked to make, yet it was typical of the way Bien did business. They refused to select those I had to lose, hiding behind the old standby that "I knew the needs of the district better than anyone else." This wasn't true and I knew it; it was quoted now to defend this latest directive. When I had fought for approval of Dalton's and Jackson's extensions, no one at Bien Hoa defended my position by saying I knew the needs of Di An better than anyone else; to do so would have been counter to "Department of the Army policy."

But I was accustomed to such maneuvers, having gained much valuable knowledge of the games played at the higher levels. So I made the decisions, choosing to keep Sergeant Adams because I needed a medic, and Lieutenant Garland because he was a hard worker and the Vietnamese liked him. In time he would be a first-rate advisor; he reminded me of myself a long time ago, when all I wanted was a chance to do a worthwhile job. I think this was the real reason why I let him stay.

Major Chau would be informed through his own channels, officially, in a day or two, but I couldn't let him wait. I told him a few minutes after the team was told. He was in his office going over the ambush locations for that night, making last-minute changes before giving them to the operations officer. He motioned me to a seat and continued his review. The only sounds were the slow revolving of the overhead fan, and his pen scratching on the thin overlay paper. It was siesta time, and nearly everyone was asleep. It was time for Major Chau to be asleep and I knew that was his next planned event after lunch. His wife was probably waiting for him, with food on the table, waiting patiently for his arrival, yet accustomed to his tardiness.

Satisfied with the ambush locations, Major Chau handed them to his aide, who had been standing quietly by his desk. The aide left the room with an air of urgency, leaving the district chief and me alone.

"What is it, Dai Uy?" he asked, directing his gaze at me.

I told him about the latest decision from Bien Hoa. There was no need to explain why it was being done, that we had been chosen as a test case due to our success; he knew this better than I. He was also familiar with the phase-down of American forces, of which this was a part. Its happening was inevitable, and if the concept of a three-man advisory team was to work, he would be as responsible as I was, to make it work. If it did succeed, it would obviously enhance his image, being a positive reflection on his ability. It wasn't necessary to explain this either. From a purely pragmatic point of view, we should have both been pleased, but we weren't. He displayed no outward emotion, yet I knew his involuntary reactions well enough to know he wasn't pleased. There was a slight twitch over his right eye, and he tapped his left foot against his desk. I remembered the times when Hau had reported an assassination or a bombing and Major Chau had sat quietly listening, and his right eye would twitch, and he would tap his desk.

"And which advisors will stay with us, Dai Uy?" he asked.

I told him who I had picked to stay and why. Then we discussed the immediate impact this would have on our daily routine. It would be impossible to send advisors on every operation now. Nor would we be able to man the radio room twenty-four hours a day. In effect, this change would reduce the team's primary function to that of simply maintaining liaison with the district chief and his staff, assisting him whenever we could. I would be pushed farther behind my desk, becoming more of a slave to the endless reports that had to be submitted to Bien Hoa. The reporting task would not decrease just because the team was getting smaller; in fact, it would increase, for now I was required to write an additional report each month entitled *The Impact on the Advisory Team Reduction*. I would have to chart each development, problem and success of this venture as carefully as the heart surgeon who had just removed the major portion of a patient's heart and still expects him to recover.

I would be even more dependent on the Vietnamese to answer my questions than before, since I would not have the time or the people to collect my own information. Again, Major Chau promised the full support of his staff to aid me. The pending reduction of my advisory team had done nothing to disrupt the "united front" in Di An and, as long as we had this, we could survive anything. The details of the reduction would be worked out gradually, as problems presented themselves. It would be useless at this point to attempt to cover every possible contingency brought on by this change. The fact that it was happening and I had been directed to make it succeed was enough at this point.

We talked a long time, with him asking questions I tried to answer. Some—such as "what will happen if the three-man team does not succeed?"—I had no answer for. This was not to be the case, as far as Bien Hoa was concerned. It would be far more damaging to have the concept fail than to never attempt a reduction at all. Aside from the tactical considerations, I knew the real thrust behind this decision was political. It would look good for the senior officials at all levels, American and Vietnamese, to be able to point at Di An and say, "there is a success story." Our real job was now to insure this would happen.

And it wasn't something I was entirely opposed to. I realized that real success had to be of the political kind, the kind that would generate publicity or propaganda for us. But it was the attitude that we were only a pawn in some giant chess game that made me feel bitter. I was searching for something more personal than this, something that would publicize more than our rating on the Hamlet Evaluation System. I wanted the story of the people in Di An told—which was the real story behind our success—but I knew this would never happen. The computer could not handle personalities, and the people in Saigon and Washington were not concerned about individuals. It wasn't important to them that Major Chau had been wounded four times or that Quy had a theory, negative in nature, yet it justified our being there.

These things were only important to me, and my importance to the system reached only to the point of making the political connection between what was desired and what could be accomplished. Beyond this, I was only a social security number in a most impersonal system. Success was taken for granted; only failure drew attention. Because of this and because I was human, I saved my strongest loyalty for the district, selfishly divorcing our achievements from the other two hundred and thirty-five districts in Vietnam, refusing to allow what was happening in them to influence what I was doing. It was a search for identity that could only be satisfied by identifying with the district's needs. And I secretly hated the computer in Saigon that clustered us all together, passing judgment on us collectively in some thirty different areas.

The Vietnamese suffered the same fate. Major Chau's position depended on how well he pleased his superiors in Bien Hoa and how well he solved the problems in Di An, in that order of priority. As always, we would follow the orders given and do the best we could. When the reduced advisory effort succeeded, which it no doubt would, there would be much rejoicing all the way up the line. And eventually, there may even be rejoicing in Di An. But not now—the death of our Advisory Team was preventing this from happening.

Before the fourteenth of May, which was the date of our reduction, most of the details affecting our future operations had been worked out. Some guidance had filtered down from Bien Hoa, but not much. The only thing Bien Hoa insisted on was that I call them three times a day for a communications check. This would make constant monitoring of the radio unnecessary, yet still allowed communications at predetermined intervals.

I had deliberately limited the use of advisors on operations during this period, in an attempt to determine where the weak points of this reduced system would appear. I soon discovered that communications was a major problem, just as we had predicted. The problem was to find a simple, effective way for the Vietnamese on an operation to relay their situation to the advisors. A wounded soldier, for example, was a situation requiring immediate attention. Something such as this could not wait for the Vietnamese channels to function—not with a man dying and a helicopter required to save him. Preventing a situation such as this from developing was the thing that worried me most. The routine, administrative details were of little concern to me, and if they never worked themselves out, it would be just as well.

Sergeant Chi and I worked out a solution to this problem, but it was time-consuming. It involved using Chi as the go-between, relaying any request for assistance from Vietnamese in the field to one of the three remaining advisors. The problem was that it required Chi to stay in the Vietnamese Operations Center during an operation. Even though this system worked, it reflected a trend that was growing stronger every day in South Vietnam—it pushed the advisor one step away from the action in the field. It forced us to receive our information second hand, and effective as it was, it

278

consumed vital time. But the argument that justified such things was growing all too familiar.

Those who favored reduction said it was time for the Vietnamese to fight their own battles, something they had been doing all along, but it was never largely publicized. They said it was a Vietnamese war, and if it was lost, it would be a Vietnamese loss. The thousands of Americans lost were used as additional ammunition to support American disengagement, not justification for continued resistance. On the home front, Vietnam was being promoted as the wrong war in the wrong place at the wrong time—a tiny country that was not vital to the interests of the United States under any conditions.

The voices raised in opposition to this popular philosophy were lost. Those who pleaded for a little more time to prepare the South Vietnamese for their own defense were branded as warmongers, subhuman animals whose only ambition was prolonging the war. And the massive anti-war campaigns on the home front had their impact, also. It was to the advantage of the Viet Cong that the battlefield was shifting from the rice paddies and elephant grass to the streets and Congress of the United States. They would have a much better chance of winning there, and they knew it. When the very real possibility of a North Vietnamese take-over was offered as a last ditch effort to stall the American pullout, it was shouted down as a "scare tactic" dreamed up by the military. And when it was pointed out that if a take-over happened, there would be large scale massacres on the scale committed by Mao Tse-tung when he gained control of China, there where those in very high places—who should have known better—that said the North Vietnamese embraced a "different kind of communism that wouldn't allow this to happen." It was easy for these simple-minded men to overlook the fact that Communist China supplied a major portion of Hanoi's ability to wage war.

Now, the decisions that had been made long before in Washington, were being implemented in Di An. I tried not to think of these things, since four of my advisors were preparing to leave, but it was hardly the sort of thing I could be optimistic about. Being at the bottom gave me an advantage those above me did not have; I could see the difference between what was supposed to happen and what was actually happening, and the two had very little in common. But I had been taught, in no uncertain way, that whenever there is a conflict between what is tactically sound and that which is politically expedient, the latter wins every time. This irreversible truth came to mind on the fourteenth of May, when I said goodbye to the largest part of my team.

It was difficult to establish a routine among the three of us, but it evolved slowly. The first, most striking change I noticed was the awful emptiness around our compound. This was most noticeable at mealtime when there were only four of us, including Chi, at the table designed to accomodate at least ten people. It was incredible, but each of us still retained possession of our original place at the table even though there was no longer any reason to justify this. And for the first couple of days following the reduction, Tom made the mistake of setting the table for a full team. He would quickly notice his mistake and rectify it, but not before it had been noticed. And I would plan on sending someone to the base camp for a needed item, only to discover that the "someone" I had in mind was no longer with me. And things grew much more quiet. At night there was hardly any point in setting up the projector, unless the movie was something special one of us really wanted to see. Usually at night, each of us would retreat into his own little world to read or write letters or listen to the radio.

But it was working, just as I had known it would work. I had several visitors during those first few days, some from Bien Hoa, others from Saigon, and even a couple who claimed they were from Washington. They all wanted to know how the "great experiment" was going, and I told them how wonderful everything was. They were looking for no other answer, and it would have changed nothing if another answer had been given. It was easier to tell what I did, and it was all true.

The things that were not wonderful were beyond measure, making it impossible to relate. I couldn't even put a finger on it myself, much less put it in language they would understand. I had no proof that the district was threatened with impending doom, nor could I prove that a three-man effort was insufficient to handle the advisory functions in Di An. What I felt and knew were invisible and silent, just as all things worth fighting and dying for are. Peace, stability, happiness, and freedom can neither be seen nor heard yet, when they're missing, the void is readily apparent. In the flexible, fluid world that surrounded me, concrete facts were at a premium.

What passed for facts supporting our efforts were read to my visitors from my multicolored briefing charts, covering everything from the disposition of the district forces to the number of blackboards in Binh Tri school house.

Because the charts were real, it was easy to relate to them and accept the knowledge they contained. I soon discovered I could say almost anything to almost anybody and make it believable—not because I was that convincing, but because my visitors felt neither the inclination nor desire to go below my level and see the things I spoke of for themselves. Naturally, this made my job easier, but it also confirmed a fear I had harbored for some time: reported results were more important than what actually happened and, if things I said were proven at a later date to be untrue, then it was my fault. This didn't bother me; I was well prepared to defend the reports I gave my visitors. What did bother me was the fact that my superiors were perfectly content with the "report," the spoken or written word. It wasn't easy to get them out in the hamlets where the real work was going on to inspect such projects as the dam at Binh Tri or the dependent housing going up at the outpost. These were the things I was proud of—these things gave the district its individuality, separating it from the other districts and projects in South Vietnam. These were the things that defied the computers and the multicolored briefing charts and gave purpose to the American presence.

On occasion, I would be pleasantly surprised by a request to see where the "taxpayers money was going," but it wasn't very often. I would rationalize it away by telling myself it was a tribute to the faith they had in me, but this wasn't very convincing. On the other hand, it was just as well they were easily satisfied—if they hadn't been, my ability to wheel and deal would have been severely limited.

Most of the interest shown by our visitors was generated by the operation of the Intelligence Coordination Center. This had been the case long before the team's reduction. It was this organization that gave Di An its distinction and paved the way for progress in other areas. Nearly every visitor was taken on a tour of the Center and shown exactly how the intelligence reports were processed and evaluated.

The Center was the source of my greatest pride in the district for many reasons. It was here that I had first been allowed "to do my thing" as an advisor. I had been put to the test here, and it was here that I had first felt bitter disappointment. And the Center had taught me how sweet success can be, and how much it costs. It had given me the background and experience that allowed me to become the youngest senior advisor in Vietnam, and I would never forget it.

Representatives came from places such as Thailand and Singapore to study the methods we used to eliminate the Viet Cong infrastructure, and we tried to make their journeys worthwhile. No less than eighty-five hard-core members of the infrastructure had been rendered neutral by this organization. No quarter had been asked, and none was given during the "heydey" of our campaign which covered the period from 1968 through mid-1969. No matter how the rest of the briefings had gone, whenever I discussed this organization, I was happy.

By the first of June we had grown accustomed to the changes. And the Vietnamese had accepted them, also. When the units gathered at dawn in the compound for the day's operations, the absence of the Americans no longer generated attention. Tinh was forced to give up the good life of carrying the advisor's radio and was returned to the ranks. He still retained the additional and very rare duty that had once taken all his time, but this additional duty was growing rarer with each passing day. We continued to feed him occasionally, which he considered our obligation for past service, and his special privilege to ride to Bien Hoa with whoever went after mail was retained. These were hard-earned status symbols, and Tinh wasn't about to give them up easily.

By not going on the operations, we were at a disadvantage as far as evaluation went. If there was no contact, we had no way of assessing the Vietnamese's performance, and their familiar report of "negative, negative" had to be accepted. There was no way of determining the intensity or aggressiveness of the operation. Had they conducted a well-supervised search of the area, fully prepared to flush a squad of VC into the open, or had it been a "walk in the sun" to meet the requirements set forth by Major Chau? There was no way we could answer these questions. Again, the multi-colored charts could not tell us exactly what happened out there in the rubber trees; they could only tell us how often the soldiers had gone, which unit, the date, and the results. And if there was a slow ebbing away of the soldiers' spirit, there was no way it could be reflected. It simply would not compute.

And so it went. On the surface everything looked rosy, and I had nothing other than my instincts to tell me anything to the contrary. Our team was performing as well as could be expected, if not better, and the assistance Major Chau promised was freely given. Di An was praised in all the seats of power leading to Saigon, and Saigon was no exception.

From all indications, I would be leaving Vietnam riding a great wave of success, and this should have made me happy. All the things I had dared to hope for came to pass, and much more. The enemy's structure in Di An had been shattered, at least for the present, which is all one can reasonably expect. Travel about the district was unrestricted, and our pacification program was leading Three Corps, if not all of Vietnam. The rice farmers were no longer plagued by the tax collectors of the Viet Cong terrorists, for they were no longer in operation. The greatest threat to life in Di An in June 1970 was from U.S. Convoys passing through the district, bound for Lai Khe or Chu Chi. Our success was undeniable, supported by every accepted method used to gauge progress and success. Of our thirty-six hamlets, thirty were rated *A*; the top of the scale. The remaining six were *B*. No other district could make a comparable claim.

Yet all this failed to make me happy. I still felt something was not quite right, that more could be done and should be done. I couldn't forget the conversation with Hau in Saigon. He had told me that I expected too much from the Americans, that I expected them to feel the way I felt. It was simple for Hau to understand, even then, and he had laughed at my naivete. At the time, the mere suggestion of an American sellout or the weakening of our commitment would have been inconceivable. But now, the possibility of something such as this happening, shrewdly disguised as "Vietnamization," was gnawing at the back of my brain. During the months I had been senior advisor, I was exposed, on a limited scale, to the political operations that governed the war. If the same was true nationwide, then there was a strong reason for the gnawing at my brain. And it increased every day.

283

Chapter Thirty-Three

GOING HOME

June brought a time for change. This was the month I would have to leave; this time it was certain. There was very little chance another extension would be approved for me, even if there was an emergency in Di An. It was becoming increasingly difficult to extend, due to the change in policy, and I had been told in December, when my last extension had been approved, that there would be no more. And from the conditions in Di An, another extension could not be justified. There was very little left for me to accomplish; it was time I left.

Yet I was not looking forward to my departure. For the past two years I had give little consideration to leaving. The day to leave would come and I would go—that much was accepted rationally. And the assignment that was still waiting for me, a teaching assignment at Fort Holabird, was accepted the same way. But it failed to excite me.

The round of parties that marked the departure of those who went before me was the mark of my departure, also. Major James Barnett was sent down from Bien Hoa as my replacement. He seemed a little heavier than he should have been, but otherwise, he was in good condition. This was a good time for him to arrive. The parties would allow him to meet the people he would have to work with under ideal conditions—everybody would be half drunk. The first test he would have to pass would be with the bottle; if he proved to be a strong drinker, he would be off to a good start right away. Barnett seemed to be in good shape in that department, probably because of the conditioning at Bien Hoa.

The parties started in earnest about a week before I was to leave, and lasted right up to the last night I was in Vietnam. I had often wondered how I would react to the "leaving process"; would it be a painful experience, or would I simply accept it as I knew I must? I discovered that the most painful part of leaving was not the parties but the complete sincerity of those giving them, making it a complete, all-out effort. I collected several gifts, including Vietnamese dolls, lacquer-covered paintings, oil paintings, and various sized plaques.

Three days before I left, I was invited to Bien Hoa for a farewell party. They gave me a cigarette lighter and a small plaque and told me I had "done a good job." I had to spend the night there due to the lateness of the party, the first night I had spent in Bien Hoa in two years.

As always, the last party was given by Major Chau at his house. This occasion was smaller than those in the past due to the reduction. It was raining hard that night, which seemed fitting. I didn't feel in a festive mood, and the rain only served to emphasize the gloomy atmosphere. Before the party was over, the lights went out, and by the time Adams and I had the generator going, we were soaked from the driving rain blowing in through the generator shed. But we continued with the party.

It was late when we left Major Chau's house, but I still had some packing to do. In over two years, a lot of things accumulated, things that weren't valuable but impossible to part with; souvenirs that had charted the months and years, each with a background worthy of remembering. I had a large vase from an abandoned schoolhouse in Binh Tri; a copper incense burner picked up in the bombed-out ruins of a pagoda just south of Tan Hiep. A large bullet hole in the side was proof the burner was a combat veteran. And there were war souvenirs, too—Viet Cong flags, propaganda leaflets, the K-54 pistol that had belonged to Chin Hien, and a CKC rifle captured in an ambush at Dong Hoa.

The next day promised to be beautiful. The early morning air was fresh and sweet, cleansed by the heavy rain the night before. But more rain would come before darkness. It would come in torrents, shutting off the bright sunshine without warning and sending people caught in the open scurrying for cover. It always happened like this during the rainy season, yet it wasn't something you could ever quite adjust to. Yet there was always hope for that special day, the day when the promise of early morning with the sun shining through would hold until night. Maybe this day would be it.

But even if it wasn't, the sixteenth of June was still a special day. This was the day I had to leave Di An District, South Vietnam. My time, all twenty-five months of it, was now up. All I had to do now was say a few last-minute goodbyes and be on my way.

I found Major Chau in his office. This was where he usually was early in the morning, trying to get a head start on the "paper war," the war none of us would ever win, but had to fight nonetheless. If the South Vietnamese Army ever decides to give medals for pushing paper, this man will have a sackful. But it really didn't matter—he had enough of the other kind.

He was bent over his desk when I entered, the way he had been bent over it so many times in the past when I had needed to discuss something important. When he looked up, a tiny trace of shock registered on his face, then he smiled. I guess the khaki uniform was a shock to him—he had never seen me in it before.

"I have to say goodbye, sir. It is almost time for me to go," I said.

At the farewell party the night before we had talked a long time about the things that had happened to us in the past two years. The party had been a formal goodbye, or as formal as we could get in the district. But now, with just the two of us in his office, I had come to say goodbye.

"Please sit down, Dai Uy."

I took the large brown chair near his desk.

"You have been with us a long time, and it is sad to see you go," he told me. "You will be missed."

This was the kindest thing he could have said, far kinder than anything I could think of.

"Thank you sir. And I will miss all the people here that I have worked with."

He asked if there was anything at all he could do for me, and I told him there was. I asked if he would say goodbye to the hamlet chiefs and village chiefs I had missed during the past few days, and he promised that it would be done.

"Is there anything I can do for you, after I get home?" I asked.

"Yes, Dai Uy, there is one thing maybe you can do. I read very much in the American newspaper about the bad things that happen in Vietnam, but everything here is not bad. You have seen much good and caused much good. You have seen bad, also, because we are at war. You know it is all not—how do you say—one way. Perhaps if your friends ask about Vietnam you can tell them."

I told him I knew only of one district, but he said that was enough.

"Most of those who say bad things about us do not know that much," he reminded me.

I told him I would tell the truth about Di An if anyone asked, and this satisfied him.

There was a lot more I wanted to say, but there was no time. Sergeant Adams was waiting in the jeep to take me to Saigon. And besides, I doubted if the words would come. What do you say to a man that you had lived with for over two years in a war zone? That I was ready to die for this crippled little man on any given day? That we were fighting for the same thing in a war that most people had already written off as hopeless? That neither of us would be satisfied until the war had been won? He knew all of these things already; they went deeper than mere words could go, and it was embarrassing to talk of them.

So when I told him I had to go, he stood up and extended his crippled hand for me to shake for the last time, thus terminating a long partnership. He limped along behind me to the door and watched me get in the jeep beside Sergeant Adams. He waved as the jeep started to move out of the compound and continued to wave until it was out of sight.

Adams and I drove the fifteen miles to Saigon in relative quiet. He hadn't been on the team very long, so there were no old "war stories" for us to recount. I didn't feel much like talking, anyway. My mind was busy turning over the past two years, making it difficult to think of anything else.

At the MACV annex in Saigon, Adams dropped me off, and I told him to take care of himself. The outprocessing went routinely enough, even though it was slow. After it was finished and the long wait at the airport was over, I finally boarded the Trans World 707 for the flight to San Francisco. After the plane was high above the South China Sea, I leaned back against the seat and tried to sleep, but my mind kept reliving the past twenty-five months.

I tried thinking about the teaching assignment waiting at Fort Holabird and wondered if it would be interesting. Rationally, I knew that I would now have to construct my world around something else, for Di An was far behind me. But it was no use. No matter what was waiting for me, I knew it would be second-rate. It would have to be, because I'd already been through the best.